DATE DUE

JE 19 '01			

DEMCO 38-296

Edison's Kinetoscope and Its Films
—— A History to 1896 ——

**Recent Titles in
Contributions to the Study of Popular Culture**

Edison's Kinetoscope and Its Films
—— A History to 1896 ——

Ray Phillips

Contributions to the Study of
Popular Culture, Number 65

GREENWOOD PRESS
WESTPORT, CONNECTICUT

Published in the United States and Canada by
Greenwood Press, 88 Post Road West, Westport, CT 06881
An imprint of Greenwood Publishing Group, Inc.

English language edition, except the United States and Canada,
published by Flicks Books, Trowbridge, England

First published 1997

Library of Congress Cataloging in Publication Data

Phillips, Ray.
  Edison's kinetoscope and its films : a history to 1896 / by Ray
Phillips.
     p.   cm. -- (Contributions to the study of popular culture,
ISSN 0198-9871 : no. 65)
  Includes bibliographical references and index.
  ISBN 0-313-30508-0 (alk. paper)
  1. Kinetoscope--History--19th century. 2. Edison, Thomas A.
(Thomas Alva), 1847-1931. I. Title. II. Series.
TR885.P48   1997
778.5'34--dc21
                                                     97-12290

Library of Congress Catalog Card Number: 97-12290

ISBN: 0-313-30508-0

Printed in Great Britain

Contents

Acknowledgements

I started this project several years ago as only a serious amateur, with serious doubts about my ability to complete it to even my own satisfaction. If it is successful, it is due to the generous help of some wonderful people, living all over the world, who have been generous and thoughtful with their time and their talents.

In completely random order, let me thank the late Wes Lambert, Kirk Bauer, Glenn Grabinsky and Harvey Dunn. Linda Harris Mehr, Director of the Margaret Herrick Library, Academy of Motion Picture Arts and Sciences, and her staff. The Baker Library at Harvard University. The National Museum of American History, a part of the Smithsonian Institution. In its archives are Gordon Hendricks' notes and manuscripts, generously donated by Guido Castelli. Leah Burt, until recently with Edison National Historic Site, long-time friend and every Edisonia collectors' favourite person! True friend of over 50 years, noted photography collector, Marian Carson. Friends formerly at Eastman House: Phil Condax, Jan-Christopher Horak and Grant Rohmer. William Pretzer of the Henry Ford Museum. David Francis, formerly of the British Film Institute, now Chief of the Motion Picture, Broadcasting, and Recorded Sound Division of the Library of Congress. Allen Koenigsberg, long-time phonograph collector, author and publisher. Eileen Bowser, recently retired from the Museum of Modern Art. Teachers and authors, Ray Wile and Charles Musser. William Radke, of Sydney, Australia. Paul Spehr, formerly of the Library of Congress. Noted collectors, Lawrence A Schlick and Carey Williams, now head of the International Cinema Museum, Chicago. Prolific author of books on coin-operated machines, Richard Bueschell. Collector, author and long-distance friend in Cornwall, England, John Barnes. Noelle Giret and the late Olivier Meston of the Cinémathèque Française. Michelle Aubert and her staff at the Service des Archives du Film. The staff at the National Film and Television Archive, and at the Science Museum (the latter is where I first saw a Kinetoscope, on 10 August 1937), and Stephen Herbert of the Museum of the Moving Image – all in London. The staff of the National Museum of Photography, Film and Television, Bradford, England. Richard Koszarski, of the wonderful new Museum of the Moving Image in Astoria, NY. English collector and author, Richard Brown. Chris Long, Australian author of articles and books on the fascinating early history of motion-pictures in his country. Professor David Shepard of the University of Southern California. "Professor" George Hall and his friend, Bob Martinique, both of Tucson, AZ. Sylvie Robitaille, of the Moving Image and Sound Archives of the National Archives of Canada. David Flaherty of the Flaherty Brothers, who deposited a wealth of early films there. The many members all over the world of the Fédération Internationale des Archives du Film (FIAF) who helpfully answered my questions.

Most of all my thanks go to my wife, Nancy, who loves me, is unbelievably patient with me, and is proud of what I do. To those that I have not specifically thanked, thank you also.

This book is dedicated to the memory of Thomas A Edison, whose life and inventions have fascinated me since I was a boy of ten; his assistant in the development of motion-pictures, W K-L Dickson, and his crew that machined the parts, operated the camera, and developed the film, all in anonymity. Also to the memory of author Gordon Hendricks, whose books gave the first complete account of this beginning of motion-pictures, the Kinetoscope.

Introduction

It was in 1985, when I was trying to find appropriate films for two Kinetoscopes which I was rebuilding, that I found out how little was known about Kinetoscope films or Kinetoscopes themselves. I had assumed that there would be an index of Edison Kinetoscope films readily available, and that film archives would have their copies of these films carefully restored, identified, dated and catalogued. How little I knew!

An astonishing book was Kemp Niver's book, *Motion Pictures from the Library of Congress Paper Print Collection, 1894-1912*, published by the Library of Congress in 1953. Because all the information in this book came from copyright records, and because Edison did not copyright his films until 23 October 1896 (after other people's duplicating of them became a problem), his entire output of films for 1893, 1894, 1895 and most of 1896 – more than 200 films – was omitted. Only two films, copyrighted by Dickson in 1894, were included. The book first lists Edison films under the date 1896, making Edison appear a latecomer to his own invention. As Edison's films before 23 October 1896 were not copyrighted, no paper print copies of them were deposited with the Library of Congress. Consequently, Kemp Niver's study did not include any of these earliest films, and the earliest film restored from a paper print dates from well into 1897.

To fill this gap and to enhance knowledge of Edison and his works, I decided to attempt to compile my own index of Kinetoscope films. As part of my research, I found Gordon Hendricks' books, *The Edison Motion Picture Myth* (1961) and *The Kinetoscope* (1966). A footnote in the latter book said that Hendricks was planning such an index. I looked for one carefully, as I certainly did not want to duplicate work already done, but found none. Indeed, in researching Hendricks' files in the archives of the National Museum of American History, I found no indication that he had even begun such a project. While *The Kinetoscope* was of great help to me, particularly in providing filming dates, and I am grateful to Guido Castelli for permission to draw from it, my index is compiled from more than 30 sources, some never before available to the public.

While working on the index I realised that, although many of us have seen one or more Kinetoscope films projected, as part of a "History of the Movies" or the like, few people now living have ever seen a Kinetoscope, much less viewed a film in one. It seemed to me that a description of Edison's "machinery" used in filming and viewing these films, and of the circumstances surrounding their use, was vital to an understanding and appreciation of the films themselves.

Over the last 59 years, I have examined all the Kinetoscopes and Kinetophones known to exist anywhere in the world, except one – in Lyon. In October 1992, I bought at Sotheby's in London what may be the earliest surviving Kinetoscope, as well as the only one to come to public attention in approximately the last 60 years. I have restored and replicated sixteen Kinetoscopes, of which seven are in museums in five countries. Since all my replicas show films beautifully, their wide dispersion should increase public knowledge and enjoyment of these machines and their quaint films. In October 1992 I also restored the missing phonograph portion of a Kinetophone at the Cinémathèque Française in Paris, thus making its machine the only complete Kinetophone on display anywhere in the world.

Consequently, I feel uniquely qualified to write on these subjects, despite being neither a professional film historian nor a professional author. Now, with the recent centennial of the public introduction of the Kinetoscope, I hope that the reader will gain an increased appreciation of these quaint but fascinating primitive films, their "machinery" and the genius of Thomas A Edison. Many want to tie the beginning of the cinema to screen projection; however, the fact remains that many hundreds of thousands of people in countries all over the world enjoyed Edison motion-pictures through the medium of the Kinetoscope before any films were publicly projected onto a screen. As Terry Ramsaye writes in his monumental 1926 history of motion-pictures, *A Million and One Nights*:

> ...mark you well this Edison peep show Kinetoscope. Every strand in the thread of motion picture destiny runs through it. It is the inescapable link between the gropings of the past and the attainments of the present. Every motion picture machine, every motion picture enterprise, every motion picture personality, screen star or magnate of the screen theatre can be traced to some connection growing out of the little black box that Edison dubbed the Kinetoscope. This is one of the absolute facts of the history of the motion picture. It must be stated most positively, in view of the hundred and one contrary and unfounded assertions of other claimants.
>
> *It is provable that there is not now and never has been subsequent to the year 1888 any motion picture film machine whatsoever of any relation to the screen art of today that is not descended by traceable steps from the Kinetoscope.*[1]

Note

[1] Terry Ramsaye, *A Million and One Nights: A History of the Motion Picture*, volume I (New York: Simon and Schuster, 1926): 72-73. Emphasis in original.

Edison's principal assistant in motion-picture work was William Kennedy-Laurie Dickson, born of English-Scottish parents in 1860. This chapter is in two parts. Firstly, Dickson relates in his own words (excerpted from an article in the December 1933 issue of the *Journal of the Society of Motion Picture Engineers*) how he joined Edison's staff. In the second part, Dickson and his sister, Antonia, are the authors of "Edison's Invention of the Kineto-phonograph", which is reprinted exactly as it appeared in *The Century Illustrated Monthly Magazine* of June 1894, the month of the Kinetoscope's first commercial showing.

*   *   *

In the year 1879 at the age of 19 I had read much of a Mr. Edison in America and his scientific experiments, and so wrote to him to inquire whether he would take me on his staff of experimenters. His reply was not encouraging. It read as follows:

> Menlo Park, N.J.
> March 4, 1879.

> William Kennedy Laurie Dickson,
> Care of Mrs. Aubin,
> 2 Tregunter Road, London W.
> Dear Sir:
> Your favor of the 17th ult. has just been rec'd.
> I cannot increase my list of employees as I have concluded to close my works for at least 2 years, as soon as I have finished experiments with the electric light.

> Very truly,
> T. A. Edison

However, in spite of this, I persuaded my mother and sisters to pull up stakes, and after a stormy crossing we landed in New York and continued down to Richmond, Virginia, by the Old Dominion S.S. Line. After residing there for two years, we youngsters made for New York City early in 1881. I took my book of credentials, etc. to show Mr. Edison at his office at 65 Fifth Avenue, in case I should be lucky enough to gain an interview.

My reception was unique. 'But I told you not to come, didn't I?' said Mr. Edison. I agreed, but told him I couldn't have done otherwise after reading about the work in which he was engaged. He watched my face while turning my testimonials over, until I had to remind him please to read them. He only replied, 'I reckon they are all right; you had better take your coat off and get to work.' I had won.

He then gave me a note to Mr. Charles Clark, chief mathematician, and another to Mr. W. S. Andrews, superintendent of the Goerk St. testing and experimental department of the Edison Electric Works, under whose able and kindly tutelage I secured a good knowledge of what was wanted. The following year, with Mr. Edison's approval, Mr. W. S. Andrews gave me his place while he traveled through the United States planning and erecting light and power stations.

My tests and experiments under Mr. Edison's direct instructions were indescribably interesting. We attempted to arrive at a fixed standardization of all electrical apparatus for home and power stations, such as type of dynamo, motors, lamps, meters, etc. One test or series of experiments stands out very clearly in my mind. I had the good fortune to help Mr. Edison to determine the meaning of the 'Edison effect,' or first concept of the famous 'valve' used now in radio apparatus.

In 1885 Edison took me away from the Electric Works at Goerk St. to assist him in his private laboratory at Newark, N.J., where I was given research problems to work on. In 1887 Mr. Edison, who knew that I was keen on photography, disclosed his favorite scheme of joining his phonograph to pictures taken photographically with a device like the 'Zoetrope'.

He was then erecting his large laboratory at Orange, N.J., in which, as soon as completed, I was allowed to select two large rooms; namely No. 5 on the first floor for the kinetophonograph experiments, and No. 14 above for magnetic ore separation work, analysis, etc.

*　　*　　*

This takes Dickson's story up to the beginning of his motion-picture experiments. Robert Conot, in *A Streak of Luck: The Life and Legend of Thomas Alva Edison* (New York: Seaview Books, 1979: 322), has a different version. He states that Dickson came to New York but made repeated, unsuccessful attempts to see Edison, and that in 1885 Dickson had been working with a group of associates on a new form of insulation. He left his associates, took his insulation with him and went to work for Edison: "Since Dickson's means of entry into Edison's service was none too commendable, Dickson in his own account obscured it and predated it by four years"!

In the following article, several statements should be treated with some scepticism. One appears towards the end of the second column on page 208, starting with "When a phonograph record..." through to the second column, third line of page 210. It is likely that this was only wishful thinking, as was the description, a few lines from the end of page 210 (starting "Projected stereoscopically...") of films in "3D", followed by a vivid description, ending at the first column, 18th line of page 212, of exquisitely synchronised sound with film! Dickson's excesses give him away, as no phonograph of that day could record a dancer's "soft-sounding footfalls"!

But give credit to Dickson's wishful thinking – even vision. Read the final column of page 214 and try to find one single thing he forecasts which has not come to pass!

*　　*　　*

Following now is the complete article entitled "Edison's Invention of the Kineto-phonograph", as written and illustrated by W K-L Dickson and his sister, Antonia, and published in *The Century Illustrated Monthly Magazine* of June 1894.

In the year 1887, the idea occurred to me that it was possible to devise an instrument which should do for the eye what the phonograph does for the ear, and that by a combination of the two, all motion and sound could be recorded and reproduced simultaneously. This idea, the germ of which came from the little toy called the Zoetrope, and the work of Muybridge, Marié, and others has now been accomplished, so that every change of facial expression can be recorded and reproduced life size. The Kinetoscope is only a small model illustrating the present stage of progress but with each succeeding month new possibilities are brought into view. I believe that in coming years by my own work and that of Dickson, Muybridge Marié and others who will doubtless enter the field, that grand opera can be given at the Metropolitan Opera House at New York without any material change from the original, and with artists and musicians long since dead.

The following article which gives an able and reliable account of the invention has my entire endorsation. The authors are peculiarly well qualified for their task from a literary standpoint and the exceptional opportunities which Mr Dickson has had in the fruition of the work.

Thomas A. Edison

THE synchronous attachment of photography with the phonograph was early contemplated by Mr. Edison, in order to record and give back the impressions to the eye as well as to the ear.

The comprehensive term for this invention is the kineto-phonograph. The dual "taking-age impressed on the sensitive surface of the shell. The photographic portion of the undertaking was seriously hampered by the defects of the materials at hand, which, however excellent in themselves, offered no substance sufficiently sensitive. How to secure clear-cut outlines, or indeed any outlines at all, to-

DRAWN BY E. J. MEEKER.

INTERIOR OF THE KINETOGRAPHIC THEATER, EDISON'S LABORATORY, ORANGE, N. J., SHOWING PHONOGRAPH AND KINETOGRAPH.

machine" is the phono-kinetograph, and the reproducing-machine the phono-kinetoscope, in contradistinction to the kinetograph and the kinetoscope, which relate respectively to the taking and reproduction of movable but *soundless* objects.

The initial experiments took the form of microscopic pin-point photographs, placed on a cylindrical shell, corresponding in size to the ordinary phonograph cylinder. These two cylinders were then placed side by side on a shaft, and the sound record was taken as near as possible synchronously with the photographic image on the sensitive surface of the shell. The photographic portion gether with phenomenal speed, was the problem which puzzled the experimenters. The Daguerre, albumen, and kindred processes met the first requirements, but failed when subjected to the test of speed. These methods were therefore regretfully abandoned, a certain precipitate of knowledge being retained, and a bold leap was made to the Maddox gelatine bromide of silver emulsion, with which the cylinders were coated. This process gave rise to a new and serious difficulty. The bromide of silver haloids, held in suspension with the emulsion, showed themselves in an exaggerated coarse-

[1] The text and pictures of this article copyright, 1894, by ANTONIA & W. K. L. DICKSON.
The photographs are by Mr. Dickson.

ness when it became a question of enlarging the pin-point photographs to the dignity of one eighth of an inch, projecting them upon a screen, or viewing them through a binocular microscope. Each accession of size augmented the difficulty, and it was resolved to abandon that line of experiment, and to revolutionize the whole nature of the proceedings by discarding these small photographs, and substituting a series of very much larger impressions affixed to the outer edge of a swiftly rotating wheel, or disk, and supplied with a number of pins, so arranged as to project under the center of each picture. On the rear of the disk, upon a stand, was placed a Geissler tube, connected with an induction coil, the primary wire of which, operated by the pins, produced a rupture of the primary current, which, in its turn, through the medium of the secondary current, lighted up the Geissler tube at the precise moment when a picture crossed its range of view. This electrical discharge was performed in such an inappreciable fraction of time, the succession of pictures was so rapid, and the whole mechanism so nearly perfect, that the goal of the inventor seemed almost reached.

Then followed some experiments with drums, over which sheets of sensitized celluloid film were drawn, the edges being pressed into a narrow slot in the surface, similar in construction to the old tin-foil phonograph. A starting- and stopping-device very similar to the one now in use was also applied. The pictures were then taken spirally to the number of two hundred or so, but were limited in size, owing to the rotundity of surface, which brought only the center of the picture into focus. The sheet of celluloid was then developed, fixed, etc., and placed upon a transparent drum, bristling at its outer edge with brass pins. When the drum was rapidly turned, these came in contact with the primary current of an induction coil, and each image was lighted up in the same manner as described in the previous disk experiment, with this difference only, that the inside of the drum was illuminated.

The next step was the adoption of a highly sensitized strip of celluloid half an inch wide; but this proving unsatisfactory, owing to inadequate size, one-inch pictures were substituted on a band one and a half inches wide, the additional width being required for the perforations on the outer edge. These perforations occur at close and regular intervals, in order to enable the teeth of a locking-device to hold the film steady for nine tenths of the one forty-sixth part of a second, when a shutter opens rapidly and admits a beam of light, causing an image or phase in the movement of the subject. The film is then jerked forward in the remaining one tenth of the one forty-sixth part of a

second, and held at rest while the shutter has again made its round, admitting another circle of light, and so on until forty-six impressions are taken a second, or 2760 a minute. This speed yields 165,600 pictures in an hour, an amount amply sufficient for an evening's entertainment, when unreeled before the eye. By connecting the two ends of the strip, and thus forming a continuous band, the pictures can be indefinitely multiplied. In this connection it is interesting to note that were the spasmodic motions added up by themselves, exclusive of arrests, on the same principle that a train record is computed independent of stoppages, the incredible speed of twenty-six miles an hour would be shown.

The advantage of this system over a continuous band, and of a slotted shutter forging widely ahead of the film, would be this, that in that case only the fractional degree of light comprised in the $\frac{1}{2720}$ part of a second is allowed to penetrate to the film at a complete sacrifice of all detail, whereas, in the present system of stopping and starting, each picture gets one hundredth part of a second's exposure, with a lens but slightly stopped down — time amply sufficient, as any photographer knows, for the attainment of excellent detail even in an ordinarily good light. It must be understood that only one camera is used for taking these strips, and not a battery of cameras, as in Mr. Muybridge's photographs of "The Horse in Motion."[1]

The next step, after making the negative band, is to form a positive or finished series of reproductions from the negative, which is passed through a machine for the purpose, in conjunction with a blank strip of film, which, after development and general treatment, is replaced in the kinetoscope or phono-kinetoscope, as the case may be. When a phonograph record has been taken simultaneously with such a strip, the two are started together by the use of a simple but effective device, and kept so all through, the phonographic record being in perfect accord with the strip. In this conjunction, the tiny holes with which the edge of the celluloid film is perforated, correspond exactly with the phonographic records, and the several devices of the camera, such as the shifting of the film and the operations of the shutter, are so regulated as to keep pace with the indentation made by the stylus upon the phonographic wax cylinder, one motor serving as a source of common energy to camera and phonograph, when they are electrically and mechanically linked together.

The establishment of harmonious relations between kinetoscope and phonograph was a harrowing task, and would have broken the spirit of inventors less inured to hardship and discour-

1 See THE CENTURY for July, 1882.

THOMAS A. EDISON, 1893.

THE FENCERS. TWO SECTIONS OF THE KINETOSCOPIC BAND,
SHOWING MINUTE GRADATIONS IN POSE.

most scrupulous nicety of adjustment has been achieved, with the resultant effects of realistic life, audibly and visually expressed.

The process of "taking" is variously performed: by artificial light in the photographic department, or by daylight under the improved conditions of the new theater, of which we shall speak. The actors, when more than one in number, are kept as close together as possible, and exposed either to the glare of the sun, to the blinding light of four parabolic magnesium lamps, or to the light of twenty arc-lamps, provided with highly actinic carbons, supplied with powerful reflectors equal to about 50,000 candle-power. This radiance is concentrated upon the performers while the kinetograph and phonograph are hard at work storing up records and impressions for future reproduction.

A popular and inexpensive adaptation of kinetoscopic methods is in the form of the well-known nickel-in-the-slot, a machine consisting of a cabinet containing an electrical motor and batteries for operating the mechanism which acts as the impelling power to the film. The film is in the shape of an endless band fifty feet in length, which is passed through the field of a magnifying-glass perpendicularly placed. The photographic impressions pass before the eye at the rate of forty-six per second, through the medium of a rotating, slotted disk, the slot exposing a picture at each revolution, and separating the fractional gradations of pose. Projected against a screen, or viewed through a magnifying-glass, the pictures are eminently lifelike, for the reason that the enlargement need not be more than ten times the original size. On exhibition evenings the projecting-room, which is situated in the upper story of the photographic department, is hung with black, in order to prevent any reflection from the circle of light emanating from the screen at the other end, the projector being placed behind a curtain, also of black, and provided with a single peep-hole for the accommodation of the lens. The effect of these somber draperies, and the weird accompanying monotone of the electric motor attached to the projector, are horribly impressive, and one's sense of the supernatural is heightened when a figure suddenly springs into his path, acting and talking with a vigor which leaves him totally unprepared for its mysterious vanishing. Projected stereoscopically, the results are even more realistic, as those acquainted with that class of phenomena may imagine, and a pleasing rotundity is apparent, which, in ordinary photographic displays, is conspicuous by its absence.

Nothing more vivid or more natural could be imagined than these breathing, audible forms, with their tricks of familiar gesture and speech. The inconceivable swiftness of the photographic

agement than Edison's veterans. The experiments have borne their legitimate fruit, and the

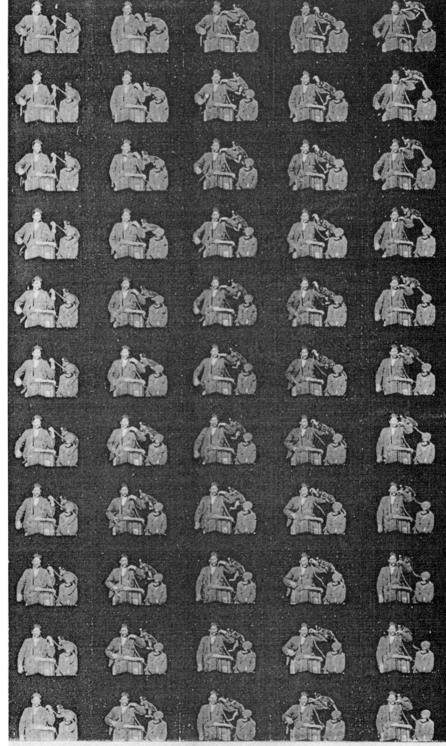

"HEAR ME, NORMA." KINETOSCOPIC VIEWS, SHOWING FIVE SECTIONS OF THE STRIP.

successions, and the exquisite synchronism of the phonographic attachment, have removed the last trace of automatic action, and the illusion is complete. The organ-grinder's monkey jumps upon his shoulder to the accompaniment of a strain from "Norma." The rich strains of a tenor or soprano are heard, set in their appropriate dramatic action; the blacksmith is seen swinging his ponderous hammer, exactly as in life, and the clang of the anvil keeps pace with his symmetrical movements; along with the rhythmical measures of the dancer go her soft-sounding footfalls; the wrestlers and fencers ply their intricate game, guarding, parrying, attacking, thrusting, and throwing, while the quick flash of the eye, the tension of the mouth, the dilated nostrils, and the strong, deep breathing give evidence of the potentialities within.

The photographic rooms, with their singular completeness of appointment, have been the birthplace and nursery of this invention; and the more important processes connected with the preparation and development of the film, together with other mechanical and scientific devices, are still carried on in this department. The exigencies of natural lighting incident to the better "taking" of the subjects, and the lack of a suitable theatrical stage, however, necessitated the construction of a special building, which stands in the center of that cluster of auxiliary houses which forms the suburbs of the laboratory, and which is of so peculiar an appearance as to challenge the attention of the most superficial observer. It obeys no architectural rules, embraces no conventional materials, and follows no accepted scheme of color. Its shape is an irregular oblong, rising abruptly in the center, at which point a movable roof is attached, which is easily raised or lowered at the will of a single manipulator. Its color is a grim and forbidding black, enlivened by the dull luster of many hundred metallic points; its material is paper, covered with pitch and profusely studded with tin nails. With its flapping sail-like roof and ebon hue, it has a weird and semi-nautical appearance, and the uncanny effect is not lessened when, at an imperceptible signal, the great building swings slowly around upon a graphited center, presenting any given angle to the rays of the sun, and rendering the operators independent of diurnal variations. The movable principle of this building is identical with that of our river swinging-bridges, the ends being suspended by iron rods from raised center-posts. This building is known as the Kinetographic Theater, otherwise the "Black Maria." Entering, we are confronted by a system of lights and shades so sharply differentiated as to pain the eye, accustomed to the uniform radiance of the outer air. Later we find that the contrasts are effected by the total exclusion of light from the lower end of the hall, heightened by draperies of impenetrable black, against which stands out in sharp relief the central stage, on which are placed the kinetographic subjects, bathed in the full power of the solar rays pouring down from the movable roof. This distribution of light and shade is productive of the happiest effects in the films, as the different figures are thrown into the broadest relief against the black background, and a distinctness of outline is achieved that would be impossible under ordinary conditions.

At the other end of the hall is a cell, indicated by an ordinary door and an extraordinary window, glazed in panes of a lurid hue, which gives the finishing touch to the Rembrandtesque character of the picture. The compartment is devoted to the purpose of changing the film from the dark box to the kinetographic camera, being provided with a special track, running from the mysterious recesses at the back of the stage to its own special precincts, where fresh films are substituted for the ones already employed. The processes of development, etc., are performed in the main photographic building.

The *dramatis personæ* of this stage are recruited from every characteristic section of social, artistic, and industrial life, and from many a phase of animal existence. One day chronicled the engagement of a troupe of trained bears and their Hungarian leaders. The bears were divided between surly discontent and a comfortable desire to follow the bent of their own inclinations. It was only after much persuasion that they could be induced to subserve the interests of science. One furry monster waddled up a telegraph-pole, to the soliloquy of his own indignant growls; another settled himself comfortably in a deep arm-chair, with the air of a postgraduate in social science; a third rose solemnly on his hind legs and described the measures of some dance, to the weird strains of his keeper's music. Another licked his master's swarthy face, another accepted his keeper's challenge, and engaged with him in a wrestling-match, struggling, hugging, and rolling on the ground.

Of human subjects we have a superfluity, although the utmost discrimination is essential in the selection of themes. The records embrace pugilistic encounters, trapeze and cane exercises, dancing, wrestling, fencing, singing, the playing of instruments, speech-making, the motions involved in the different crafts, horseshoeing, equestrianism, gardening, and many others.

We have yet to speak of the microscopic subjects, a class of especial interest, as lying outside of the unaided vision of man. In the treatment of these infinitesimal types, much

"THE BARBER SHOP."

difficulty was experienced in obtaining a perfect adjustment so as to reproduce the breathing of insects, the circulation of blood in a frog's leg, and other similar processes of nature. The enlargement of animalculæ in a drop of stagnant water proved a most exacting task, but by the aid of a powerful lime-light, concentrated on the water, by the interposition of alum cells for the interception of most of the heat rays, and by the use of a quick shutter and kindred contrivances, the obstacles were overcome, and the final results were such as fully to compensate for the expenditure of time and trouble. We will suppose that the operator has at last been successful in imprisoning the tricksy water-goblins on the sensitive film, in developing the positive strip, and placing it in the projector. A series of inch-large shapes then springs into view, magnified stereoptically to nearly three feet each, gruesome beyond power of expression, and exhibiting an indescribable celerity and rage. Monsters close upon one another in a blind and indiscriminate attack, limbs are dismembered, gory globules are tapped, whole battalions disappear from view. Before the ruthless completeness of these martial tactics the Kilkenny cats fade into insignificance. A curious feature of the performance is the passing of these creatures in and out of focus, appearing sometimes as huge and distorted shadows, then springing into the reality of their own size and proportions.

Hitherto we have limited ourselves to the delineation of detached subjects, but we shall now touch very briefly upon one of our most ambitious schemes, of which these scattered impersonations are but the heralds. Preparations have long been on foot to extend the number of the actors and to increase the stage facilities, with a view to the presentation of an entire play, set in its appropriate frame.

This line of thought may be indefinitely pursued, with application to any given phase of outdoor or indoor life which it is desired to reproduce. Our methods point to ultimate success, and every day adds to the security and the celerity of the undertaking. No scene, however animated and extensive, but will eventually be within reproductive power. Martial evolutions, naval exercises, processions, and countless kindred exhibitions will be recorded for the leisurely gratification of those who are debarred from attendance, or who desire to recall them. The invalid, the isolated country recluse, and the harassed business man can indulge in needed recreation, without undue expenditure, without fear of weather, and without the sacrifice of health or important engagements. Not only our own resources but those of the entire world will be at our command. The advantages to students and historians will be immeasurable. Instead of dry and misleading accounts, tinged with the exaggerations of the chroniclers' minds, our archives will be enriched by the vitalized pictures of great national scenes, instinct with all the glowing personalities which characterized them.

Antonia and W. K. L. Dickson.

DRAWN BY E. J. MEEKER.

EXTERIOR OF EDISON'S KINETOGRAPHIC THEATER, ORANGE, N. J.

Edison tried to take pictures firstly on cylinders, and then on photographic film wrapped around cylinders (illustration 1). He was familiar with cylinders because of his phonograph. When strips of film became available in 1889, he experimented using strips ¾" wide moved horizontally, firstly with notches across the top of the film, then with perforations along the bottom (illustration 7). By 1892, Edison had changed to the format with which we are familiar today. The film runs vertically and is 35mm wide with frames ¾" high, with four pairs of sprocket-holes to each frame. Modern sound films have a somewhat narrower picture, due to the use of a narrow strip on the side of the frame for the sound.

The Service des Archives du Film at Bois d'Arcy, France, has an original Kinetoscope film of *Barber Shop*. Once M. Courbet there realised that I knew my subject, he let me handle it carefully, so I am able to describe it at first hand. My initial impression in holding the film was that it seemed noticeably heavier than today's film. It had a solid feel to it, and I do not think that entirely came from old age or stiffness. It was sturdy and in usable condition, except for the fact that a large proportion of the sprocket-holes had been torn. Even this might not have made it unusable for a Kinetoscope, as the large sprocket-wheel engaged about twelve *pairs* of sprocket-holes at any one time, and only a few of these would have been necessary to keep the film moving.

Looking at the film was a rare and thrilling experience. Today's black and white film, unless there is light behind it, just looks uniformly dark, except for the transparent edges containing the sprocket-holes. With Edison Kinetoscope film, on the other hand, the image appears light. The film stock is not clear, but has the

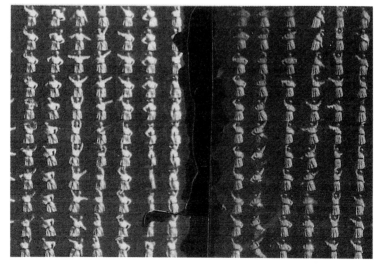

Illustration 1 · A portion of two Edison cylinder strips of 1889, printed full size

Boxing　　　　　　　　　　　Fencing

Illustration 2 · Experimental films from 1892, among the earliest in Edison's final vertical format. These would play on a modern projector. (From an Edison "house organ", *The Phonogram*, autumn 1892, from the collection of Lawrence A Schlick)

appearance of ground-glass, a sort of greyish white. One can see light through it, but one cannot see through it as through a window. This ground-glass quality reflects light so that one can see the image on the film without holding it up to the light.

Time has yellowed the *Barber Shop* somewhat. Except for the image, Kinetoscope films were entirely black. The edges of the film around the sprocket-holes were not transparent, but black. See the illustration of *The Short Stick Dance* (page 186). This frame has not had the edges trimmed off, so one can see how black they are. I described Kinetoscope film as feeling heavier than modern film. Perhaps almost-100-year-old film is simply less flexible; checking this with a micrometer, modern film is 6/1000" thick, while the Kinetoscope film is only 4/1000" thick. This comparative thinness must have contributed to the almost universal heavy sprocket-hole damage that I have since seen in these films.

I have recently obtained five original Kinetoscope films together with Kinetoscope #141. The pictures are in strikingly good condition: clear, bright and free from scratches. The film on four of them is somewhat shrunken, which makes it hard to copy, as the sprocket-holes no longer mesh easily with a modern sprocket-wheel, and are somewhat warped from not having been kept in original film cans. The sprocket-holes are in less good condition. In 1963, the National Film Archive in London (now the National Film and Television Archive) had to make extensive repairs to them before it could copy the films. The fifth film, *Bar Room Scene*, is in poorer condition. It has some tears, and, even with repairs to the sprocket-holes, the NFTVA's copy is excessively jumpy – but at least it exists. The four films in relatively good condition are *Serpentine Dance*, *Barber Shop* (with shoeshine), *Pickaninnies*, and a boxing match. Unlike the ones I saw in France, these appear black from either side. Not until looking through the film can one see the delightfully clear images, which appear to be sunlit from the slight yellowing that age has added. When I viewed the NFTVA's copies in 1991, I had no idea that the originals even existed, much less that a few years later I would own them.

According to Charles Musser, early film stock was procured from Eastman.[1]

When commercial films were begun, and Edison decided to use translucent film stock (in those days it was called "opaque", which was a misnomer, as opaque means that no light can get through), Eastman film stock turned out to be unsatisfactory. Edison then turned to the Blair Camera Company of New York City, and used its stock

Illustration 3 · Edison film-punching machine c.1889 (more likely 1891)
This rather primitive machine calls attention to the fact that Edison initially had to buy film, cut it into strips, and then add his own sprocket holes. I am sure that he soon used a more automatic type of machine, but proper punching continued to be a problem. At least into 1895, films were spoiled because of improper punches. (From the volume described with illustration 11, from the author's collection)

until August 1896, when clear stock began to be used again because it was preferable for projection; Edison then returned to using Eastman stock. "Opaque" film was still used for Kinetoscope films.

It would seem that the sprocket-hole perforations were not added until the film reached New Jersey (illustration 3). Such a seemingly simply mechanical process was not all that easy in those days. The *Index* relates how several films were spoiled by poor perforations. This is not to say that the supplied film was perfect. One reasonably frequent complaint was that the emulsion (and with it the picture) simply peeled away from the film base! Poor perforations and peeling emulsion were not the only problems; by the time films got to the exhibitors, there were also complaints of films being out of focus or lacking sufficient contrast.

The use of a translucent but not transparent film stock was – to some extent at least – following custom. From as early as the 1860s and still into the 1890s, transparent photographs were used as high-quality stereoscopic slides and, in 10x8" format or sometimes larger, were framed and hung in windows where the light from outside showed them off quite handsomely. All those that I have seen have been on a glass plate bound together with a piece of ground-glass, so that the picture could be seen without the distraction of the view beyond (which a clear glass would have provided). In the Kinetoscope's case, the distraction would have been the bright filament of the electric light barely 2" below the film. Instead, the reflector below the light and the diffusion provided by the film base gave an even illumination to the entire frame. From very early days, hand-colouring of films was available. Many films, particularly of dancers, had this done, and some have survived to this day. The cost was about $8.

All Edison's descriptions and those of others have called the length of a Kinetoscope film "50'". This statement is deceptive. I expect that the spool of film put in the camera may well have been 50', but the loop of film that reached the Kinetoscope was not 50': that amount of film could not be crammed into the Kinetoscope. The film loop in the Kinetoscope was a maximum of 42'. This is controlled by the capacity of the machine's film spools and mechanism, and it simply comes out at 42'. Only the specially constructed "fight machines" held longer

Illustration 4 · Original Kinetoscope films in their original film cans.
Thanks to William Pretzer of the Henry Ford Museum, the author was allowed in June 1988 to examine two Kinetoscopes in storage at the Museum. Found on the shelf of one were three original film cans, each with its film virtually intact. Pencilled on the two paper labels and the top of the can were the titles, *Serpentine Dance*, *Sandow* and *Blacksmith Shop*.
Two cylinders are soldered to the tin bottom. Around them the loop is wound doubled. The end, which also forms a loop, is put around the loose third cylinder, which fits into a depression that holds it in place when the lid is put on. The films were sent to the Museum of Modern Art, where they were found to be in generally excellent condition, copied and returned to the Henry Ford Museum. A fourth film was on the film spools of a second, but locked, Kinetoscope. At the time of publication, its subject had not been determined and it had not been copied.
(Photograph by the author)

films. Some films were even shorter. The example of *The Execution of Mary, Queen of Scots* that I saw was on 16mm film, but, in translating its dimensions back to 35mm film, I was surprised to find that the scene was only 28' long. "Mary" laid her head on the block, the axe came down, the head rolled away, the executioner grabbed it and held it up to the camera. In 28' of film, that was impressive. It must also have been somewhat confusing. The counting device on the Kinetoscope provided for showing more than 28' of film. Since there was no beginning and no end to the loop, the scene could have begun anywhere and the film would have repeated some of the action first seen – which was generally very confusing.

Unfortunately, the film in those days had one other quality. It was, and continued to be for many years, what is now called "nitrate film". Nitrate film is not only dangerously flammable, but also can "self-destruct" over time. Very many silent films have disappeared as a result. Film archives worldwide are trying desperately to transfer millions of feet of nitrate film to safety film, so that as many of these historic films as possible can be preserved. Just because film is "nitrate film" does not mean that it will automatically self-destruct. The five films the author acquired with Kinetoscope #141 at auction were bright and clear, as were the ones I examined at the SAF, and the ones at the Henry Ford Museum shown in illustration 4, and they are all at least 102 years old!

To illustrate that not all nitrate film self-destructs, see illustration 4. This shows three original c.1895 Edison Kinetoscope film loops still in their original tin cans and in good condition, except where the film was looped around a tin cylinder. The films are Annabelle's *Serpentine Dance*, *Sandow* and *Blacksmith Shop*. The titles are written in pencil on the labels. I discovered these in June 1988 sitting on a shelf of a Kinetoscope in storage at the Henry Ford Museum, Dearborn, MI. They seem to have been undisturbed since at least 1929, when Henry Ford bought them.

These pictures show how the film was stored: they were not on reels, as we might expect. A loop of the film was put around one of the two cylinders closest together. Then the doubled film was wrapped around both cylinders. When the looped end of the film was reached, it was put around the removable third cylinder, which sat in a depression in the tin bottom, which held it in place when the container was closed. Without these special precautions, the loop would have been in severe danger of being folded flat and thereby creased. This would have rendered the film unusable without cutting out the creased portion and resplicing the film.

In the spring of 1896 the advent of projectors required that film be made with a clear base, which Edison provided, beginning in August, so that more light could reach the screen. Soon 150' films became common. No longer were films looped, but stored on reels, as we are familiar with. Edison issued films on both film stocks, according to customers' wishes. Some exhibitors using projectors even asked for the "opaque" film, as it was called, saying that it gave a softer, pleasanter effect, and that it made faults such as scratches less apparent. With the passage of time, most Kinetoscope films wore out, disintegrated or were simply discarded. The *Index* describes how many films have no known surviving copies.

Before the end of 1896, Edison had parted company with both Raff & Gammon (the Kinetoscope Company) and Maguire & Baucus. Maguire & Baucus catalogues for 1897 indicate that they must have bought the Raff & Gammon film collection, and the Corbett-Courtney and Leonard-Cushing fight films as well, and were selling prints. A 1905 Edison film catalogue, loaned to me by Lawrence A Schlick, contains an amazing number of subjects taken ten or so years earlier for the Kinetoscope. Some subjects must have survived from these later prints. If any reader has or knows of any of the subjects listed in the *Index*, please contact the author, the Museum of Modern Art, Eastman House, the UCLA Film Archive, or a similar institution. Even if there is already a known copy of what you have found, yours may be more complete or in better condition. For those who live outside the United States, please contact the author or your national film archive.

Note

[1]   Charles Musser, *The Emergence of Cinema: The American Screen to 1907* (New York: Charles Scribner's Sons, 1990): 72.

Illustrations 5 and 6 · Edison's "strip" Kinetograph (camera)
(While conceived in 1889, and called "1889", this camera was almost surely not actually built until 1891.)
Exterior and interior of the camera used to produce the films shown in illustrations 7 and 12, which were used on the early Kinetoscope shown in illustration 11. The film moved from left to right, produced round pictures, and had sprocket holes only on the bottom side of the film, which was only ¾" wide. In the lower photograph, note the revolving shutter, behind it the lens, and, at the rear, two holders for the film. At the right are the motor and governor of an early Edison electrically-driven phonograph, most likely used to power the shutter and the gate. At left rear is another Edison electric motor, probably used to operate the take-up spool. The camera survives at the Edison National Historic Site. (Both photographs from the legal document described in illustration 11)

The oldest surviving Kinetograph is the one in illustrations 5 and 6, now in the vault at the Edison National Historic Site. While labelled (for purposes of the 1898 lawsuit) as "1889", Hendricks felt that in 1889-90 Edison was still using film-wrapped cylinders, and that this machine dates to 1891.[1] Certainly, published descriptions and illustrations of films produced by it and the patent application on its matching Kinetoscope all date from 1891. This machine used a ¾ " film, moved horizontally, with sprocket-holes just at the bottom. In 1892, Edison settled on a vertically-moved film strip 35mm wide with frames ¾ " high, sprocket-holes on each side of the film, and four pairs of holes per frame. Except for using a portion of the side of Edison's frame for the sound strip (which makes modern frames appear more nearly square), this is the standard format used today. It is Edison's equipment using this film that we now describe and illustrate.

There is only one surviving 35mm "Kinetograph", as Edison named his motion-picture camera. It is at the Henry Ford Museum, Dearborn, MI. Strangely, there are problems with its authenticity, because it is too pretty! The cabinet is of finely crafted mahogany, and shows no wear, although the machinery shows signs of use (illustration 8). The only existing pictures of Kinetographs from this era are sketches of the interior of the "Black Maria" (illustrations 47 and 48) and one photograph (illustration 10) of two smaller, lighterweight cameras apparently designed for use in the field. All these pictures show cameras in thoroughly utilitarian boxes apparently painted black. Hendricks felt that the Ford camera was made up from some original

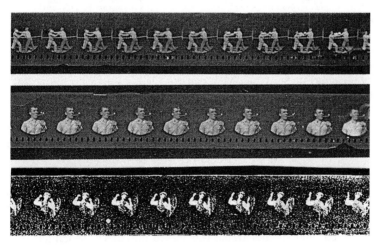

Illustration 7 · Examples of films produced by the camera in illustrations 5 and 6, and used in the Kinetoscope in illustration 11. (From illustrations published in *Scientific American*, 20 June 1891.) The date of this article reinforces Hendricks' belief that this Kinetograph (camera), film and the Kinetoscope in illustration 11 are 1891, rather than 1889.

Illustration 8 · Interior of the Edison Kinetograph (motion-picture camera) at the Henry Ford Museum, Dearborn, MI.
(Photograph by the author)

parts and used as an exhibit in a lawsuit some years after the original cameras had most likely been scrapped. Illustration 9 shows the camera closed. The near side has a handgrip at the top. In order to reach the interior of the camera, this whole side is slid upwards and lifted off. The lens has a cap to keep it clean when not in use. One wonders how many times the cameraman spoiled a film by forgetting to remove the lens cap.

Illustration 8 shows the camera with the side removed, as would be necessary to change film or to adjust the mechanism. The upper reel, which would have been loaded with 50' of unexposed film, is in place. The long tube is an eyepiece used in fine-focusing the camera. Behind it is a shaft which was apparently connected to a crank (now missing) at the rear of the camera. This camera therefore appears to be a reconstruction of a portable camera, as it is not electrically driven as the large "Black Maria" camera was.

The operation of the camera was just as to be expected, with one exception. While the revolving shutter shut off the light, a frame of film was jerked into place. In these earliest of all motion-picture cameras there were no sprocket-wheels above and below the film transport mechanism to form the "loop" with which those who have used motion-picture cameras or projectors are familiar. These missing wheels are unexpected, as virtually all machines since that day have used "loops" to smooth out the movement of the film. Once the frame was in place, the revolving shutter opened and closed, and another frame was jerked into place. Much has been made of the fact that Edison's cameras did not use the "loop". Experts claim that this is the reason why Edison limited his films to 50' – that the inertia of a larger roll would cause the sprockets to rip the film. Yet, as early as June 1894, Edison's camera was taking 150' films. If 150' films produced problems, I have not encountered them.

My opinion is that the camera was capable of taking films longer than 50', but that this usually was not required of it. The Kinetograph (camera) and Kinetoscope "matched". The Kinetograph produced what the Kinetoscope required – a film not of 50', but of 42', as that is all that would fit on its spoolbank. 50' of film, allowing for the length required to load the camera and perhaps a little to spare, would net sufficient film to fill the Kinetoscope.

Illustration 9 · Edison "Kinetograph" (motion-picture camera) at the Henry Ford Museum, Dearborn, MI. (Photograph by the author.)

The Kinetoscope and films could be manufactured and sold at a price and volume to produce a profit to Edison, and the exhibitors could make a profit at a price the public would pay.

In the *(Newark) Daily Advertiser* of 14 November 1896, Gordon Hendricks found a good description of James H White in action, taking a film called *Going to the Fire*:

> The camera was in a wagon with a black cloth wrapped around it... [The cameraman] had stationed himself in front of the Central Railroad depot. He took off his tall hat and waved it in the air. One of his assistants grabbed a crank in the rear of the kinetograph, while the other exposed the lens.[2]

Illustration 10 is the only known photograph of Edison cameramen and cameras of this period in action. The cameramen have been identified as James H White and William Heise. One may carefully discern two cameras: the one in the right rear has the side raised, almost certainly to change film. It is likely that the scene was taken on the occasion of the photographing of *New Black Diamond Express* in April 1897, since a portion of the handcar can be seen in the left rear. The filming used the new transparent film, first issued by Edison in August 1896, in the 150' length. As no batteries, wires or other electrical equipment are visible, these cameras must have been hand-cranked, as was the one in the description. Note also that in both the "Black Maria" and the field the cameras remained stationary while filming was

Illustration 10 · Edison "Kinetographs" and crew. James White leans
on the front machine, while William Heise is at the right.
This is the only known contemporary photograph of Edison Kinetographs (motion-picture
cameras). Earlier Kinetographs had electric motors, but these two apparently were hand-
cranked. Note that the side is open on the rear camera, presumably to change film. The sign in
the rear says "Black Diamond Express/Lehigh Valley Railroad". The photograph was probably
taken on the occasion of the filming of *New Black Diamond Express* in April 1897, as a portion
of the handcar used in that film can be seen at left rear.
(Museum of Modern Art Film Stills Archive)

taking place. There was no "panning" and only one scene. One might think that the rheostat shown in the sketches was used to keep the film at a standard speed, but that seems not to have been the case. Edison's literature usually describes the film as being taken at 46 frames per second. Studies of this, including tests by Hendricks, showed that no film Hendricks experimented with had an exposure rate of over 40 frames per second, and some were as low as sixteen frames. The viewing device, the Kinetoscope, also had a speed-controlling rheostat, so that films taken at various speeds could be accommodated.

There was one other use for the Kinetograph about which almost nothing is known – its use as a projector. In Edison's patent application, he states that "[t]he means for advancing the films and for operating the shutter to expose the pictures may be the same in all particulars as in the apparatus for taking pictures". In the early stages of motion-picture experiments, Dickson worked on projection until instructed by Edison to concentrate on the device that eventually became the Kinetoscope. Edison's reasons are given in the next chapter.

In *The Life & Inventions of Thomas Alva Edison* (1894), Dickson describes the projection room as hung with black draperies.[3] In Edison's suit against the American Mutoscope Company in 1900, James H White, who was working for Holland Brothers (who opened the first Kinetoscope parlour) stated that in October 1894 he saw a projecting machine at Edison's factory: "I saw the entire machine, including the film and the screen on which the pictures were exhibited. I did not see the machine in operation."[4] In a letter to Earl Theisen on 6 April 1933, Dickson states that films were projected using the Kinetograph with a smaller sprocket to allow for shrinkage of the film (note that this occurred in the developing process), and that "it acted perfectly".[5] In 1924, Edison recalled:

> I am very sure that we projected motion pictures on the screen before we stopped making the peep hole machine. One of the peep hole machines was changed so that it would project a picture about twelve inches square. Then a large screen was made and the camera was used. This screen was five feet square. Geneva stop was probably badly made, as the picture was quite unsteady.[6]

Edison did not want to manufacture projectors and did not – until competition forced him to do so in 1896.

Notes

[1]   Gordon Hendricks, *The Edison Motion Picture Myth* (Berkeley; Los Angeles: University of California Press, 1961): 143.

[2]   Quoted in Irving Deutelbaum, *Image: On the Art and Evolution of the Film* (New York: Dover Publications, 1979). This publication is a reprint of the article published in *Image* in 1959.

[3]   W K-L Dickson and Antonia Dickson, *The Life & Inventions of Thomas Alva Edison* (London: Chatto & Windus, 1894): 311.

[4]   Testimony in one of the unpublished briefs of the trial.

[5] Letter in Arthur Clarke Collection, Margaret Herrick Library, Academy of Motion Picture Arts and Sciences.

[6] Terry Ramsaye, *A Million and One Nights: A History of the Motion Picture*, volume I (New York: Simon and Schuster, 1926): 69.

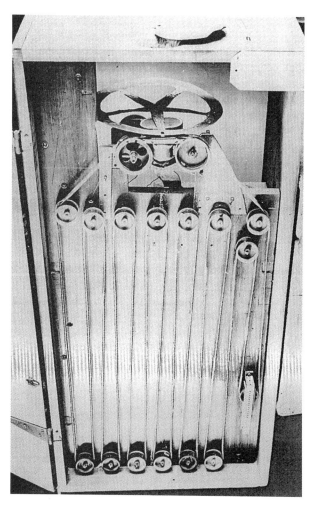

Illustration 11 · Edison's 1889 Kinetoscope
(While conceived in 1889, this machine was almost surely not made until 1891.)
From an original photograph in a volume entitled *Thomas A Edison vs American Mutoscope Co., 168/Records and Complainant's Briefs/Jno. Robert Taylor*. This is one of 34 volumes of original court documents of Edison lawsuits collected and bound for Mr Taylor's law office. While most of the cases refer to the electric light, this volume is on motion pictures, and others refer to phonographs and cylinder records. This photograph was used in 1900. There is some question about the date. Hendricks feels that this machine could not have been made before 1891. This ancestor of the 1894 Kinetoscope used ¾" film which ran sideways, so that it was viewed from the position shown. It seems that the machine has not survived, and it is likely that it was burned in the tragic 1914 fire. (From the author's collection)

Edison applied for a patent on the Kinetoscope on 24 August 1891. His patent, which was granted on 14 March 1893, included projecting a picture on a screen. Illustrations 11 and 12 show the Kinetoscope as it was in 1891. This was when the film still moved sideways, and so the picture is of the front of the machine. By the time the patent was issued, Edison had long since changed to a vertical film movement, and the film was viewed from what in this drawing would be the left side.

Dickson wanted to pursue the idea of projection, but Edison instructed him not to, and instead to develop the Kinetoscope. Edison felt that there would be sufficient demand for Kinetoscopes so that he could recover his costs of development and make a profit. His "clouded crystal ball" told him that there would be no profit in projectors, as he felt that ten of them would fill the demand of the entire United States! Can we laugh and say he was wrong? By 8 December 1899, he had manufactured and sold 973 Kinetoscopes, plus uncounted films for them. He had recovered his costs and had made a substantial profit. It must be remembered that almost all Edison's time, energy and money during this period were being expended on his ore-milling project. Even Dickson's time and laboratory space were divided between the two projects. The ore-milling project was a failure, costing Edison

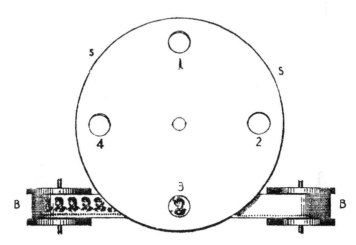

Illustration 12 · Edison's 1889 Kinetoscope, seen from the top
More likely 1891 than 1889. Note the use of ¾" film, perforated only on the bottom side. The film ran from left to right; the shutter revolved clockwise, and had to make only a ¼-turn between frames. The pictures were round, as evident in illustration 7. *Harper's Weekly* 13 June 1891 and *The Electrical Engineer* 24 June 1891, both reprinted in 1900 as part of the Complainant's Exhibit in Edison's 1898 suit against the American Mutoscope Co.
(Author's collection)

millions and almost bankrupting him. As a consequence, his – and Dickson's – time and attention to motion-pictures were severely limited, but the eventual income from the Kinetoscope was most useful.

The ore-milling project was apparently the reason why it took so long for the Kinetoscope to be introduced commercially. It was supposed to have been ready in time for the Columbian Exposition in 1893, and there is some thought that perhaps one made it. But there was no group of them for general viewing by the public.

Hendricks' *The Kinetoscope* (page 46) describes the summer 1893 letting of a contract for 25 Kinetoscopes. Ten were supplied to the first Kinetoscope parlour to open at 1155 Broadway, New York City, ten to Chicago, and five to San Francisco

THE KINETOSCOPE.

No, it is not a very handsome looking cabinet. There is nothing picturesque about it, and the ordinary passer-by would hardly give it a second thought unless he knew what it was. But when we consider *what it will do* we forget its unattractive outward appearance and are filled with wonder at the results. There is the appearance of actual life inside of that plain, unpretending cabinet; men and women moving about as if they were really alive; every gesture and expression reproduced faithfully, and nothing but their size to indicate that they are not human beings acting their parts on the "Stage of Life."

To drop a nickel in the slot and see a noted performer go through his act, exactly as he does it upon the stage, is a more wonderful thing than that which transpired in the Arabian Nights tale of "Aladdin and his Wonderful Lamp." Besides, Aladdin was the only man in the community who had such a lamp. But now-a-days any man who possesses a nickel can produce more wonderful results by dropping it in a phonograph or kinetoscope cabinet than Aladdin could in summoning a Genii by rubbing his lamp. A nickel will at any time summon the *genius* of Edison, and produce far more wonderful results.

Illustration 13 · From The Edison Phonographic News

(Bacigalupi's EDISON Kinetoscope, Phonograph and Graphophone Arcade). More were promptly made and distributed, but the first 25 were soon returned to the factory, and Bacigalupi, at least, was supplied with ten new machines, the ones shown in illustration 37. Why were the first 25 returned? Hendricks gives no reason, but I believe that the discovery of Kinetoscope #141 (see page 100) and the rare

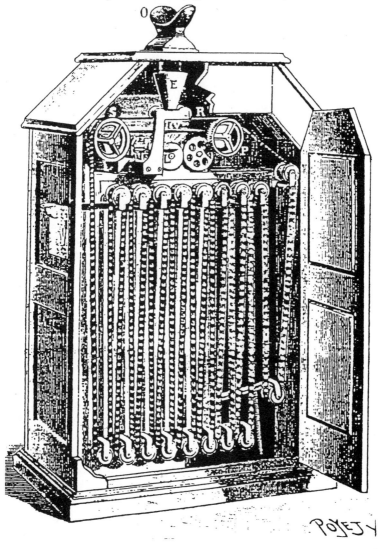

Illustration 14 · Interior of right side of the Kinetoscope
This drawing from the journal *La Nature* is clearer than a photograph would be. The upper "works" are described with illustration 18, but below them are the eighteen velvet-covered wooden spools on which the film is stored. From the sprocket-wheel (P) the film runs clockwise. At the lower right of the cabinet, the spool is on an arm which pivots, and is held down by a spring. This keeps sufficient tension on the film so that it rides smoothly under the viewer and firmly over the sprocket wheel. (*La Nature* journal, 20 October 1894)

Illustration 15 · On/off switch on rear of cabinet
The lever controlling the Kinetoscope is shown in the "off" position. To start the machine, the lever is moved to the right, where it is caught under the brass hook. When the machine's idler wheel has measured the allotted amount of film, the mechanism lifts the hook, allowing a spring to pull the lever back to the "off" position. No effort is made to start a film at its beginning, or stop it at its end. This made little difference to the earlier films, such as acrobats or dancers, but when scenes such as *Execution of Mary, Queen of Scots* came along, the result must have been most unsatisfactory.
(From machine in author's collection)

catalogue reprinted on pages 47-58 provide a likely answer to this previously unexplained event. #141 adds a previously unknown and unique type of device for starting the Kinetoscope, and the catalogue gives it a name, "the pull-rod", as in the "pull-rod Kinetoscope". See the detailed description of it on page 100, and note particularly its shortcomings.

What better reason could there have been for recalling the first 25 than to replace an unsatisfactory starting mechanism? Once the "lever-operated" starting device superseded the "pull-rod", the basic mechanism was not changed for the remainder of the Kinetoscope's existence. All surviving machines other than #141 have the lever-operation, or signs of where it had been, except the one coin-operated machine. The "first twenty-five" were renumbered and resold. Hendricks gives the new serial numbers for fourteen of them. #141 is not one of these, but it could have been one of the eleven unaccounted for, renumbered and shipped to London. Hendricks states that "[n]one of these 'original twenty-five', are, therefore, so far as we know, extant". Because of its primitive nature, #141 has a reasonable claim to be the sole survivor of the "original twenty-five".

Once the Kinetoscope had gone from "pull-rod" starting to what may be called "lever-operated" starting, it remained virtually unchanged – except for those adapted to coin slot operation, those to which phonographs were added to convert them into Kinetophones, and those made particularly to show "fight films". These last had an extra-long cabinet in order to hold the approximately one-minute films, each of which showed one round of the fight (illustration 41). None is known to have survived.

The Kinetoscope (see illustration 13) did exactly what it was designed to do. It showed to the patron a bright, clear, reasonably steady motion-picture, sufficiently long so that the patron could understand and enjoy the action, and sufficiently short so that he/she would want to see the subjects on the adjoining machines.

Illustrations 16 and 17 · On/off switch on rear of cabinet, and interior of motor compartment.
Upper The lever controlling the Kinetoscope is shown in the "on" position, held there by the brass hook. At the end of the allotted time, the machine lifts the hook, allowing a spring to return the lever to the "off" position at the far left. *Lower* At the upper left appears the inside of the controls, showing the resistance coils. In the centre is the 8-volt motor, made by the Edison Manufacturing Company. The pulley wheel on its right is missing its belt which drives the 'works'. It can be seen in illustration 18.

Illustration 18 · Kinetoscope interior - left side

On the left side, the upper compartment is completely concealed by the cabinet, so again a drawing shows what a photograph cannot. As in illustration 14, "O" is the viewer. The patron would be standing at the right. "E" is the funnel, to keep out extraneous light. Below it are two brass spools, covered with black velvet to protect the film, as are all the wheels and spools over which the film passes, except the sprocket wheel. These two spools hold the film steady while it is being viewed. Below them is the circular shutter, which spins clockwise. The ⅛" slit through which the film is seen is at "F". The light is below the shutter at "L". "R" is the film, being pulled to the left by the sprocket wheel "P". "S" is the idler wheel. The worm gear assembly would be just this side of it on the same shaft, but is not shown.

The lower compartment has a door, so most of what can be seen here would be visible with the door open. On the left wall, not shown here but visible in illustration 17, are the on/off controls, which would be used if the machine illustrated were operator-controlled. However, this machine is coin-operated; the mechanism is at "B". I have never seen a machine with a coin device like this one.

On the right side of the motor, the wheel drives a round leather belt which goes up and around the pulley wheels, sending it over to the drive-wheel just to the right of "D". This shaft rotates the shutter and, through a series of gears, drives the sprocket wheel "P", so that the shutter makes one complete revolution each time a frame of the film is centred under the viewer. "D" is a flat coil of resistance wire, by which the speed of the motor and the brightness of the lamp can be altered. Reading the "DIRECTIONS FOR SETTING UP AND OPERATING THE EDISON KINETOSCOPE" in illustration 19 will enable a better understanding the parts and the operation of this machine. (*La Nature* journal, 20 October 1894)

Therefore, while viewing one film for about 30 seconds cost a nickel, the average customer probably parted with 25 cents (perhaps six tickets for 25 cents), and the interested affluent patron with 50 cents!

Let us now travel back in time and space to a Kinetoscope parlour and see what happened. Bacigalupi's in San Francisco is a good example (illustration 37), with a large group of phonographs and some good selections. My favourite is "The Little Bird on Nellie's Hat" and its refrain, "'You don't know Nellie like I do', said the cute little bird on Nellie's hat"! But we came in to look, not to listen! It is 1894 and Bacigalupi's does not yet have a Kinetophone. The phonographs are on the right. On the left is a bank of ten Kinetoscopes, sufficient to present a good choice of films. From the lady near the door you buy six tickets for 25 cents. You walk up and down the row of machines looking at titles. One of the attendants waits for your signal. You decide to see a brand new film of Mme. Alcide Capitaine, "The Perfect Woman", doing her trapeze act. You signal to the attendant and hand him one ticket. He thanks you, takes hold of a small wooden knob on the back of the machine (illustration 15) and, as you peer down into the viewer, he moves the knob from left to right. You hear noises, but do not yet see anything. What is going on? Actually, quite a lot! In a compartment at the bottom of the cabinet are wet batteries producing a total of 8 volts of electricity – only about twice that of a modern flashlight, but with many more amperes. In a compartment above and on the left side of the machine is a large electric motor, made by the Edison Manufacturing Company (illustration 17). It has no cover, and therefore with the door open you can see the coils of wire and the black enamelled metal parts decorated with gold striping. It is amazing that 8-volt batteries can propel a motor of that size and also power the light!

Just to the left of the motor is the inside of the controls, shown in illustrations 15 and 16. Seen from the inside, the lever moved by the knob started with the button on the right and moved to the left. As it touched the second button, a surge of electricity was sent to the motor. As it had to pass through the two coils of resistance wire shown, the electricity was too weak to start the motor, but it did tighten the drive belt, sprocket-wheel and loop of film. A moment later, when the lever left the second button and moved to the third, one coil of the resistance wire was bypassed, and the motor slowly began to move one drive belt, three pulley wheels, seven gears and the shutter. One of the gears started the sprocket-wheel, thus causing the 42' of film to move. The movement of the film started up twenty spools and the large idler pulley (S) (shown in illustration 14). As "S" turned, it started a measuring device that eventually would turn off the machine.

As the lever passes from the third button to the last, the last resistance coil is bypassed, leaving nothing between the full power of the battery and the motor except the rheostat, the little card wrapped with wire just under (D) (illustration 18). This is set by the management to control the speed of the film so that the speed of the performers' motions are appropriate. The rheostat could also be used to vary the brightness of the lamp to suit the wildly varying density of the films.

As the film reaches its viewing speed, the light is turned on and you see Alcide Capitaine in the middle of her trapeze performance. The last thing that happened was that when the lever reached the last button it also lifted a brass hook (illustration 16), which then came down and held the lever in place, so that when the operator released the knob a spring could not immediately pull the lever back, turning off the machine.

All of the above happened in a fraction of a second! Now you are watching Mme. Capitaine's daring feats – but not in silence! The motor is humming and twenty pulley wheels are clacking away while the several wheels, whose bearings could use some oil, are squeaking! You are caught up in the magic of the moment and do not notice. All too soon the light goes out, there is a loud "whack" as the spring pulls the start lever back to "off" and it hits a stop, then silence. You lift your head, slightly dazed to be pulled back so suddenly into the world of reality. You are filled with a sense of wonder, and the feeling that you have seen the birth of you know not what, but something fascinating! You think of Edison, the phonograph, the electric light, and now this!

What, meanwhile, was going on inside the machine? See illustration 18 again. The motor turned the pulley on its right, moving the belt which passed over the pair of pulleys above and rotated "D" clockwise. The vertical shaft above "D" spun the shutter, and at the same time moved a series of gears ending at "P", which combines a gear and the all-important sprocket-wheel. This linkage ensured that, for every time the edge of the sprocket-wheel moved ¾" (one frame), the shutter wheel made one complete revolution. As the mechanism reached viewing speed, the light "L" was turned on. It was not like the ordinary electric light bulbs of the day; they were much larger, perhaps 5" long, and used around 110 volts. This bulb used 8 volts, had a smaller base, and was only about 3½" long. The filament, instead of being a long loop of carbon, had a short, tightly coiled filament to concentrate the light, just as bulbs used in projectors have done ever since.

On the shutter wheel, of black-painted tin about 11½" in diameter, is a ⅛" slit at "F". The sprocket-wheel pulled the film under the viewer "O" with its magnifying glass "E". The shutter is adjusted so that the slit passed over the continuously moving film at the exact moment that each frame was centred under the viewer. The slit permitted the light to shine up through the moving film, but so briefly that the film appeared stationary and the image was bright and clear.

This technique of showing a moving film with brief flashes of light was both a blessing and a curse. It was beautifully simple and gentle on the film, which was far from perfect at this point. The curse was that this technique could not successfully be adapted to projection. The movement of the film, imperceptible at the low level of magnification of the Kinetoscope, became intolerable at the magnification required for projection. In addition, the extremely brief flash of light required produced an unacceptably dim picture when projection was attempted. Several experimenters did make the attempt; all failed.

Now comes a description of how the machine timed your viewing of the film and turned itself off. Read it and believe that Rube Goldberg (the popular American cartoonist of the 1920s and 1930s) must have examined a Kinetoscope at the beginning of his illustrious career of describing wildly improbable mechanical devices! I like to think that perhaps Edison was wintering in Florida when this part of the machine was invented! Unfortunately, he was more likely to have been trying desperately to keep his ore-milling project from failing.

On the same shaft as the idler-wheel "S", which is revolved by the film coming up from off the bottom of the cabinet, is a worm gear. The usefulness of a worm gear is that the shaft with the "worm" on it can turn many times for every turn of the "worm wheel". In this case, the idler pulley (and the "worm") revolved about 40 times in order to give the worm wheel a half-turn. Sticking out from opposite sides of the worm wheel are two ⅛"-long steel pins. The last few of the 40 turns of the worm made one of the steel pins push a lever, which in turn pulled on a thin steel wire. This assembly, at "S", is at the upper front of the cabinet. The on/off mechanism is at the very back of the cabinet, and down in the motor compartment.

In order to send the "off" signal, the wire had to go from the front of the cabinet to the back. Near the back of the cabinet it pulled the top of the back of an "L" shaped piece of brass to the left. This pulled the "toe" of the "L" up, along with a wire fastened to this "toe". The wire goes down through a hole into the motor compartment where it pulled a lever fastened to the brass hook on the back of the machine that is holding the on/off lever to "on". When the hook was pulled up, releasing the lever, a spring pulled it back to "off".

While you have been enjoying yourself, I have been getting hungry. I convince you that we should lunch at one of San Francisco's famous restaurants, and come back later to use the balance of your tickets.

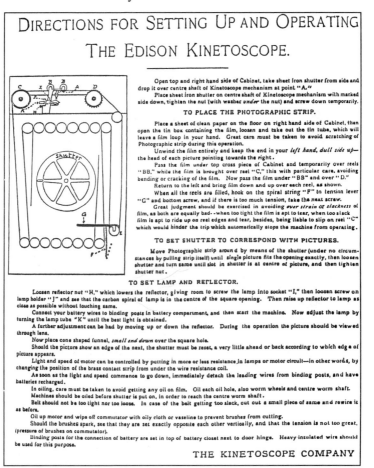

Illustration 19 · From a damaged original found pasted inside the Kinetoscope at Eastman House, Rochester, NY. Restored by the author. (Author's collection)

Illustration 20 · Interior view of 1889 photographic studio (taken in 1894). Studio construct by Dickson while Edison was in Europe (US Department of the Interior, National Park Service, Edison National Historic Site).

In late 1892, progress in motion-picture experiments rendered out-of-date the "photographic building" (illustrations 20 and 21) that Dickson had caused to be built in 1889. As a consequence, the building which came to be famous as the "Black Maria" was built on part of Edison's West Orange laboratory grounds. Work began in December 1892 and was completed in the following February.

The building was about 15' wide and 50' long, very lightly constructed of lumber covered with black tar paper outside and painted black inside. It was designed to turn on a central pivot, with steel wheels underneath each end running on a circular wooden track. It was hand-pushed to follow the sun so that light shone through the roof, which was opened for the purpose, directly onto the stage. Much of the time it must have been miserably uncomfortable, hot and without ventilation in the summer, and bitterly cold in winter.

Illustration 21 · The 1889 photographic building, exterior, winter 1894
Many early experiments and films were made in this building, which was a predecessor of the "Black Maria". Some films made here, such as *Sandow*, were reshot in the "Black Maria" for commercial release. After the latter was built, the building illustrated here was used for film processing and storage. In the interior photograph (illustration 20), notice that the entire roof was of glass, not just the side window. On the left and right are Kinetoscopes in cabinets (and on the left a viewer), differing from the style settled upon when production began. (*Photographic Times* January 1895, in Gordon Hendricks, *Origin of the American Film*)

It was originally without heat, but one small stove was added later. Since Kinetoscope films were taken at up to 40 frames per second, the rather "slow" film available required full sunlight to obtain adequate exposure. So began the world's first motion-picture studio. The name "Black Maria" came from the black tar-papered building's resemblance to the big black patrol wagons used by the New York Police Department, which were called by that name. In it, new films were made in preparation for the introduction of the Kinetoscope, followed by large-scale production to satisfy the exhibitors' demand for new product. Several old subjects were reshot when the original negatives wore out.

In illustration 26 of the "Black Maria", inside, at the right end, was a darkroom where the camera was opened and the film changed. This room had a small window with a sliding shutter. The glass was dark red "ruby" glass. The faint red light that entered allowed the cameraman to see dimly without affecting the film of that time, which was quite insensitive to red light.

The large black-painted camera sat on a large wooden stand equipped with steel rollers (illustration 22). When the darkroom door was open, the entire camera and stand combination could be pushed on a track leading into the centre station and up towards the stage. On the left was the stage, illuminated by the sun through an

Illustration 22 · A typical scene in the "Black Maria"
Annabelle performs her *Serpentine Dance* for the Kinetograph. Gordon Hendricks tentatively identifies the man on the far right as W K-L Dickson. Note the roof opened to the sky, the "MB" on at the right front of the stage, signifying that this film is being taken for Maguire & Baucus. The men are wearing not only coats, but also hats. It was probably most uncomfortably cold, as this sketch was probably made not long before it appeared in the February 1895 issue of *Frank Leslie's Popular Monthly*.

Illustration 23 · Earliest known photograph of the "Black Maria"
Taken between 5 and 8 March 1894. The man on the left shows how the building is revolved.
Near the door is William Heise, staff cameraman. On the roof is Fred Ott, and standing with
one of his fighting cocks under his arm is Fred Devonald. Behind him is the wire cage in which
the birds fought for several Kinetoscope subjects.
(US Department of the Interior, National Park Service, Edison National Historic Site)

---

open roof. Several times in his writings Dickson refers to illumination by electricity, but there is no physical evidence that this ever occurred.

Many famous films were taken in the "Maria". Hendricks says that even what he describes as the first outdoor film, *Caicedo, the Rope Dancer*, was taken by turning the Black Maria's camera sideways and shooting through the open door! The building provided electricity to operate the camera. In the sketches of the interior can be dimly seen two wires leading from the wall to the camera. I have never found any description of the camera that indicated what voltage motor drove it. I conjecture that 8 volts was used, supplied by batteries stored elsewhere, perhaps in a closet. 8-volt battery-powered motors were made by the Edison Manufacturing Company at that time, and they were used in every Kinetoscope. However, motors using other voltages were made, and eventually those using the 110 volts with which we are more familiar in the United States. In a picture of February 1895, Hendricks saw wires which presumably came from the laboratory's central power plant. If that is the case, they may have been added during the winter 1894 expansion of the building, and brought in higher voltage. A more elaborate electrical system is shown in a sketch illustrated in the description of the "Kinetophone".

In the winter of 1894-95 the building, including the stage, was enlarged (illustration 24). The railings at the sides of the stage, with their ornamental newel posts, were removed and replaced with the other cruder railings shown in illustration 25, with the four stage hands standing on the brightly illuminated stage. In the foreground, notice the barely visible camera tracks and, hanging from the left, the ropes with their counterweights. These ropes probably controlled both the hinged roof and backdrops like the one partly visible behind the stage. The films taken in the

Illustration 24 · The expanded "Black Maria", winter 1894
Note the door, enlarged to facilitate the use of "sets", and the lengthened building. In this picture, the roof is opened to the proper place for photographing. Note that the tree appears to have moved to the other end of the building; the result of the buildings having been turned halfway round compared to the photograph in illustration 23.
(National Park Service, Edison National Historic Site)

"Black Maria" were not processed in it; the darkroom was only for unloading and reloading the camera. Developing and printing took place in other buildings of the laboratory compound.

The first picture of the "Black Maria" is illustration 23, the earliest known photograph of it. I chose it not only because of that, but also because of the activity shown. Taken between 5 and 8 March 1894, according to Hendricks,[1] it shows at the far left a man demonstrating how the building was revolved. In Hendricks' copy of the photograph, he said: "Through the open door could be seen the sign used in the film the *Barber Shop*". My copy seems too dark, as no sign is evident. On the roof is Fred Ott, and near the door may be seen William Heise, who built some Kinetoscopes and was the staff cameraman. Towards the right, Fred Devonald holds one of his fighting cocks under his arm. He stands before the wire cage in which the birds fought in *Roosters*, one of the ten films shown at the introduction of the Kinetoscope that April, and in at least one other similar film.

When filming was underway, the roof, shown in a vertical position, rested on the framework at the right end of the building. This is shown in the second exterior photograph of the building (illustration 24), taken after the building was enlarged in the winter of 1894. Notice how the main door was enlarged, at the expense of losing the window, to facilitate the use of "props" and stage sets. Another door was added towards the right.

Note the enormous timber leaning against the building, and notice that it appears also in the earlier photograph (illustration 23). I have never read a description of the "Maria" that described the use of this timber, and I must have looked at similar photographs a hundred times before I suddenly realised its purpose. This timber is fastened to the two steel I-beams on which rest the centre of the building and the pivot on which the building turns. The upper end of this huge timber is meant to be swung out and down until it is parallel to the ground, and the inner end locked between the I-beams. Then it and probably a matching timber on the other side of the building can be pushed to assist in turning the building. Without them, pushing at opposite ends of the lightly constructed 50' long building would almost certainly have twisted it out of shape.

As time passed, the "Black Maria" fell out of use, and virtually all references to it in motion-picture history books cease. I have found only one mention of its later use. F H Richardson in *What Happened in the Beginning* (New York: Motion Picture World, 1910) states that it was "used for a time to develop films for the Vitascope". This could have been as early as autumn 1896, when the Vitascope was introduced (see illustration 27). This conjecture is reinforced by a statement in *Before Hollywood*, edited by Jay Leyda and Charles Musser. In describing the film there entitled *Blackton Sketching Edison* (see the *Index* under its formal title, 97. *SKETCHING MR. EDISON*. BLACKMAN [sic], THE "WORLD" ARTIST AT WORK), the authors state that the film "was probably shot at Raff and Gammon's

Illustration 25 · Stage-hands on the "Black Maria" stage
Notice the railings. Their crude shape was a result of the winter 1894 remodelling. The camera's tracks are just visible leading up towards the chair. The counterweights at left and right probably helped to control the open roof, as well as the backdrop. Backdrops were seldom used in the "Black Maria". Most acts had a black background supplied not by a black canvas, but by the "black tunnel" (illustration 26) which began directly behind the brilliantly lit stage.
(US Department of the Interior, National Park Service, Edison National Historic Site)

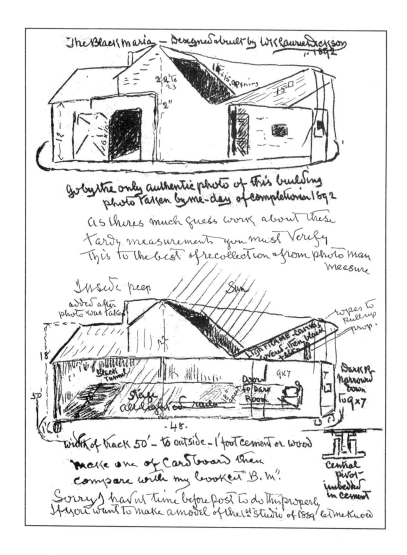

Illustration 26 · Exterior and interior sketches of the "Black Maria"
This was sent by W K-L Dickson to Earl Theisen on approximately 5 July 1933. The interior sketch appears to be the only known illustration of the entire interior. Note that the "black tunnel" was used instead of a painted backdrop to give the black background seen in so many early Kinetoscope films. (Earl Theisen Collection, Margaret Herrick Library, Academy of Motion Picture Arts and Sciences)

makeshift rooftop studio on West 28th Street, New York City, in July or August, 1896". I knew that filming did not stop, so if the "Black Maria" was abandoned, there had to be another studio, and this apparently was it. The "Black Maria" was demolished in 1903. By this time Edison had a studio in downtown New York on 21st Street, and in July 1907 he moved into a handsome new studio in the Bronx (illustrations 28 and 29). Here millions of feet of film were produced until the studio closed in February 1918, a victim of competition.

When the current replica of the "Black Maria" was built in 1953, it had to be built from photographs, sketches and probably some recollections. No blueprints could be found, and the arrangement of the rooms is conjectural. For many years it was on exhibit, but I was told that it has been closed in recent years. In June 1994 it was not a part of the public tour. The guide explained that it was small inside, which made it inconvenient for tours, and, as it was a hot day, the inside would be excessively hot. However, upon my shocked protests, he kindly sent the rest of the tour back to the lobby and unlocked the door for me. He was correct; the heat was truly intolerable for more than a few seconds at a time. It is no wonder that 100 years ago some artists refused to appear there! These few seconds showed that there were no replicas of the stage, the camera, its stand or the tracks on which they travelled. On the far wall was the electrical wiring and meter, as shown in the sketches. The ends of the wires lay on the floor. Other than that the building contained nothing but some metal folding chairs and scrap lumber. Nevertheless, the building itself seemed in good condition, and it was a thrill to see it.

Illustration 27 · Film processing at the Vitagraph plant, 1897
The interior of the "Black Maria" would have looked just like this after filmmaking ceased and *it* was used for film processing. Visible are several cylindrical drums made of wooden slats. The film was wrapped around them in a spiral for processing. The man on the right is revolving a film-covered drum, the lower half of which sits in a trough of water to wash the film.

Illustration 28 · Edison Studio, Bedford Park, Bronx,
New York (1908)

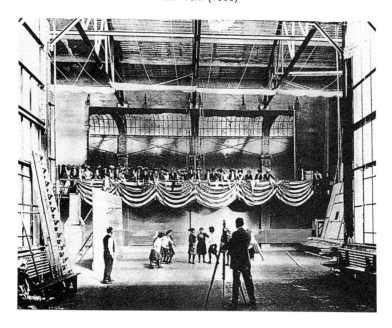

Illustration 29 · Interior of the Edison Studio, 1908
Henry Cronjager filming *A Country Girl's Seminary Life and Experiences*.

Recently, a fascinating sketch came to my attention. In the early 1930s Earl Theisen wanted to build a model of the Black Maria. Dickson was still alive and living on Jersey, in the English Channel. Theisen wrote to ask him for help, and was sent the sketches in illustration 26. The lower sketch is the only known depiction of the entire interior layout of the building. The script may be a bit difficult to decipher. In the sketch the wording reads as follows, from left to right: "Black Tunnel", "Stage all lighted", "Rails 18" apart", "Doors to Dark Room", "9x7" and, at the extreme right, "Dark R narrowed down to 9x7". At an angle and above to the right are the words "Light FRAME-canvas covered-then black felt-" and in very light script, "ropes to pull up prop". The original is in the Earl Theisen Collection at the Margaret Herrick Library, AMPAS, and this may well be the first time it has been reproduced for publication.

Note

[1]   Gordon Hendricks, *The Kinetoscope: America's First Commercially Successful Motion Picture Exhibitor* (New York, 1966): illustration 5.

Selling in quantity, especially a new product, requires advertising. The best kind of advertising is publicity, and Edison was an expert at this. At the beginning of motion-pictures, in the form of the Kinetoscope, a stream of books and articles in magazines and newspapers began that has long since become a flood! To describe the new product, a catalogue was required.

Edison already had a network of Phonograph wholesalers in place, each with a "territory". When Kinetoscopes and films became available, these dealers – of which the Ohio Phonograph was a prominent example – began to stock and sell them. They solicited their customers with catalogues such as the following rare (and very possibly unique) example. This is reprinted here as a facsimile through the courtesy of its owner, Lawrence A Schlick. The catalogue is a survivor from August 1895 and, while it bears the Ohio Phonograph Company name, it is most likely that it was produced by Edison or by the Kinetoscope Company, and that a certain number were imprinted for the Ohio Phonograph Company. On page 12 of the catalogue there is reference to an article in *The Century Illustrated Monthly Magazine* of June 1894 for more general information. Pages 5-13 of this book contain that article.

Many things about this catalogue hint that it is largely a reprint of one issued a year earlier, at the very beginning of the Kinetoscope. Two machines are offered, "pull-rod" or "nickel-in-slot", although the "pull-rod" feature had been abandoned almost immediately. Although New *Barber Shop*, *Blacksmith Shop* and the *Barroom* films had been taken months before, they are not substituted for the originals. Hand-tinting of films, particularly dance films, was very popular, but is not offered. Even though Kinetophones had been introduced in the spring, no cylinders are offered for them. The only updating seems to be that many early films had been dropped.

*　　*　　*

The Edison Kinetoscope.

Price-List, August, 1895.

⊹THE OHIO PHONOGRAPH CO.⊹

411 ELM STREET, - CINCINNATI, O.

EDISON'S LATEST WONDER.

———➤➤◉◅◅———

THE KINETOSCOPE.

———➤➤◉◅◅———

MR. EDISON had proven, in his laboratory, that the perfected Kinetoscope was only a question of time, and he hoped to produce a practical exhibition machine in time to exhibit at the great World's Columbian Exposition. Vague rumors of a new marvel emanating from Edison's inventive brain spread like wild-fire, and, as a consequence, thousands of visitors to the Fair inquired daily at the Edison exhibits concerning the new machine, which was to reproduce moving figures and scenes before the eye, as the Phonograph reproduced sounds to the ear. But great inventions take time, extended experiment, and large expense before reaching perfection, and thus it was that the Kinetoscope was not perfected in time for the great Fair, and the eager anticipations of numberless Americans and Europeans were, for the time, doomed to disappointment.

But after years of experiment, test, and detail work, the Kinetoscope has been perfected, and is now being exhibited throughout the world.

≼ DESCRIPTION. ≽

This machine is in the shape of a handsome hardwood cabinet, about the size of a coin-slot Phonograph. This cabinet contains a mechanical device, operated by electricity, which is so constructed as to run the films (containing the views photographed from life by the Kinetograph) past a given point at a speed of about 46 each second of time. The films pass over a series of rollers, which hold them steady and secure accurate results.

In the top of the cabinet of the Kinetoscope is a small window covered with clear glass. The person who desires to witness the reproduction of the views looks down through this window, and the film passes before his eyes with such rapidity that he beholds one continuous view, which we will endeavor to explain in a practical and easily understood way.

Perhaps the most simple method of explanation will be to describe an actual scene. Among many subjects thus far secured for the Kinetoscope is

....THE FIRE SCENE....

The beholder, looking through the window of the Kinetoscope, sees a burning building, with volumes of smoke rolling upward. The firemen, in uniform, have placed the ladders in position, and are throwing a stream of water from the hose upon the conflagration. One fireman ascends the ladder, and, fastening himself to it with his belt hook, receives in his arms a young lady in her night dress, and also a boy, who are passed from the window of the burning building by another fireman, and he in turn passes them to a fireman standing upon the ground; thus they are saved from the flames.

A scene from Hoyt's "MILK WHITE FLAG"

shows thirty-four persons of both sexes in their stage costumes, reproducing their evolutions precisely as they appear upon the stage of the theatre, and showing every motion accurately and true of life.

This is the largest number of figures ever shown on a Kinetoscope film.

—3—

...THE BUCKING BRONCHO...

is a typical Western frontier scene, and shows a cowboy in his accustomed garb, attempting to ride a vicious bucking broncho, while a crowd of curious lookers-on are standing idly by. Another cowboy, standing on a high fence, repeatedly fires his revolver; and so faithful and accurate is the portrayal of this scene that even the puff of smoke which darts from the mouth of the pistol, at its discharge, is distinctly seen.

These are but three from nearly a hundred interesting subjects now exhibited through the medium of the Kinetoscope. As our list of these "Subjects" is being constantly added to, we issue it in the form of bulletins, which are mailed to owners of Kinetoscopes throughout the United States and Canada.

OF INTEREST TO EXHIBITORS.

Replying to the numerous inquiries regarding the earnings of the Kinetoscope, we will give a few reports of earnings which have come to us from exhibitors :

From one exhibit of eight machines, a total of over $8,000 was taken during a period of less than three months, when the machines were moved to another city. This rate, continued through the year, would amount to about $25,000 from eight machines.

Holland Brothers, well-known exhibitors of the Kinetoscope, report receipts from ten machines as follows:

First day, ... $155.70.
Second day, ... 150.70.
Third day, ... 152.60.

After these three days the receipts, although not so phenomenally large, continued very high for quite a period.

The same firm also reports from four machines, in two days, $241,70 or for each day $120,85; and for six machines in one day, $141.35.

WEIGHT, DIMENSIONS, ETC.

Kinetoscopes are shipped almost entirely set up. The very little work required to put them in running order can be done by any person of ordinary intelligence, from the printed directions which accompany each machine.

The machines are incased in handsome oak cabinets, 42 inches high, and occupying about 15x24 inches floor space. The weight complete, crated for shipment, is 185 pounds; boxed, they will weigh about 200 pounds.

An Electric Motor operates the mechanism, and a special Electric Lamp, of about four candle power, is used to light the subject or film.

The Motor and Lamp, combined, take a current of 8 volts and about 7 amperes per hour of actual working time.

The Standard Kinetoscope is made with or without nickel-in-the-slot attachment, and stops automatically at the end of about thirty seconds. One person at a time should look into each machine. In ordering, indicate whether you want pull-rod or nickel-in-slot machine.

The Films containing the pictures are about fifty feet long, and are in form like an endless belt. Each film contains about 800 pictures of the same subject in 800 different positions.

It takes but a few minutes to remove one film and place another upon the machine.

No expert knowledge is required to successfully operate the Kinetoscope, as the machines are simple in construction and very rarely get out of order.

PRICE-LIST.

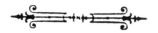

KINETOSCOPES.

Complete (without battery or film) . . . $250 00
Discount on two machines or more.

FILMS.

(Subjects for Exhibition) $10 00 each and upward.
See list and prices attached.

BATTERIES.

These are put in special "Nests" (Hard Wood Cabinets) of 4 cells each, giving a voltage of over 8.
Each "Nest" will run **one or two** Kinetoscopes.
By special arrangement with the manufacturers, we
are enabled to offer cells at the lowest market
price.
"Bradbury-Stone" (capacity about 150 ampere
hours) per "Nest," $50 00
Full directions for re-charging and care of Batteries
accompany each shipment.

COMPLETE OUTFIT.

Consisting of one Kinetoscope, set of Batteries (4)
and two films. $300 00

SPECIAL.

We shall be pleased to quote **Special Prices** on
"outfits" of from two to ten machines, including
battery, films, and everything necessary to a first-
class and complete exhibit of the machine.

PRICE-LIST OF FILMS.

―――(SUBJECTS FOR EXHIBITION.)―――

This list cancels all previously issued by us.—The prices quoted herein are subject to change WITHOUT NOTICE.

DANCES.

The following dance subjects are all first-class exhibits, and are arranged in about the order of their popularity among our customers.

Price, per Film.

Carnival. Skirt Dance by 3 young ladies of the "London Gaiety Girl Company." $15 00

Trilby Quartette. The latest. Burlesque from David Henderson's "Aladdin, Jr." A decided hit, ... 15 00

Lucy Murray. Of the "Gaiety Girl Co." in an attractive Skirt Dance, ... 15 00

Trio. A lively, eccentric dance by Frank Lawton and Misses Williamson and France, of Hoyt's "Milk White Flag." Attractive costumes, ... 15 00

Wilson & Waring. An eccentric dance from "Little Christopher Columbus," by John Wilson, the famous "Tramp," and Miss Bertha Waring. 15 00

Serpentine,   **Butterfly,**   **Sun,** By the famous "Annabelle." These dances are among the finest for the effects of costume, light, and shade, and are very popular. Each, ... 12 50

Sioux Ghost Dance. By genuine Sioux Indians, in full costume and paint. A weird and interesting scene, ... 15 00

Jamies. A burlesque Scotch Dance, in full Highland costume, by Richard Carroll and the Jamies, from the Whitney Opera Company's "Rob Roy." 12 50

Paddle Dance.   **Dance of Rejoicing.** Native dances by Samoan Islanders, as produced at the famous "Midway Plaisance." Each, ... 12 50

―7―

Imperial Japanese Dance. By three
Japanese ladies in full native costume, . 12 50

May Lucas. Eccentric Skirt Dancer, of
the " London Gaiety Girl Company," . 12 50

Elsie Jones. "The Little Magnet," in
her famous Buck Dance, ... 12 50

James Grundy. Buck and Wing Dance,
from "South Before the War," . . . 12 50

Grundy & Frint. "Breakdown," also
from ' South Before the War," . . . 10 00

Pickaninnies. By 3 lively negro boys,
from "The Passing Show," a characteristic dance, ... 12 50

Skirt Dance Dog. A serpentine dance
in costume, performed by one of Prof.
Tschernoff's marvelous trained dogs.
(From Koster & Bial's), ... 10 00

DESCRIPTIVE SCENES.

Bucking Broncho. An out-of-door scene
from "Buffalo Bill's Wild West," showing
an interesting bout between a cowpuncher
and an unruly broncho, ... 15 00

Annie Oakley. The " Little Sure Shot "
of the "Wild West," in an exhibition of
rifle shooting at glass balls, etc., fine
smoke effects, ... 15 00

Buffalo Bill. The noted proprietor of the
" Wild West," in an exhibition of rifle
shooting, ... 12 50

The Dentist's Chair. Represents Dr.
Colton, the famous inventor of "Laughing
Gas," in the act of administering same.
Also shows method of extracting teeth. 10 00

Trilby Death Scene. From David Henderson's Burlesque. Represents Trilby,
Svengali and the Laird. Svengali hypnotizes Trilby and the Laird, then falls dead
across a table. Very funny. The dramatis personæ of this act are made up in
exact imitation of the illustrations given
in Du Maurier's book, ... 15 00

Fire Rescue Scene. Showing uniformed firemen rescuing people from a burning building. Fine smoke effects, . .   15 00

Trilby Hypnotic Scene. Svengali hypnotizes every one in sight, and causes them to go through sundry burlesque performances. Very popular, ...   15 00

Milk White Flag. This scene represents the grand assembly march from the finale of the first act in Hoyt's "Milk White Flag, and contains thirty-four figures in full costume, including Bands, Vivandieres, Drum Corps, Messenger Boys, etc., etc. A very fine subject. 15 00

Band Drill. From Hoyt's "Milk White Flag." Represents the march of the band, with leader at their head playing popular airs, ...   15 00

War Council. Representing Buffalo Bill and a number of his Indian warriors in council, smoking the famous Pipe of Peace.   12 50

Barber Shop. Represents the interior of a "Tonsorial Palace," with customer getting a "shave"; meanwhile "next" is having his shoes polished by the usual darky attendant. This is one of the most popular films ever produced, ...   12 50

Barroom Scene. Presents a barroom with all the accessories, including a barmaid, who serves a policeman with a glass of beer at the side entrance. Two men are smoking and having a quiet game of "draw," when a couple of "toughs" lounge in and a quarrel arises, in which the policeman takes a hand and forcibly expels the crowd. A very popular and realistic subject of this kind, ...   12 50

Blacksmith Shop. Shows two men at anvil. A third is repairing a wagon wheel. Incidentally a little liquid refreshment is passed around as the work progresses. .   12 50

Opium Den. Scene represents section of the interior of a Chinese Opium Den, .   10 00

Chinese Laundry Scene. Represents the pursuit of Hop Lee by Policeman O'Flannigan, in, out, and around Hop's laundry cabin, ...   12 50

Political Debate Represents Messrs. Topack & Steele impersonating Cleveland and Harrison in a lively political discussion, which progresses from words to blows. Burlesque, ...   15 00

COMBATS, ETC.

Glenroy Brothers. In a one round burlesque boxing bout, ...   15 00

Walton & Slavin. The "Long and Short of It," from Rice's "1492," representing a burlesque boxing test between 6 ft. 4 and 4 ft. 6. Very amusing, ...   15 00

Mexican Knife Duel. Between Pedro Esquirel and Dionecio Gonzaies. Full of action, ...   15 00

Hornbacker & Murphy. A five round glove contest, showing knockdown in the third and fifth rounds. Lively sparring throughout (each film), ...   15 00

Billy Edwards and the Unknown. A spirited five round sparring contest between this well known pugilist and a skillful antagonist (each film), ...   15 00

NOTE.—Each film of the above fights contains one round.

Broadsword Combat. Between the far-famed Capt. Duncan Ross, Champion of the World, and Lieut. Martin. An exciting contest in full armor, ...   15 00

Cock Fight. An exciting contest between lively game birds, in which the feathers fly freely. The owners of the birds are seen in the background exchanging bets.   12 50

Wrestling Match. A Græco Roman match, between Pettit and Kessler, . .   12 50
(The former is Champion of New Jersey.)

Lady Fencers. Exhibiting the Englehart Sisters in an exciting broadsword contest.   12 50

MISCELLANEOUS SUBJECTS.

Boxing Cats. An interesting and scientific bout between two trained Thomas Cats.   10 00

Wrestling Dog. Wrestles with his trainer.   10 00

Bertoldi. The marvelous lady contortionist and acrobat. in one of her inimitable performances. 10 00

Caceido. "The King of the Wire." A marvelous slack wire performance. in which Caceido turns somersaults in the air while balancing on the wire. . . .   10 00

Luis Martinetti. The famous gymnast and contortionist. performing on flying rings. 12 50

Somersault Dog. This trained animal turns backward somersaults in the air A wonderful performance. 10 00

Mlle. Capitaine. "The Perfect Woman," exhibiting in a graceful trapeze performance. 12 50

The Rixfords. Exhibiting the Brothers Rixford in a difficult and interesting head balancing feat, ...   12 50

Guyer. The famous clown. in an exhibition of grotesque tumbling. 12 50

Human Pyramid. Marvelous acrobatic performance by seven members of "Beni Zoug's" famous Arab troupe, ...   12 50

Cake Walk. By James Grundy, from "South Before the War." 12 50

Hindoo Fakir and Cotta Dwarf. From Barnum & Bailey's "Greatest Show on Earth." 10 00

Attila. The world-famous athlete and trainer, ...   10 00

Weimar. The Champion Light-Weight Dumb-bell performer of the world, .   10 00

Lasso Thrower, Vincente Oro Passo. The Champion Lasso Thrower, gives an interesting exhibition of lasso twirling and throwing, from "Buffalo Bill's Wild West," 12 50

All the foregoing Films are made for exhibition on the standard size Edison Kinetoscope; are about 50 feet in length, and each is composed of about 750 different views of the same subject. They are neatly and securely put up in tin spool boxes, and can be safely shipped by express to any point.

Prices quoted include packing. We do not prepay express charges, nor do we guarantee safe delivery of goods after they have been accepted by Transportation Companies.

Our terms are strictly **CASH WITH ORDER,** or goods will be sent **C. O. D.** on receipt of sufficient funds to guarantee express charges both ways.

The illustration on the first page of this price-list, shows an Edison Kinetoscope ready to be operated for public exhibitions. A full description of the principle of taking and reproducing photographs of moving objects by means of this instrument, was given in the Edison Phonographic News, Cincinnati, O., for July and August, 1894, and in The Century Magazine, for June, 1894, and we refer to those publications for such information. The present circular deals only with the kinetoscope as presented to the public as an exhibiting machine, and from a business standpoint, and is not intended to cover other points.

For further information, and in placing orders, address

The Ohio Phonograph Co.

411 ELM STREET, ÷ CINCINNATI, O.

Some comments on the catalogue.
(note: page numbers given are those of the catalogue)

Page 2
The question of whether or not Kinetoscopes appeared at the Columbian Exhibition of 1893 is still being debated. Current thought is that there might have been one, but it is agreed that there was no commercial-scale exhibition.

Page 3, line 3
This catalogue continues the claim that the film speed was 46 frames per second. It seems never to have been that fast, at least on commercially distributed films. If the claimed 750 frames were exhibited at 46 per second, the film would have lasted only a little over 16 seconds, and that simply was not the case. As noted elsewhere, Hendricks studied film speeds, and found them to range between 16 and 38-40 frames per second, with the majority falling in between.

Page 4, line 6
This makes clear that both nickel-in-the-slot machines and attendant-operated machines (here called "pull-rod") were made at the same time. The "pull-rod" description is apparently left over from the text of a very early catalogue, and did not describe the machines of 1895. By the time of the manufacture of Kinetoscope #69, and probably considerably earlier, the machines were operated by a lever as described in chapter 4.

Page 5, paragraph 7
This carries on the fiction that the films were 50' long. Perhaps in the camera, but in the standard Kinetoscope only 42' of film could be accommodated. Amusingly, page 5, paragraph 7 claims that 800 frames in 50', while page 12 claims "about 50'", but only 750 frames!

The story of Kinetoscope parlours starts with the parlour opened by Holland Brothers at 1155 Broadway, New York City, on 14 April 1894. As shown in the drawing (illustration 30), it had ten machines, five in a row back to back, with a brass railing to direct the public to the fronts of the machines. A ticket booth is at the far right. Between the two rows of machines, attendants stand ready to turn on a particular machine upon receipt of a ticket. The rather small converted shoe store is decorated with potted palms, a bust of Edison and, up in the corners, small dragons illuminated with miniature electric lights.

Illustration 30 · The first Kinetoscope parlour
Opened at 1155 Broadway, New York City, on 14 April 1894 by Holland Brothers, eastern agents of the Kinetoscope Company, which had its headquarters in Chicago. There were ten machines, arranged in two rows of five, with room for the attendants to walk between them in order to operate the machines. Note the lady on the left reading a title, and the young attendant ready to turn on a machine for her. (Gordon Hendricks, *The Kinetoscope*)

The films shown at the opening were *Sandow, Horse Shoeing, Barber Shop, Bertholdi (Mouth Support), Wrestling, Bertholdi (Table Contortion), Blacksmiths, Highland Dance, Trapeze* and *Roosters*. Several of these remained popular for some time and at least two, *Barber Shop* and *Blacksmiths*, were rephotographed when the original negatives wore out.

The parlour in the Bowery (illustration 32) seems to have used a layout similar to the first parlour, if less elaborately decorated.[1] In this illustration, from *Leslie's Magazine* of February 1895, there is a board just visible at the upper right. It lists the following films: *A Knock Out Fight in Five Rounds, Gaiety Girls, Carmencita* and *High Kicking*. The *Knock Out Fight in Five Rounds* was the set of films, one round on each, titled *Billy Edwards and the Unknown*, probably taken in January 1895, and

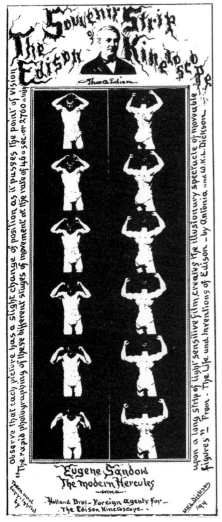

Illustration 31
Dickson's "souvenir strip"
In 1894, Dickson copyrighted this "souvenir strip" containing a photographic copy of a film with the perforations trimmed off. I assume that it was designed to sell to patrons of the Kinetoscope parlours. The few surviving examples are highly prized! This strip was copyrighted by Dickson; the copyright quite promptly transferred to Edison!

would have taken up five machines. *Gaiety Girls* and *Carmencita* were regular Edison titles. *High Kicking* is an example of an exhibitor inventing his own "improved" title for a film, a rather common occurrence, particularly as no titles appeared on Edison's Kinetoscope films.

By 8 December 1899, Edison had made and sold 973 Kinetoscopes and 45 Kinetophones worldwide, almost all before the end of 1895, after that time Kinetoscope parlours rapidly disappeared. Photographs of them are extremely scarce, but photographs of several are shown here. I hope that this book will encourage owners of other similar photographs to make them known. Owners of two of these arcades went on to make their fortunes from motion-pictures – Charles Urban as a filmmaker, and Thomas L Tally as an exhibitor.

The photograph of Urban's Phonograph and Kinetoscope Parlor, Detroit 1895 (illustration 34), shows the more usual arrangement of a row of coin-operated phonographs and a row of Kinetoscopes. Coin-operated phonographs were introduced in 1890 and were reasonably common by 1894. They were sold by Edison's phonograph sub-companies, such as the Ohio Phonograph Company, to the exhibitors. When Kinetoscopes came along, they also were sold by Edison's phonograph wholesalers, and in many cases added to existing phonograph parlours. It appears that most "parlours" used attendant-operated machines, since coin-operated machines were pretty much restricted to locations where single machines were exhibited, such as hotels, bars and even steamships.

Charles Urban's interest started when he became a phonograph salesman, and he introduced them into offices for dictation purposes. After 1894 he managed a phonograph and Kinetoscope parlour on Woodward Avenue, Detroit. By 1896, he had obtained the rights in Michigan to the Vitascope projector, but by 1897 was in

Illustration 32 · The Kinetoscope on the Bowery, New York City
(*Leslie's Magazine* February 1895)

England as London manager for Maguire & Baucus, the distributor of Edison films in England. Soon he was making his own films, and later produced films in Kinemacolor, the first successful colour motion-picture process.

This photograph not only is one of the very few interiors of a Kinetoscope parlour, but also has two other distinctions. Because of Urban's early move to England, it is highly likely that it has never been published in the United States. It comes from the Science Museum, London, and was published by them in a 1969 monograph called *The First Colour Motion Pictures* (reprinted in 1983). The fourth Kinetoscope is not in fact a Kinetoscope, but a Kinetophone, and this is the only confirmed photograph of one in a "parlour". It can be identified by the white rubber eartube arched over the top of the machine, and (if that is not readily visible) by the towel hanging from the front of the machine. As the earpieces were black hard rubber that fitted inside the patrons' ears, towels were frequently provided so that the earpieces could be wiped clean before using. Strangely, the two phonographs on the left and the row on the right, each with its set of eartubes, show no towels, but some can be seen in a later photograph. Note that each phonograph and Kinetoscope has a raised signboard behind it to announce the selection. Urban's short stay with the "parlour" is indicative of the Kinetoscope's short commercial life. Actually, coin-operated phonographs started earlier – 1890 – and lasted longer. They could be found in penny arcades into at least the 1940s. I can remember playing them myself, eartubes and all!

A highly successful merchandiser was Peter Bacigalupi of San Francisco. He advertised as "Founded 1893" and may have opened a phonograph parlour by then. He opened his Kinetoscope, Phonograph and Graphophone Arcade on 1 June 1894, starting with five of the first 25 Kinetoscopes produced, later increasing the number to ten. In 1895 he bought at least one "conversion kit" to turn a Kinetoscope into a Kinetophone.

By far the best existing photographs of a Kinetoscope parlour are several (at least three) of Bacigalupi's, of which one taken from the rear of the Arcade is the most inclusive (illustration 37). The front door is in the centre of the picture. The wall to the left is lined with coin-operated phonographs. To the right of the front door is a partly hidden phonograph with multiple eartubes, enabling several people to listen at one time. Notice that each phonograph has its towel.

Six Kinetoscopes plus the corner of a seventh are shown, out of the total of ten. Each machine has a framed board on the slanted front saying "EDISON'S LATEST INVENTION/THE KINETOSCOPE/PRESENTS", and on the fourth line the title of the film. In one photograph these first three lines can be made out, but none of the titles is legible. Set into the panel on the front of the machine is what I am sure is a piece of ¼" plate glass with a crackled pattern formed on the back, "EDISON KINETOSCOPE" painted on, and the whole backed with gold leaf. These additions must have added colour to otherwise rather drab-looking machines. What is not apparent is that the row of Kinetoscopes is set sufficiently far out from the wall to allow the attendants to move up and down behind the machines in order to respond to the patrons' requests (illustration 38). Edison produced coin-operated Kinetoscopes, but I have not seen any photographs of a "parlour" using them.

Bacigalupi was nothing if not a survivor. Besides his arcade, he had a store where he sold Edison phonographs and records, Columbia "Graphophones" (as Edison's

Illustration 33 · The Kinetoscope on exhibition
This is a strange combination: the sign offers tickets, yet there is no sign of attendants to take the tickets, and no room between the rows of machines for attendants to work. The machines are set up as they would be for coin operation, but in that case the sign should offer change, not tickets! (*The Electrical World* 16 June 1894)

Illustration 34 · Phonograph and Kinetoscope parlour
On the left are two coin-operated phonographs, followed by a row of Kinetoscopes, except for the fourth machine, identified by the author as a Kinetophone. This may be the only known photograph of one in commercial use. It can be identified by its white rubber eartube arching over the top of the machine and ending in the black hard-rubber earpieces visible as a black dot on the slanted front of the machine. Also a clue is the white towel hanging from the front of the machine, which was used by the patron to wipe off the earpieces before using them. There may be a second towel, identifying a Kinetophone, but it is not possible to be sure. At the far right is a row of coin-operated phonographs.
Charles Urban managed the parlour for a time in 1895. Later he went to England for Maguire & Baucus, and shortly after the turn of the century was involved with Kinemacolor, the first successful natural colour process for motion pictures. (Science Museum, London)

biggest competitor called its version of the Phonograph), music boxes, slot machines, phonograph cylinders, and films. Slightly later, he added Edison projectors and X-ray equipment. Besides selling Edison cylinders, he recorded his own (on Edison blanks) and sold them.

The San Francisco city directories of 1895 and 1896 list the "Edison Phonograph and Kinetoscope Arcade", but already in 1897 the listing changed to "Edison Phonograph Parlor, 946 Market, sales 933 Market". Here again, the short life of the Kinetoscope parlour is illustrated. Bacigalupi survived the 1906 earthquake and fire, although both of his locations were destroyed. Later, with his sons, he dealt in "talking machines", cylinder records giving way to discs. Soon the listing was for "musical instruments", and in 1918 and 1919 it was "Peter Bacigalupi & Sons, Electric Pianos".

According to Ramsaye,[2] Thomas L Tally first became acquainted with the Kinetoscope when, as a cowboy, he found "Winnie Brothers' Kinetoscope Parlor" in Waco, TX, sometime in 1896. Soon he was working for the Winnie Brothers. This did not satisfy him long, apparently, as by August 1896 he had opened Tally's Phonograph & Kinetoscope Parlors at 311 South Spring Street, Los Angeles (illustration 40). In the drawing, it is in the left edge of the three-storey Hotel Ramona. Across the top of the storefront the sign reads "TALLY'S PHONOGRAPH PARLOR". On the left window are the words "EDISON VITASCOPE", and on the right window "EDISON KINETOSCOPE".

Ramsaye says that Tally provided "Kinetoscope pictures, the American Mutoscope, the Casler peep show machine, and on the screen as presented by the Vitascope".[3] Ramsaye must have been a little confused, as the Mutoscope *was* Casler's "peep show machine", and he does not mention the long bank of phonographs on the right wall where the ladies are sitting listening (illustration 41). It is interesting to see chairs provided: this was unusual, as is the tall phonograph cabinet with projecting horn at the extreme right of the picture.

At the left is a row of Kinetoscopes. Particularly unusual is the opportunity to see a picture of one of the extra long Kinetoscopes built specially to hold a complete, although short, round of boxing matches produced for them. Five of the Kinetoscopes each held 150' of film, and the rounds were shortened to fit – one minute each. The

Illustration 35 · New Vine Street Parlor, Cincinnati, OH.
From an article on "Phonograph Parlors" in the November/December 1895 issue of *The Edison Phonographic News*. The electric lights in the windows flashed so as to make it appear that the lights revolved! (Collection of Lawrence A Schlick)

Illustration 36 · Front and back of Bacigalupi's advertising card of 1896
Even two years after it took place, the Corbett-Courtney fight was still a "drawing card"!

Corbett-Courtney fight was the second fight put on by the Kinetoscope Exhibition Company, which was established solely to film prize fights. The sign on the side of the Kinetoscope says "SEE THE CORBETT FIGHT". In the centre is a row of what eager collectors now call "clamshell Mutoscopes", made of massive elaborately shaped metal castings. In the rear are chairs and an opening so that persons (ladies, presumably) who would feel uncomfortable sitting in a darkened theatre can watch the Vitascope project a picture on a screen. It appears that Tally was truly trying to offer something for everyone!

The author has owned the little "flyer" headed "EDISON X RAYS" (illustration 42) since the 1950s, and it introduced him to the vast knowledge of Gordon Hendricks. I sent Beaumont Newhall, at that time at George Eastman House, a copy of it in autumn 1958. He forwarded it to Hendricks, who answered on 1 January 1959, and graciously provided the following information:

> The Holidays referred to on this sheet are clearly those of 1896, placing the date of this sheet as closely before Christmas of that year.
>
> The manufacture of Edison's 'wonderful penetrating light' [i.e. the X-ray] began between March 11, 1896 and March 27, 1896, but these machines did not reach the Kinetoscope parlour stage for several months thereafter. (a letter dated March 11 says ... not yet started to manufacture, and one dated March 27 says 'fluoroscopes are made by ...') A letter to Edison's vitascope agents dated October 16, 1896 ('...the Chicago people are advertising an X-Ray machine...') suggests that at that date the X-Rays had not yet reached the Los Angeles Kinetoscope parlours.
>
> The frame enlargement from 'The Great Corbett Fight' is obviously from the subject shot in Edison's Black Maria in West Orange, New Jersey at noon on September 7, 1894. ... Corbett is on the right and Pete Courtney is on the left...
>
> 'Niagara Falls..etc.' is apparently one of the group copyrighted by Edison on December 12 and 24, 1896. A shooting date of late November, 1896 is strongly suggested – though I have not yet dated these subjects precisely. 'Employees leaving the great Clark Thread Mills' was apparently shot in October, 1896 (and previously [sic] to the 20th) outside the Clark works in Newark, New Jersey, and probably by Edison's man James H. White. It was Edison's 'answer' to the Lumière subject 'La Sortie d'Usine' which had made such a sensation at Keith's Union Square Theater in New York the previous summer. 'Arrival of the Local Express' is apparently the subject called 'Chicago and Buffalo Express' described in the Maguire and Baucus catalog of April, 1897 as showing 'the arrival at a station, and passengers alighting from and boarding the train.' It was apparently shot in Buffalo on the visit which resulted in the Niagara Falls group from which the above subject was selected for this Los Angeles Kinetoscope showing.
>
> 'The Famous Muscle Dance' is apparently an older subject, and could be any of several – *except* the well known Fatima subject, which was shot the following spring.

Chris Long, motion-picture researcher in Australia, says that exhibitors there gave a "muscle dance" type title to Sandow's exhibition of strength! I do not think Hendricks would have thought of that, nor would I!

Tally later became a successful motion-picture exhibitor. In 1902 he opened the Electric Theater at 262 South Main Street, Los Angeles, and had a long and successful motion-picture theatre career.

The above are just a few well-illustrated examples. Besides these, Kinetoscopes were shown both singly and in groups in reasonably permanent "parlours" or by travelling exhibitors who would set up in small towns and move on when demand dropped. This was the case not only in the United States, but also all over Europe and Australia. I have not heard of any in South America or the Far East, but that does not mean that they were not there.

While reading Hendricks' *Origins of the American Film*, Glenn Grabinsky of Montville, NJ, suddenly realised that the newspaper article quoted in the book

Illustration 37 · Bacigalupi's Kinetoscope and Phonograph parlor
Taken from the rear, this view shows many coin-operated phonographs down the angled wall on the left and in the centre. On the right are five more phonographs, including one with multiple eartubes, a mechanical singing bird in a cage, and six of the ten Kinetoscopes, plus part of a seventh. Bacigalupi converted at least one of his Kinetoscopes to a Kinetophone, but there is no visible evidence of one in this picture. At the extreme left, the sign says "Edison Kinetoscope Films for Sale". The large poster on the right says "Edison Kinetoscope, The Life Producing Marvel". On the front of each Kinetoscope, the sign reads "Edison's Latest Invention, The Kinetoscope Presents", then below is room for a title, unfortunately none of which is legible. (US Department of the Interior, National Park Service, Edison National Historic Site)

(describing the interest caused by Edison Kinetoscope #457 being exhibited at a New Jersey coastal resort hotel) was in fact describing his machine! Indeed, he had found an empty Kinetoscope cabinet, but with the plate containing the serial number intact, and had the author restore it to a complete functioning machine. Now he even has the name of the original owner.

Perhaps the overseas parlour best known to history is the one that two Greeks, Georgiades and Trajedis, opened on Old Broad Street, London, with Kinetoscopes purchased in New York in August 1894. When their success made them want more machines, they persuaded the instrument-maker, Robert W Paul, to make copies for them, rather than pay Edison's price. Paul refused until he discovered that Edison had not patented the Kinetoscope in England, nor indeed throughout Europe. He then proceeded to make about 60 exact copies – exact even to the incised decoration on the left-hand side of the cabinet. An examination of the only known surviving Paul Kinetoscope reveals Paul's name and address, "R. W. PAUL/HATTON COURT/

LONDON", cast into the machine's bedplate, and invisible unless the machine is opened. This survivor is at the Conservatoire des Arts et Métiers in Paris. Unfortunately, in recent years part of the viewer has been removed and the interior mechanism terribly mangled, apparently by some inexperienced person trying to make it operate.

Paul used some of his machines to open a parlour in Earl's Court, London. The unusual London demand for films alerted Edison's people. When they found out what was going on, they refused to sell any more films to supply Paul's Kinetoscopes. Paul then invented his own camera, and in March 1895 hired Birt Acres to take films for him, thus starting film production in England.

This rather untidy beginning to motion-pictures in England has had amusing results down to the present day. One British film historian begins his book in 1895, neatly avoiding the subject. Patricia Warren's *The British Film Collection 1896-1984* manages to avoid any mention of Edison or of the Kinetoscope, even though Robert Paul's first film, *A Rough Sea At Dover*, of February 1896, was made for his copies of Edison's Kinetoscope! The above is not typical of England or the English. For many years the Science Museum displayed an original Edison Kinetoscope, now at the National Museum of Photography, Film and Television, Bradford; and the Museum of the Moving Image, London, displays my two operating replicas.

Illustration 38 · Peter Bacigalupi's Edison Kinetoscope, Phonograph and Graphophone Arcade, 946 Market Street, San Francisco, CA.
This view, from the rear of the room, shows part of a coin-operated phonograph at the far left, and, on the right, eight of the total of ten Kinetoscopes, with three of the "operators", each ready to turn on a machine upon receipt of one of the tickets purchased at the front door. There is some opinion that the figure on the right is Mr Bacigalupi himself. (US Department of the Interior, National Park Service, Edison National Historic Site)

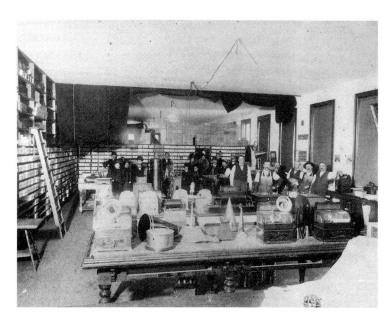

Illustration 39 · Peter Bacigalupi's Store, 933 Market Street, San Francisco, CA, 1896-97

The boxes on the shelves around the room held cylinder phonograph records. On the front table are three Columbia Graphophone coin-operated phonographs. In the centre, the dark box with the eyepiece is an X-ray viewer, almost surely Edison-made. On the right side, just behind the table, can be seen the distinctive top of a Kinetoscope. Just behind it, a man rests his arm on a "Hand Kinetoscope" (see chapter 10 on Kinetoscope competitors). On the second table, the two dark horizontal cylinders are X-ray equipment. At centre left is a large vertical tank, and, to the right of it, an early film projector (almost certainly an Edison Vitascope) with a man standing behind it. The tall tank held gas (probably Acetylene) so that the projector could be lit by gaslight for showing films in towns not yet equipped with electricity. Also in the scene are phonograph horns, mechanical novelties, and several slot-machines. (From an original photograph in the author's collection, a prized gift from Robert Halgrim, retired Curator of the Edison Winter Home Museum, Ft. Myers, FL, and never before published.)

History certainly repeats itself. In 1991 I had some correspondence with the Museum of the Moving Image about a third Kinetoscope replica to join my two already there. Then the correspondence stopped. When I next visited the Museum in October 1992, I found that the Museum had created a third machine by copying my cabinet and adding a viewer to the interior, although not an Edison-type one, I regret to say. Stephen Herbert seemed a little concerned that I might be offended at this. I was not offended, but I certainly was amused. I had never experienced such a good example of history repeating itself. In 1994, Stephen ordered some additional Edison films from me. About the same time I learned that the Museum had created a second British-made machine. I suggested to Stephen (without malice) that he should run *A Rough Sea At Dover* and a companion film on the two British-made Kinetoscopes!

At least one of the Greeks appears in recent records. *A Fotografia Animada em*

Portugal 1894, 1895, 1896, 1897, by Antonio J Ferreira (1986), reports that George Georgiades introduced the Kinetoscope to Lisbon at the Tabacaria Neves on 6 March 1895. It does not say how many machines were there. Paul's copies were used, and the cost per viewing was "100 reis". On 24 November 1896, Joaquin Dunes opened an exhibition there that included the Kinetophone and the X-ray. The Edison Kinetoscope Parlor opened at 85 rue de Richelieu, Paris, in October 1894. It is likely that this is where the Lumières and the Pathés first saw motion-pictures.

In Mexico, the President of the Republic attended the introduction of the Kinetoscope on 17 January 1895; in Italy, the Continental Phonograph Kinetoscope Company was selling Kinetophones, films and cylinders for them in 1896 (illustration 51).

Australian researcher and author, Chris Long, informs me that ten machines (#118-127) were shipped from the Edison works on 13 September 1894 to Irving T Bush in London. Bush was the financier behind Maguire & Baucus. Five machines were then trans-shipped to Australia. It was done that way because

Illustration 40 · Tally's Phonograph Parlor
Opened in August 1896 and located at 311 S Spring Street, Los Angeles, CA, in the corner of the Hotel Ramona. The sign on the left window reads "Edison Vitascope", and on the right window, "Edison Kinetoscope". Listed in the Los Angeles City Directory as "Tally's Phonograph and Kinetoscope Parlors". (Author's collection)

Illustration 41 · Interior of Tally's Phonograph Parlor

At the far left, in front, is a coin-operated phonograph with its eartubes hanging down. Next is a row of Kinetoscopes. The first, at least, is one of the enlarged "fight Kinetoscopes" designed to hold 100 feet or so of film – an abbreviated "round". The sign on the side advertises the Corbett-Courtney fight film. In the centre is a row of Mutoscopes. Today's collectors call this style the "clamshell" model because of the pattern on the elaborate cast-iron cabinet. In the rear is a room where the Vitascope was used to project films. Visible are chairs for patrons fearful of sitting inside a darkened room. At the right are ladies sitting listening to coin-operated phonographs. At the far right is an Edison coin-operated phonograph, unusual because of its having a horn, rather than eartubes.

Maguire & Baucus were Edison's exclusive agents in Australia. On 30 November 1894 the machines were placed on exhibition at 148 Pitt Street, Sydney (the building survives). Remarkably, this was only a few weeks after the London opening! A Sydney reporter who attended the opening gave a rare eye-witness description of a visit to a Kinetoscope parlour. Note that the procedure used differed from that customarily used in the United States – that of giving customers a choice of machines to view:

Patrons paid their shilling at the door to file past each of the five electrically-operated machines. They looked down into a window in the top of each to view a clear but tiny image. The machines contained a 50-foot loop of film running at the surprisingly high speed of about 40 pictures a second and lasting about 30 seconds. In spite of the brevity of the loops, one film at the premiere explored the story-telling potential of the medium. [Here follows a description of the first *Barber Shop*, which is quoted under that title in the *Index*].

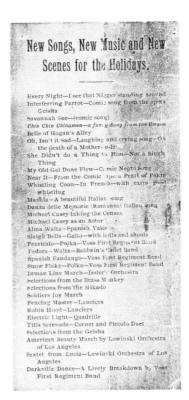

Illustration 42 · A Tally's advertising "flyer" of December 1896
Edison invented an improved fluoroscopic "viewer for X-rays", which were discovered by Roentgen only the previous year. The Edison Manufacturing Company made X-ray equipment, and the X-ray was demonstrated to an amazed public until its harmful possibilities were realised. Near the bottom of the list are two selections by "Lowinski Orchestra of Los Angeles". I have not been able to find any information about this group, but these could well be the first commercial recordings made in Los Angeles! (Collection of the author.)

This group toured all the major cities in Australia over the next couple of years and was later joined by two other exhibitors. By February 1896, there were about 25 machines in the country, including six Kinetophones, and, in addition, several extended-capacity "fight machines" (see the photograph of Tally's parlour in Los Angeles [illustration 41]). One of the Kinetophones survives today, in a private collection in Sydney. It was its owner's kind permission to examine the machine that gave the author the knowledge required to restore the Kinetophone in the Cinémathèque Française, Paris, in October 1992. Richard Brown of England and Chris Long of Australia compiled this Australian information. Long goes on to say that the Edison Electric Parlour, Sydney, was trying to sell these machines in 1898 and was still (at greatly reduced prices) offering them in 1901! Sic transit gloria mundi!

1   In 1990, the Kinetoscope exhibit at the Deutsches Filmmuseum in Frankfurt, Germany, replicated this format.

2   Terry Ramsaye, *A Million and One Nights: A History of the Motion Picture*, volume I (New York: Simon and Schuster, 1926): 276.

3   Ibid: 277.

Illustration 43 · The realistic Kinetoscope! By gosh, it is amazing! It is a picture of the sea. Is it real? It must be, because I already feel my feet getting wet!

EDISON KINETOSCOPE.

THE MOST RECENT AND MARVELLOUS PRODUCTION OF THE GREAT INVENTOR'S BRAIN.

This instrument presents to the view, photographs of living and moving objects at the rate of 46 per second (2760 per minute), each photograph representing a distinct phase of motion. The speed with which they pass before the vision is greater than makes it possible for the human eye to detect the change from one to the other, hence the effect of absolutely perfect motion.

Now on Exhibition for the FIRST time at 1155 Broadway, near 27th Street, New York.

(over)

KINETOSCOPE

KINETIC:—Moving: Causing motion.

KINETOSCOPE:—"An instrument for producing curves of the combination of circular movements."—*Webster*

KINETOSCOPE:—"A kind of movable panorama. An instrument for illustrating the results of combinations of arcs of different radii in making curves."—*Century Dictionary.*

This last and most wonderful invention of Thos. A. Edison is now having its first and only public exhibition at 1155 BROADWAY, near 27th St.

(over)

An amazing discovery! Shown are both sides of a small handbill advertising the first Kinetoscope parlour, the one in illustration 30. The earliest known – perhaps the *first-ever* – piece of motion-picture advertising, and never before published, dating from c.May 1894 (From the collection of Allen Koenigsberg)

Although Edison was a great inventor, not all his inventions were commercial successes. His Kinetoscope was a great success, and heralded the beginning of motion-pictures, but when he added a phonograph in an attempt to produce talking pictures, the Kinetophone, as he called it, failed rapidly and completely. Edison wrote in *The Century Illustrated Monthly Magazine* of June 1894:

> In the year 1887 the idea occurred to me that it was possible to devise an instrument which should do for the eye what the phonograph does for the ear, and that by a combination of the two, all motion and sound could be recorded simultaneously.

In that year Edison was just beginning experiments with wax cylinders for his phonograph, experiments that would put the phonograph on the market just two years later. Why not record pictures on a cylinder, as well as sound? He put W K-L Dickson in charge of experiments of this nature. The motion-picture part of the experiments made progress; the sound portion did not. Articles and interviews over the next several years confirm his continued interest. As it turned out, this seemingly simple combination was amazingly difficult to put into practice.

Illustration 44 · The Kinetograph
A. Recording horn; B. Phonograph; C. Kinetograph; D. Battery. (From *The New York Herald* 28 May 1891, in the Hendricks Collection at the American History Museum of the Smithsonian Institution, Washington, DC)

Illustration 44 shows the appearance of the camera and recording phonograph in 1891 – or does it? The connection between the machines seems so logical, but the chances are that this drawing is only a concept and that there never was such a machine, because it would never work. The difficulty was in trying to link closely two mechanisms with widely varying requirements. The camera required that the subject(s) be at such a distance that a reasonable picture could be obtained, and that allowed room in the picture for the actors to move around a stage. Look at Dickson in illustration 45, recording his violin which is within inches of the recording horn. Even a brass band would have had its dozen or so members grouped directly in front of the horn, with the loudest instruments perhaps 10' away. There is no way a scene of several people moving and talking could have been taken.

There is at least one hint that Edison considered what is now known as "dubbing". Many scenes in modern motion-pictures are taken with the actors speaking, but without the sound being recorded. This is commonly done in scenes taken outside the usual sound-stage, where there may be undesirable background noise, where the actors are at a great distance from the camera, or where an actor is singing and dancing at the same time, and so on. Later, the silent film is shown on a screen while the actors and the sound-effects staff add sound to match the requirements of the scene. If Edison did consider this, he did not pursue it in practice.

In 1892, the combination of picture and sound was still talked about, but when the Kinetoscope was demonstrated in 1893 and introduced commercially in 1894 it was silent. Unfortunately, the "state of the art" of both the Kinetograph (camera) and the phonograph was too primitive to allow Edison to reach his goal. We cannot fault him for failing. Experimenters around the world worked for the next 35 years before advances in technology made sound motion-pictures commercially successful.

The only surviving film that appears to have attempted synchronisation is an obviously experimental film of 1894-95, commonly called *Dickson Violin*. In this film (illustration 45), Dickson plays his violin into an enormous recording horn, while two of Edison's young workmen in shirtsleeves dance to provide motion. It is likely that the phonograph in illustration 46, recently identified at the Edison National Historic Site by George Frow, an English author on phonographic subjects, was the phonograph that did the recording. It would have been just outside the picture to the left, attached to the recording horn. If the cylinder survives, it has not been identified. To illustrate the informal nature of the film, towards the end a man walks into the scene from the left rear and partially disappears behind the recording horn as the film ends. This film is a graphic example of how unlikely successful synchronisation was.

Take illustrations 47 and 48, each supposedly a representation of a Kinetophone film being taken. Each shows an excellent view of the camera and its operator. The problem here is that the camera and the tracks on which it slides have been moved from the centre of the room to the far right in order to improve the view of the stage. Other than the camera and the building interior, the scene is pure fiction. As the illustrations clearly show, a phonograph placed anywhere near the one shown would have picked up no sound at all, probably not even the whirring and clicking of the camera.

When Kinetophones were introduced in spring 1895, there was no attempt at synchronisation. Kenneth Chew, of the Science Museum, London, kindly sent me a

Illustration 45 · Frame from *Dickson Violin*

In this frame from the experimental film usually called *Dickson Violin*, W K-L Dickson plays his violin into an enormous recording horn while two Edison workmen dance in a circle to provide "motion". Although the cylinder recorded with this film seems not to have survived, it was almost certainly recorded on the phonograph shown in illustration 46, which would have been attached to the horn, but just out of the scene to the left. The phonograph survives in a vault at the Edison National Historic Site.

This film, taken in late 1894 or early 1895, seems to be the only surviving film with which sound synchronisation was attempted. When the Kinetophone was introduced in 1895, its records provided only background music. This frame comes very near the end of the film, where an unidentified man walks in from the rear left. The film ends with his face hidden behind the horn. The scene demonstrates why synchronisation was not possible at this time. Later, probably after the failure of his 1912 Kinetophone, Edison said: "The problem of actual synchronisation was the least difficult of my tasks. The hardest job was to make a phonographic recorder which would be sensitive enough to sound a considerable distance away, and which would not show within the range of the lens." This problem was not really solved until electrical amplification came along many years later.

(Frame still from film in the author's collection)

---

unique eye-witness description of the Kinetophone upon its arrival in France in spring 1895. It reads in part:

> We have seen a ballet dancer dance the Serpentine [Annabelle?]. None of her graceful movements passed unnoticed, and the orchestra music was heard very clearly. In a different machine we were present at a performance of military band

Illustration 46 · Phonograph probably used in filming *Dickson Violin*
(Photograph taken in the Edison National Historic Site by George Frow.)

music [see *Band Drill* on pages 118-119]. We saw the conductor wave from the podium and spread both his arms to give the signal for the instruments to begin playing. The music immediately began playing softly. Through this unusual experience one senses the imperfection of the apparatus The phonograph can accompany fairly well at a distance the movements of a ballet dancer, or a conductor, but the synchronization of music and motion is still not perfected.

What the reporter did not realise was that Edison had given up on synchronisation and settled for merely suggesting that certain films might have appropriate regular-issue cylinders played along with them as accompaniment (illustration 51): dance music to accompany a film of a dancer, or a choice of several military band pieces to accompany a film of a parade, are two examples. The *Index* provides many specific examples. All Edison's work and great expectations had come down to only this. He gave up for the time being, tried again in 1912, and failed again.

Physically, the Kinetophone was a Kinetoscope which had had the motor moved from its compartment at the middle of the cabinet down into the battery compartment at the bottom. Then an altered version of the 1889 phonograph and a repeating attachment were mounted in the motor compartment; the phonograph was driven by a belt connected to the drive-shaft of the Kinetoscope's shutter. A rubber tube led the sound to the patrons' ears while his eyes looked through the cast-iron viewer. Illustration 49 gives a good view of the exterior of a Kinetophone. The client watches the film while the rubber tube conveys the sound to his ears.

Of the three surviving Kinetophones (described more fully on pages 2, 73, 80 and 98-103), the most nearly complete unrestored machine is the one of which the phonograph is shown in illustration 50. This nearly complete machine is the only one in private hands, and is in Sydney, Australia, and not on display. Its custodian has most kindly allowed me to examine it and photograph it on two different occasions. It is quite complete, missing only the phonograph's repeating attachment and its connections to the machine, which had been removed. His generosity, plus the

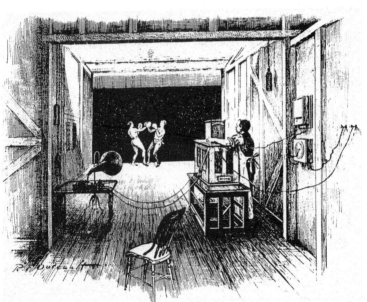

Illustrations 47 and 48 · Scenes in the "Black Maria", supposedly of
Kinetophone films being taken with sound.
To improve the scene, the camera track and camera have been moved from the centre of the
room to the side. That is just "artistic licence". Note the appearance of a recording phonograph
at the left. As is apparent in illustration 47, successful recording at the distance shown is
impossible.

willingness of an English collector to sell me the phonograph portion he had rescued from a scrap heap some years ago, the thoughtful gift of my friend Steve Oliphant of the repeating attachment which he had recognised in a pile of phonograph parts in northern California and realised its importance to me, and the public-spirited decision by the Cinémathèque Française to have their machine restored, have all combined to produce the only reasonably complete Kinetophone on public display anywhere in the world.

The author owns a phonograph and repeating mechanism still on its original mounting-board. The only thing still missing from the Cinémathèque's machine is the connection between the machine and the repeating mechanism, which allowed the cylinder to be replayed with each viewing of the film. As these parts are also

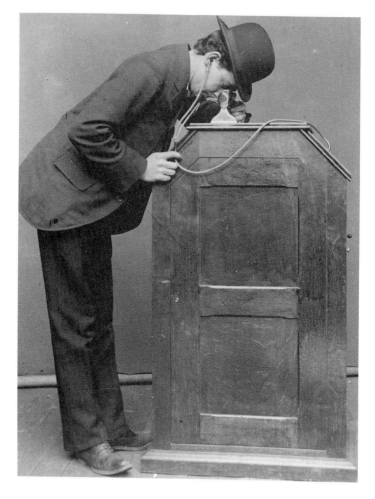

Illustration 49 · A Kinetophone in use, c.1895
The patron is looking through a magnifying glass at the 35mm film. He hears the sounds through eartubes extending down to the phonograph in the bottom of the cabinet. (US Department of the Interior, National Park Service, Edison National Historic Site)

missing from the Australian machine, they could not be copied, and how they operated is not clear. There are no known drawings or plans of a Kinetophone and, indeed, no photographs of the interior of one, except that of the author. In fact, illustration 50 appears to be the only photograph of the interior of a Kinetophone ever published.

Many years ago, the Science Museum, London, placed a phonograph in the battery compartment of a Kinetoscope and photographed it there, which was completely in error. This is not to criticise the Science Museum, but to illustrate the complete lack of information about Kinetophones available until now. The phonograph went in the motor compartment; the motor was dropped to the battery compartment at the very bottom of the cabinet, where the museum had photographed the phonograph. The Science Museum's machine, now transferred to the National Museum of Photography, Film and Television, Bradford, is the least complete machine of the three, at least for the present time. I am encouraging them to restore it – so far without success.

Tragically few artifacts or documents of the Kinetoscope or Kinetophone remain at the Edison National Historic Site, Almost everything was stored in one of the buildings that was destroyed in an enormous fire on 9 December 1914, which burned down a number of Edison's factory buildings.

Illustration 50 · The phonograph portion of a Kinetophone
In a Kinetoscope, the motor sits in the left side of this compartment. To convert the machine to a Kinetophone, the motor is shifted to the battery compartment at the bottom of the machine, and this hinged board, with its phonograph and repeating attachment, is substituted. For power, the phonograph is connected to the drive shaft of the shutter, and the hose conducting the sound is connected to a brass tube going through the rear of the cabinet, with another hose going from this tube to the front of the machine, where the customer can put on eartubes. On the front of the phonograph, the gold letters says "FOR USE IN CONNECTION WITH THE EDISON KINETOSCOPE ONLY". A brown wax cylinder record fits on the brass mandrel at the right of the machine. In front sits the repeating mechanism. This photograph, by the author, is the only known photograph of the interior of a Kinetophone published.

The phonographs used in the Kinetophones were not models current in 1895, but rather primitive machines dating back to 1889, which were adapted for use in the Kinetophone. Parts used in recording were eliminated, for example. A small "K" was stamped in front of the serial number, and in two places "FOR USE IN CONNECTION WITH THE EDISON KINETOSCOPE ONLY" was added in gold paint. One apparent reason why Edison used these machines was that in 1894 he had thrown into bankruptcy the North American Phonograph Company, which owned the rights to the phonograph in the United States, and he was forbidden by the court to manufacture phonographs. The other possible reason is that he had sold to others the right to sell the phonograph in countries other than the United States and Canada. He was dissatisfied with their efforts, and did not want to have to sell Kinetophones through them. Indeed, after he shipped one Kinetophone to England to trigger a test case, he was promptly enjoined from sending others. If the first possibility was the reason, he could honestly claim that, indeed, he did not manufacture new phonographs for the Kinetophone. If the second possibility was the reason, he might have felt that by using a type of phonograph no longer sold he could skirt around the terms of the contract.

Modern authors have made much of the fact that only 45 complete Kinetophones were sold. They seem not to realise that adapter kits were also sold, so that existing Kinetoscopes could be converted to Kinetophones, and there is no record of the number of these that were sold. To cite just two examples: the Raff & Gammon records at Harvard University mention a Kinetophone sold to P L Richardson of Austin, TX, for $400 on 23 April 1895; and a "phonograph attachment with instructions" was sold for $55 on 12 April, buyer unidentified. It is known that at least one kit was sent to Bacigalupi in San Francisco. Chris Long, researcher and author in Australia, informs me that in 1896 in Australia, in addition to about 30 Kinetoscopes, there were six Kinetophones. The January 1896 list of the Continental Phonograph Kinetoscope Company of Milan, Italy (illustration 51), shows that Kinetophones were in use in Europe at that time. These demonstrate that Kinetophones did receive worldwide distribution.

Of the almost 1000 Kinetoscopes made, only nine survivors are known in the form of Kinetoscopes, all in museums (except that of the author), whereas there are three survivors that were Kinetophones. At least five ex-Kinetophone phonographs are known, and it is likely that more survive unidentified. From this surviving physical evidence, it would seem there must have been a respectable number of Kinetophones.

Illustration 51 is the only known list of films with appropriate cylinders suggested. It was discovered by Allen Koenigsberg of New York City, a distinguished phonograph historian. In it, *Carmencita*, for example, has three possible cylinders listed: "Santiago Waltz", "La Paloma", and what is possibly translated as "Spanish Fandango". Edison had issued two versions of the "Santiago Waltz" – one by the Edison Grand Concert Band, and the other by the Edison Symphony Orchestra. "La Paloma" had been recorded by the Edison Symphony Orchestra, and "Spanish Fandango" by the Edison Grand Concert Band. Most were available as musical cylinders from Edison's regular catalogue, as were most of the other cylinders on the list. A few may have been recorded by the Columbia Phonograph Company, Edison's bitter competitor, or by phonograph companies based in Europe. No cylinders were recorded to match or even accompany specific films, and all of the recommended cylinders were instrumental.

Lista delle films
accordate coi cilindri musicati da adoperarsi nel Kinetofono

Films	Cilindri	Musica
L. 150 Cad.	L. 10 Cad.	
Carmensita	Valse Santiago	Orchestra
	La Paloma	»
	Alma-Danza Spagnuola	»
Anna Bell, la Farfalla	Tobasco, Valse Mio	
	Sogno	»
	Padrone Feming	»
Bertoldi, Contorsionista	Cav. Rusticana	»
	Padrone Feming Valse	»
	Danza Agile	Piccolo
Danza Pickainnies	Danza del ventaglio	Orchestra
	Polka Eloisa	»
	Barkies Tukle	»
	Piccolo Kenkies	»
Rob Roy, danza Scozzese	Nulla troppo buono	
	per l'Irlandese	Orchestra
Giuocatore di Coltelli?	Belle di New Jork, Marcia	Banda di Gilmore
	Cav. Rusticana	Orchestra
Daino e ventaglio	Parkies Tukle	»
	Danza del Ventaglio	»
Warring e Vilson	Soirée al Club Lione	
	Kiln	»
May Leuas fanciulla		
Gaiety	Ridda irlandese	Piccolo
	Danza di Nozze Africana	Orchestra
	Polka Eloisa	»
Danza Carnevalesca (3		
Danzatori	Duetto Banjo	»
	Danza del ventaglio	»
Lucy Murrag	Ridda irlandese	Piccolo
	Indugia più a lungo,	
	Lucy	Orchestra
	Danza di Brownies	»
I. atto del Milk White	Marcia della luna di	
Ilag	miele	Banda
	Marcia del Centenario	Banda di Gilmore
	Marcia Arcadica	Orchestra
Band Drill	Marcia del Centenario	Banda di Gilmore
	Marcia Liberty Bell	
	Marcia Tommy Atkins	Orchestra
Trio, Whie Milk Ilag	Marcia Arcadica	»
	Danza del ventaglio	»
Elsie Jonee Spagnuola	Faudanze Spagnuolo	»
	» »	»
Danza del remo	Marcia di Nozze Afri-	
	cana (Dal Museo di	
	Barnum e C.)	»
Principessa Ali	Danza del Ventre	»

This one-page list was copied precisely (including typo's) from a January 1896 Catalog of the Continental Phonograph Kinetoscope Co. of Milan, Italy. No speech synchronization was attempted, as all the cylinders above are musical selections.

Illustration 51 · List of films with appropriate musical cylinders for use on the Kinetophone
The only known list of its type, this is reprinted courtesy of Allen Koenigsberg.

What caused the Kinetophone's rapid demise? I believe that there were three reasons. The most obvious one is that it did not synchronise picture and sound, which was a disappointment; however, the public seemed indifferent to sound motion-pictures until the late 1920s. Another reason is purely commercial. Kinetophones cost $50 more than Kinetoscopes at a time when $50 was a considerable amount of money. The phonograph portion was primitive and difficult to keep in adjustment; the cylinders were fragile and expensive. Exhibitors usually got a nickel per film from their patrons. It is likely that they could not get more for a film with sound accompaniment.

A third possible reason is that the Kinetophone was introduced in a market that was declining drastically. The sales, even of new Kinetoscopes, were already tapering off, and the Kinetophone was not sufficiently a novelty to revive the market. No Kinetophones were produced after the spring and summer of 1895, although the ones already sold continued to be used. If the surviving machines at the National Museum of Photography, Film and Television, Bradford, and at the Cinémathèque Française, Paris, are an indication, when the novelty of sound wore off, the phonograph portion was removed from at least some Kinetophones and they continued to be used as Kinetoscopes.

This advertisement in *The Phonoscope* of November 1896 illustrates the approaching end of the active lives of both the Kinetophone and the Kinetoscope:

FOR SALE.–Six Edison Kinetophones, practically as good as new, for $100 each. They cost $300 each. Also 2 Kinetoscopes at $67.50 each. In splendid condition. Will divide the lot if desired. Address, K., care of "The Phonoscope," 822 Broadway, New York.

Announcement.

REDUCTION IN PRICE OF KINETOSCOPES AND KINETO-PHONES.

E take pleasure in announcing that, in consequence of advantageous arrangements having been made with the manufacturers, the price of Kinetoscopes hereafter will be $250.00 per single machine ; former price, $350.00. In lots of four or more, $225.00 each ; former price, $325.00.

The Kineto-phone, which reproduces both music, articulate speech and moving figures and objects (this being Mr. Edison's own combination of the Kinetoscope and Phonograph), we now offer at $300.00 ; former price, $400.00.

The marvelous earning power of the Kinetoscope has been fully demonstrated by practical tests, and the new Edison Combination has fully doubled the receipts of some of the parlors in which it has been shown. Mr. Frank Harrison, of Atlanta, Ga., says : " I have the Phonographic Attachments in. They are working nicely and giving perfect satisfaction, and my receipts have run up to more than three times what they were before." The Kineto-phone (the new combination machine) is indeed a wonder and a marvel. The exhibition of Kinetoscope subjects in conjunction with appropriate music makes the Kineto-phone a complete and most attractive exhibition device.

One of the new machines is now in operation in the Company's office. The film is the First Act of "The Milk White Flag," and as the band is seen coming into view in the Kinetoscope, the music bursts forth with a volume and melody that is truly wonderful and realistic.

While those heretofore listening to the Phonograph have been compelled to draw upon their imaginations in forming an idea of the artist or specialist who rendered the music or dictation listened to, and while those looking at the Kinetoscope have seen the figures acting in pantomime only, this combination machine reproduces both the sounds and motions of the subject in a life-like manner.

Illustration 52 · From the Kinetoscope Company

This entire section is based on articles by and original newspaper clippings collected by Australian researcher and author, Chris Long, from cities all over Australia – a remarkable collection. The only problem is that I thought I had the subject quite well covered until Chris came up with some quite astounding information.

The first Kinetoscopes in Australia were exhibited in Sydney on 30 November 1894, and were shown in city after city to much acclaim. They were part of an early shipment to England, and were then trans-shipped to Australia, as previously described. In September 1895 they were joined by the Kinetophone.

Australian newspaper reporters greeted the arrival of these machines with enthusiasm, and often gave quite detailed synopses of the films shown. This seems not to have been the practice in the United States, although there appears to have been little research in newspapers outside New York City. These synopses provide a great deal of information on films which have been lost, as well as useful descriptions that accompany several films in the *Index*.

Now comes a truly remarkable report of Kinetophone films with, apparently, synchronised cylinders. Edison seems never to have issued any, yet several of these films would appear to have been American-made. A couple might have been Edison films with sound provided on cylinders recorded in Australia, but other films appear distinctly Australian. While phonographs capable of recording on cylinders were readily available, no motion-picture camera is known to have been in Australia at the time these films were shown. I am confident that if anyone can discover where, how and by whom these films and cylinders were made Chris Long can, but meanwhile they remain a challenging mystery!

The films are listed in the chronological order in which they appeared in Australian newspapers. The first film reported is from the *Rockhampton Bulletin* of 4 October 1895: "Mr. Harry Rickards, in his coster-song, 'E dunno where 'e are'". Rickards was an Australian. I cannot think of an Edison film that might fit this description. The same paper for 5 October 1895 reports:

> Mr. A. Chevalier sings 'Mrs. 'Enery 'Awkins'. Mr Chevalier is seen exactly as he appeared on the stage. He starts singing, and while every note and indeed, every word can be heard with the utmost distinction, the movements and gestures of the singer are seen as clearly as ever they were witnessed by those in the stalls of the music halls where he appears.

Mr. Chevalier was English. The reporter's description makes it quite clear that the film and cylinder were made for each other. The question is: who did it? I cannot believe that it was Edison:

> The next subject was Madame Patey [Adelina Patti, it would appear] singing a verse of 'The Holy City.' This impression was taken in Melbourne when Madame

Patey was singing there. To watch the singer just as she appeared on the stage, to see her little gestures and movements, note her turning the sheets of her music, finally rolling it up as she reaches the concluding bars of the song, and all the time to hear her wonderful voice singing this fine song, fills one with amazement at this supreme triumph over time and distance.

In the same paper, same date:

It was an American auctioneer selling a mob of cattle. He is seen in his rostrum calling the attention of buyers to the cattle he was about to offer, and he announces that he will put up one animal, but the purchaser will have the right to take as many of the mob as he chooses at the price at which the one is knocked down. The sale begins with a bid of twenty dollars, and soon runs up to thirty, where there is a slight halt. The auctioneer throws out his hands, knocks on the box, asks if it is possible that is all they mean to bid for such remarkably fine animals, and at length gets his patrons started again, when they run the price up to thirty-five dollars, at which figure the hammer falls. The scene closes with the auctioneer asking the purchaser how many he will take, and the reply that he will take the lot.

The *Adelaide Register* of 18 January 1896 describes the same film, but with some additional information:

The first item was a kinetoscope view of an auctioneer earnestly selling a prime lot of bullocks from somebody's estate on Lake Michigan. He did his work so well, and his voice was so clear and vehement, that the only regret was that the shutter obliterated him before the *Register* representative had time to raise the bid another dollar or two.

A remarkable film; most likely a moderate close-up, as is the definitely Edison film, *Layman, Man of 1000 Faces*. It is impossible to imagine this film without the dialogue.

The same paper for 12 October 1895 mentions "The Alabama Coon". On 29 February 1896, Broken Hill's *The Barrier Miner* lists an untitled song by "George J. Gaskin, America's Leading Vocalist". Indeed, he was one of Edison's regular recording artists for many years; Allen Koenigsberg's *Edison Cylinder Records, 1889-1912* lists him as recording "Little Alabama Coon". This is getting close to Edison, but I cannot link the cylinder to any known film. In the same paper, same date:

a man who sang a Tyrolean song with an Irish accent, but a distinct 'yodel,' and every time he moved and his coat flapped one could catch a glimpse of the gold medal he wore on his watch chain...Then came a dancer, whose sinuous limbs in all their muscular changes could be marked under the thin veil of the black skirts, and the music to which she danced was, as an Irishman would say, 'clearly visible.'

The same paper for 27 January 1896 states:

The tonsorial artist is seen lathering his customers and during the whole of the scene is to be heard addressing the usual small talk to his victim.

Of these four films, the first two seem to have no connection with Edison; the dancer does not give enough description to tell. The last sounds like one of the two Edison *Barber Shops*, with perhaps an Australian cylinder added – an extremely easy task and one not requiring any synchronisation, since the barber is in the background with his lips not clearly visible. Broken Hill's *The Barrier Miner* for 24 February 1896:

> The FRENCH DANCING GIRL (also called 'a French danseuse.') To watch the French lady artist as she glides along in her white satin dancing costume, keeping time to her accompaniment, to see her movements throughout the dance – it is wonderful indeed...SALVATION ARMY CAPTAIN (with full band accompaniment) (also listed elsewhere as Salvation Army Captain Heckled at a Meeting).

In the same paper, same date: "George J. Gaskin, America's Leading Vocalist" (note: no song was announced). Of these three films, I cannot identify the *French Dancing Girl* as Edison. In none of the several dance films I have seen is the dancer wearing "white satin". *Salvation Army Captain* poses a real puzzle. In the *Index* is an entry for "Miss Isabelle Coe as 'The Widder'", one of five Edison filmings of subjects from the musical, *The Milk White Flag*. In the film, her costume certainly looks as if it could be a Salvation Army costume. The only problem is that, according to Hendricks in *The Kinetoscope*, a note from Dickson to Raff & Gammon said that the film was faulty, and it was to be deleted from the list of films. As for George J Gaskin, see the listing of these Australian films under the date of 12 October 1895 for "The Alabama Coon". The cylinder could well be Gaskin's, but I have never heard of an Edison film of any man just singing, much less Mr Gaskin!

In the same paper, 4 March 1896: "THE COLDSTREAM GUARDS (with conductor)". This could well be *Band Drill* from Edison's series of films of the musical, *The Milk White Flag*, with a band cylinder accompaniment. I suppose a marching band in costume could be given almost any desired name. In the same paper, 9 March 1896:

> Mrs. Shawe – the beautiful lady whistler (with piano accompaniment) of New York. "I Can't Change It," (song).

Edison recorded a number of whistling solos, but no known films of Mrs Shawe or any other whistler. "I Can't Change It" does not appear in any list of Edison cylinders. In the same paper, 25 July 1896:

> Call and see Mr. Frank Lawton, the famous whistler, dance, and actually hear the orchestra accompaniment at the same time.

No specific selections were listed until the 1 August edition. In the same paper, 1 August 1896:

> Call and see Mr. FRANK LAWTON, the Great American Whistler, of the 'Trip to Chinatown' Company in the Trio Dance, and hear him whistle 'Ben Bolt,' the 'Canary Polka,' etc.

Coincidentally, Frank Lawton not only was one of the three dancers in Edison's *Trio, A Lively Eccentric Dance by Frank Lawton and Misses Williamson and France, of Hoyt's 'Milk White Flag'*, but also he was performing in Hoyt's 'A Trip to Chinatown' in Sydney at this time! What a wonderful opportunity for him to record an appropriate cylinder for the *Trio Dance*. He is not known to have recorded for Edison.

If any reader has or obtains any information about this remarkable work, a letter to the author would be appreciated.

Edison did not invent the Kinetoscope in a vacuum. Men had been working on "moving pictures" for many years in this country and abroad. There were spinning discs, rotating slotted cylinders and similar devices in various combinations with wonderful names such as "Zoetrope" and "Praxinoscope". At least one was successfully projected (see illustration 53). These devices used a series of drawings, such as a girl skipping rope, which repeated a simple action at about one-second intervals.

Some experimenters used photography. The most noted example was Eadweard Muybridge, who used a series of 24 cameras to take pictures of a trotting horse. When viewed in a Zoetrope or the like, the photographs gave a good representation of a trotting horse. The major problem was that the horse appeared to be trotting in place, with the earth flying by underneath him! He did not appear to trot from one place to another, as he actually did in life, and as Edison's Kinetoscope would show him doing. Others tried multi-lensed cameras and other variations.

Illustration 53 · "A curious adaptation of the Praxinoscope"
Projection of moving pictures in 1884. The lens on the right projected a background, in colour, onto the screen, while the lens at the left projected figures in motion. London's Museum of the Moving Image demonstrates to visitors a replica of a similar but larger machine.

The earliest of Edison's competitors actually preceded him in the market. In 1891, Siemens & Halske, the German electrical company, produced a machine called the "Schnellseher", invented c.1887 by Ottmar Anschütz (illustration 54). It had a

Illustration 54 · A German "Schnellseher" of 1891

Originals are in the Deutsches Museum, Munich, and in the National Technical Museum, Prague. The latter has two extra reels, one of which seems to be on a large sheet of celluloid. In operation, the large wheel turns counter-clockwise. As each image appears behind the viewer on the left, a Geisler tube gives a brief bright flash of light, stopping the action. The machine merely repeats the same action over and over again. (The Siemens Company)

large wheel with transparent photographs mounted around the edge, as in the illustration. Upon depositing a coin, the patron could turn a crank which spun the wheel. As the wheel spun, each picture in turn was momentarily lit by a Geisler tube mounted behind the viewer, and the series of pictures showed motion, such as a horse running, repeated with every turn of the wheel. There was no film, and the machine could show only about one second of motion, repeated over and over again. It was really only an elaborate Zoetrope. However, these machines were produced commercially and at least one was in New York City at the Eden Musee at the time the Kinetoscope was introduced. According to Ramsaye, it operated until pictures were no longer available.[1]

As Edison's experiments were widely publicised, with diagrams and detailed descriptions of the Kinetoscope appearing in magazines and newspapers at least by 1891, it is surprising that he did not have more competition. More did appear, but not until Edison had introduced the Kinetoscope publicly in April 1894.

One problem arose because Edison, possibly because he was deeply involved with his magnetic ore separator project at the time, badly underestimated the appeal of the Kinetoscope. As a result, probably combined with his increasing disgust at the lack of protection which patents were giving him, and the cost of filing them, he decided not to patent the Kinetoscope in Europe. Two Greeks bought several of the first Kinetoscopes, took them to London and opened an exhibition. The venture was highly successful, and they wanted more machines. Rather than paying Edison's price, they decided to have copies made. They found an Englishman, Robert W Paul, who discovered the lack of patents and proceeded to make some 60 copies, thus severely damaging the European market for Edison. Paul initially bought Edison films, as there were no others. When Edison's agents found out what was going on, and refused to sell him more film, Paul invented a camera and made his own films, in spring 1895. At least one of Paul's Kinetoscope copies survives. It is on display in the Conservatoire des Arts et Métiers in Paris, France (see its description on page 100).

In the United States, a man named Chinnock had a camera made for him by autumn 1894 and manufactured "Kinetoscopes" that were somewhat extensively sold and used, at least in the eastern United States, beginning early in 1895. While called "Kinetoscopes", his machines used no film for viewing. They used a series of photographs on paper, glued to canvas and wound in a spiral around a large drum. Gordon Hendricks, author of *The Kinetoscope*, was unable to find either a Chinnock "Kinetoscope" or a picture of one to use for an illustration, and I have not heard of a surviving machine.

Note from the above description and from the following paragraphs that others besides Edison used the term "Kinetoscope" to describe their machines, although only those of Paul were direct copies. The index of Hendricks' *Origins of the American Film*, a compilation of his three books on early motion-pictures, lists ten Chinnock "films".

The fact that these pictures were not on film, but paper prints fastened to canvas, leads me to the next machine, the American Parlor Kinetoscope (illustration 55). This machine was patented on 24 August 1897, and used a paper strip of photographs about 1½" high and 1¾" wide in a 25' loop. The pictures were not printed photographically, but in halftones on ordinary paper in sections about 13" long, glued end to end. The only illumination was a window on one side, and the mechanism was a rocking-mirror device. At one cent per view, it was not asking too much to require the patron to turn the crank! This machine had no sprocket-holes or any other device to keep the pictures in registration. However, on display at the Cinémathèque

Française, Paris, is a strip of paper prints, perhaps mounted on canvas. At the outer edges of the paper, and between each frame are two brass grommets. There was no machine on display with it, but the grommets indicated that registration was provided for.

Illustration 55 · American Parlor Kinetoscope
Patent applied for 1 June 1896, granted 24 August 1897. It used a paper loop 1¾" wide and about 25 feet long, not on photographic paper, but printed in halftones on pieces of paper 13" long, which were then pasted together end-to-end.

The machine most like Edison's appears to have been the "Hand Kinetoscope", manufacturer unknown (illustration 56), but the date would appear to be 1897 or 1898. An ad for it appeared in a catalogue of Ogden & Company, Chicago. The same issue advertised "Edison's new 1898 Home Phonograph", and among the films recommended for the "Hand Kinetoscope" was a *Bull Fight*, which was copyrighted by Edison in 1898. The machine looked very similar to the upper 18" of an Edison Kinetoscope, except that the left side was glass, which allowed for illumination and also showed that the film was allowed to lie in a jumble instead of being stored on spools. This saved both money and space, but must have shortened the useful life of the film. The type of action is unknown to the author at this time, as he knows of no surviving machine.

At an early stage, Edison had competition in the film business as well. Until 23 October 1896, he did not copyright his films; he probably felt it an unnecessary expense, as he controlled the only machines – except Paul's – capable of using them. Films taken in the Black Maria did use an identifying device, as Edison made the films for several corporate entities, which then sold copies. The device was to put a small card on the front corner of the stage, so that it appeared in every frame of the film. For the Kinetoscope Company (Raff & Gammon) it was an "R"; for Maguire & Baucus an "MB"; and for the Continental Commerce Company it was a "C". These are the only ones known so far. However, unauthorised and unpaid-for duplication by the International Film Company and others finally forced Edison to copyright.

THE HAND KINETOSCOPE.

GREATEST, EASIEST AND QUICKEST MONEY MAKER IN THE WORLD.

Size, 18 x 18 x 10 inches.

Is a moving picture machine showing each subject as if it were alive and in real life. Every move can be seen as plainly as if you were watching the subjects themselves. IT USES ANY STANDARD MAKE OF FILMS. The film moving mechanism does not injure the film, and the results much better than the $150 Electric Kinetoscope. The nickel-in-the-slot attachment is simple, and so constructed that it is impossible to operate machine without a nickel. We guarantee the workmanship and material on this machine to be first-class throughout, and will gladly ship it C. O. D., privilege of examination, on receipt of $10.00 to guarantee express charges. Place one of these machines in a store, saloon, hotel, depot or any public place, with a good prize fight, Midway dance, foreign street scene, bull fight, where the bull kills the horse, etc., and you will be surprised at the receipts.
If in good location will pay for itself in two weeks.
Drop a nickel in the slot and by turning the handle or crank puts the machine in motion. French plate glass covering the entire one side of the machine, it is therefore free from any complicated electric connections for lighting connections.
We carry in stock a full assortment of EDISON FILMS at lowest market prices.

NEW HAND KINETOSCOPE.

With Nickel-in-the-Slot Attachment.

$30.00 COMPLETE WITH EDISON FILM.

No Battery.   No Electricity.   No Expense to Run.

Illustration 56 · From a Samuel Nafew mail-order catalogue of 1897-98
(From the collection of Richard Bueschell)

Lumière and others started producing films *and* copying each other's (illustration 57). Raff & Gammon were selling Lumière films by late August or early September 1896. Edison candidly admitted doing his share of copying!

Now back to competing machines and the Kinetoscope's nemeses; plural because it took double blows to "kill" the Kinetoscope. Projection was one blow, killing the "upper-class" market, which was already failing as the novelty wore off. Skirt dances and speeding locomotives became boring. Projection did not kill Edison's interests. He adapted, and produced projectors (illustration 58) and films until 1918, very profitably. On 29 January 1900, he testified that he still occasionally sold 1918, very profitably. The other blow was the introduction of the Mutoscope (illustration 59). It captured the arcade business by doing everything the Kinetoscope did, only cheaper

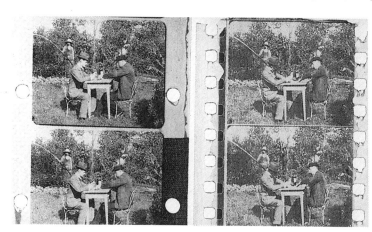

Illustration 57 · The Lumière film, *Quarrel Over a Game of Cards*
The first Lumière films in the United States (August and September 1896) used the standard Lumière sprocket holes – one round hole on either side of each frame. This limited them to Lumière projectors. As shown here, they were soon copied on film with Edison perforations, and became major competition. (Seaver Center, Natural History Museum of Los Angeles County)

HEADQUARTERS FOR

Thomas A. Edison's Projecting Kinetoscope

"'97 MODEL."

AND ORIGINAL EDISON FILMS.

Buy Direct and Get the Latest Genuine Edison Apparatus,

WRITE FOR NEW LIST OF 75 EDISON FILMS JUST TAKEN IN THE WEST. THEY ARE THE BEST OF MR. EDISON'S PRODUCT.

MACHINES
—AND—
FILMS
IN STOCK,
And Can be Shipped
Promptly.

Special Calcium
Light Jet
—FOR—
EDISON
Projectoscope

Write for Complete List of more than 800 Genuine Edison Films.

Enabling Machine to be Operated Independent of Electricity and with equal results.

EDISON '97 MODEL PROJECTOSCOPE.   WRITE FOR CATALOGUE.
Samples of all Edison apparatus may be seen, and purchasers instructed in use of same, without charge, at Show Room in Edison Building.

EDISON CONCERT PHONOGRAPH.

To be used in Combination with the projectoscope, the Records Harmonized to Films, REDUCTION IN PRICE Edison Class M Phonograph, $75.00; Edison Home Phonograph, $30.00
For Complete Catalogue and prices of everything manufactured at the Edison Laboratory, address
J. O. PRESCOTT, Edison Building, New York, N. Y.

Illustration 58

When the Kinetoscope "died", Edison switched to projectors, and for many years they were considered the finest available. Edison's earliest projectors provided for the use of his Kinetoscope-type looped films. Early instructions suggested that each film be run through the projector three times: once to get the audience used to the idea of the film; again to let the audience actually enjoy the subject; and a third time only because after that the audience would become bored!

---

and better. Instead of playing for about 30 seconds, a Mutoscope played for about one minute. Cast-metal cabinets (illustration 60), later replaced by cheap sheet-metal boxes, replaced the oak cabinets. A simple crank replaced the batteries, electric motor, gears and belts. A reel of almost indestructible cards (illustration 61) replaced the scratchable, breakable film. Today, in the few Mutoscopes still in arcades rather than in collectors' hands, many of the reels are originals of the 1920s – and they never seem to wear out!

It is strange to note that W K-L Dickson was largely responsible for the Mutoscope. After working for Edison for many years, Dickson sadly left under difficult circumstances. On 2 April 1895, after a dispute involving Edison's new general manager, William E Gilmore, Dickson resigned. The fact that he was doing some outside work for a competitor of Edison likely contributed to the disagreement. A few days later, Dickson returned to pick up his personal effects. The group of the famous Edison notebooks pertaining to the Kinetoscope and to motion-pictures, according to Edison's sworn testimony, disappeared at this time. Within a matter of months, Dickson had joined the firm which became the Mutoscope and Biograph Company.[2] By September 1895, a Mutoscope camera had been produced (one is on display in the National Museum of American History). By December, Mutoscopes were on the market, and by February 1897 were so prevalent that the Kinetoscope's doom was at hand. While many Kinetoscopes were still in use, sales of new machines dropped to only a few per month, and almost all new films were made for projection.

When, in 1909, Edison and his major competitors formed the Motion Picture Patents Company, a grand formal dinner was held. At the dinner, a film was made showing Edison standing while each guest filed by and shook his hand. A copy of the film was given to each guest as a souvenir (illustration 62). The gift was not even an Edison product. The Biograph film was transferred to reels of Mutoscope cards, and given to the guests in decorative table-sized Mutoscope cabinets! I suspect that Edison just laughed at the irony of it all![3]

Notes

[1] Terry Ramsaye, *A Million and One Nights: A History of the Motion Picture*, volume I (New York: Simon and Schuster, 1926): 183.

[2] For a detailed history of this company, see Richard Brown and Barry Anthony, *A Victorian Film Enterprise: The History of the British Mutoscope and Biograph Company* (Trowbridge: Flicks Books, forthcoming).

[3] At least one, and perhaps two, of these table Mutoscopes survives. A gift from Charles G Clarke, it is in the collection of the American Society of Cinematographers, 1782 N Orange Drive, Los Angeles (Hollywood), CA. Another, in the 1960s, was given to what was supposed to be the Hollywood Motion Picture Museum, which never came to pass. It may still exist in storage somewhere.

Illustration 59 · A "table" Mutoscope of 1898

Most coin-operated Mutoscopes of this period were huge floor-standing machines like those in the photograph of Talley's (illustration 41). However, table models were built, and one similar to that shown above was given to each guest at the banquet on 18 December 1909. One of them is on display at the American Society of Cinematographers headquarters, 1782 N Orange Drive, Los Angeles, Hollywood, CA. On it is the original reel, showing Edison greeting the other guests at the banquet. A film has been made from this reel, although I do not know its location.

MUTOSCOPES

"BACKBONE OF THE ARCADE BUSINESS."

The average town or city will readily support as many "Automatic Vandevilles" as it does theatres. Dozens of Arcades were opened last year by men of no previous experience with coin-operated machines, and all are coining money.

Do you know of a good location? If so, don't hesitate. The Autumn months are the very best of the year. We have a splendid new model Mutoscope at $50.00, and bargains in used machines as low as $32.50.

AMERICAN MUTOSCOPE & BIOGRAPH CO.,

TYPE E.   116 NO. B'WAY, LOS ANGELES.   11 E. 14th ST., NEW YORK

Illustration 60 · A typical large, cast-iron Mutoscope of the late 1890s

Illustration 61
A complete card from a Mutoscope reel. Notice the worn top-centre of the card, the rather typical "girlie" subject, the hole just below the picture which was used to keep the pictures in registration, and the triangular cuts towards the bottom, which enabled the card to be held firmly by the metal reel. Note: this may be the first published illustration of a complete Mutoscope card.

Illustration 62 · Edison and some of his competitors, 18 December 1909
An enlargement of one card of a Mutoscope reel, further described in the text.

There is only one surviving Kinetograph (camera), and only nine known Kinetoscopes and three Kinetophones. Only a few of these are on public display. Let me describe the machines I know of, beginning with those on public display. I may have missed one, as the list is shockingly brief.

Kinetoscope #1026, on display at Eastman House, 900 East Avenue, Rochester, NY, is the best preserved machine I have seen, and I have seen all those described, with just one exception. It is virtually complete, even to having traces of the original gold striping barely visible on the black-enamelled viewer. On no other machine I have seen has this decoration survived. Also at Eastman House is a modern device on which one can view a Kinetoscope film. Although it is not available to the public, Eastman House has a large collection of Kinetoscope films.

The library of the Academy of Motion Picture Arts and Sciences (AMPAS), in its handsome new building at 333 S La Cienega Blvd., Beverly Hills, CA, has a Kinetoscope on display, and a request to the librarian may allow one to view a hand-coloured *Annabelle Serpentine Dance*. The viewing portion is original except for the eyepiece, which I provided for it recently. The motor and some other parts were replaced early this century, so that it now operates on 110 volts. The original nameplate is missing, so that its serial number is unknown. This machine and the next have been altered to 5-cent coin operation, probably at the same time as the motors on both machines were changed.

Nearby, in the collection of the American Society of Cinematographers (ASC), 1782 N Orange Drive, Hollywood, CA, is a companion piece to the one at the Academy. Both were found in storage in Oakland, CA, in 1936 by Charles G Clarke, and given to the two institutions. The one at ASC has had the top and one side replaced with plexiglass. It could probably operate, but does not.

On display at the Henry Ford Museum, Dearborn, MI, is the only surviving Kinetograph (camera). Since it is described in chapter 3, I will only mention that it is on display. Also at the museum, but in storage, are two Kinetoscopes. One is damaged and incomplete. The other, #1018, was locked when I saw it in 1988, and keys were unobtainable. Even then, I was able to determine that it had an original film on its spoolbank, and on a shelf in the incomplete machine were three more original films, each still in its original film can, as described elsewhere. When I visited the museum in May 1996, the keys to #1018 had been found and the film removed for safe-keeping. For the first time in many years, the interior could be examined.

It had a coin slot on the exterior, so it had definitely been a coin-operated machine at one time. An examination of the interior showed that the Kinetoscope works in good condition, but with an unusual adaptation that enabled the machine to use the clear film that Edison introduced in summer 1896. It had an elaborate but primitive coin-slot mechanism from which all the electric wiring had been removed. With a shock I recognised the machine. I have had a copy of a c.1896 photograph of it for many years. It is so unique that there is no question about it. The photograph was taken in Edison's library. All the machine's doors were open, giving a clear view of the parts unique to this machine. I would surmise that this machine was never sold, but was an experimental model given to Ford in the 1920s together with thousands of other items destined for Ford's museum.

There are several interesting machines in Europe. The Cinémathèque Française in Paris, has a superb collection, and one of only three known surviving Kinetophones. Restored in October 1992 by the author, it is the most complete Kinetophone on public display. It has the lowest serial number (#69) of any surviving machine, and is unusual in that its history has survived. According to Richard Brown, it was supplied to Holland Brothers in New York in August 1894. Along with two other machines, it was bought by two Greeks, ostensibly for use in the United States. Instead, the three machines were shipped to England. Besides being exhibited there, they were used by Robert Paul as models when he was making copies of the Kinetoscope. Later, #69 was sold by the Greeks to a mobile exhibitor in Halifax, in the north of England, and was purchased from his widow by Will Day, possibly c.1919. It was then placed on show in London's Science Museum for many years. It was sent to France when the Will Day Collection was sold around 1959. This Collection forms a major part of the Cinémathèque Française. Unfortunately, this history does not describe #69's conversion to Kinetophone, or state when the original phonograph was removed.

In 1994 the Cinémathèque acquired one of my working Kinetoscope replicas so that visitors may see it in operation and view films on it.

The Musée du Cinéma de Lyon in France (69 rue Jean Jaurès, 69100 Villeurbanne) has what is reputed to be a machine in excellent condition, although missing the nameplate, for which I recently supplied a replica.

In Denmark, Det Danske Filmmuseum has a large collection of early film apparatus, including Kinetoscope #211. Unfortunately, none of this collection is on display at the present time, although the Museum hopes to exhibit it eventually. It is in storage at a branch of the Technical Museum at the Trafikmuseet, Ole Rømers Vej 15, 3000 Helsingor (Elsinore), a charming town twenty miles north of Copenhagen. After advance arrangements, I was allowed to inspect #211. It is in basically good condition, with the nameplate and original motor surviving. Exceptions are that the original lamp and its fitting have been replaced by a small modern 220-volt bulb not connected to the Kinetoscope's wiring, and the viewer and its magnifying lens have been modified. The stop mechanism survives almost intact, but a missing spring makes it inoperable. On the spools is a modern copy of a tinted Annabelle dance which was apparently obtained from Prague. This is a puzzle, as this film is identical to the one on the Kinetoscope at the Academy Library, Beverly Hills, CA, and, since they gave me a copy, I also have one. Obviously an original either exists or existed until modern colour film became available, but I know nothing further about it.

As it happened, the day I saw #211, 10 August 1993, was 56 years to the day after I first saw a Kinetoscope in the Science Museum, London. This machine survives, and is one of two recently transferred to the National Museum of Photography, Film and Television. Richard Brown sent me the following information, obtained from the Science Museum's files. The first machine obtained was actually a somewhat incomplete Kinetophone. It was purchased in 1930 for £6. The Science

Museum's Keeper wrote to his Director about copying the missing parts from Will Day's machine (then in England, and now in the Cinémathèque Française, Paris), but this never occurred. Missing were the patent plate and all the phonograph parts except for two small fittings which serve to prove that it was once a Kinetophone. The Museum has a separate phonograph, Serial #K1268 (the "K" indicating that it was for use in a Kinetophone), but there is no indication that it came with the Kinetophone, nor has it ever been installed. I have offered to complete the machine, but have received no reply to my letters. The second machine was Kinetoscope #509, purchased in 1948, and reasonably complete and on display. However, at the time of writing, title to the photography collection had been turned over to the National Museum of Photography, Film and Television, Pictureville, Bradford, West Yorkshire, England, and the Kinetoscope and other material has been moved to Bradford.

There is a tragic ruin at the Conservatoire des Arts et Métiers, 292 rue Saint-Martin, Paris, France. There is located the only surviving example of more than 60 copies of Edison's Kinetoscope made by Robert Paul of London in 1894-95. Not visible from the outside but cast into the iron bedplate are the words "R. W. PAUL/ HATTON COURT/LONDON". When I saw it in 1961, it was in excellent condition, but by 1990 it had almost been destroyed. Half of the two-part exterior viewer had been removed. Inside, the partitions had been removed, the wooden spools had been replaced with brass, the whole lower part of the spool-bank replaced with sheet-metal, and so on. It appeared that someone had tried to make it operate by removing much of the original mechanism and replacing it with a modern device, and, sadly, in doing so virtually destroyed the machine.

The author purchased Kinetoscope #141 at auction at Sotheby's, London, on 2 October 1992. It is an unusual machine, differing in its starting mechanism from any other surviving Kinetoscope. The August 1895 brochure reproduced on pages 47-58 gives a name for it at the bottom of page 5. It is a "pull-rod" Kinetoscope, and that is how the machine is actuated. When pulled, a knob on the back of the machine pulls a rod attached to the starting switch. The motor is started and the lamp turned on, all in one operation. This requires the patron to watch a flickering beginning as the film gets up to speed. Even Kinetoscope #69 at the Cinémathèque Française, as well as all other surviving Kinetoscopes (except the one coin-slot machine at the Henry Ford Museum), have the lever-action described on pages 30-35 or the holes in the cabinet showing where the lever-action had been. The lever action was a great improvement, reducing damage to the sprocket-holes and turning the lamp on only when the film was up to speed, and it must have been introduced very early, despite its serial number, #141. Kirk Bauer suggested a likely explanation: that it was an early machine that had been returned to Edison, refurbished, had a new nameplate (and serial number) added, and was then sold overseas. Hendricks' *The Kinetoscope* reports that, indeed, the first 25 Kinetoscopes were returned, refurbished, renumbered and resold. This machine's number does not fall within the series of new numbers Hendricks cites, but he gives only fourteen numbers, leaving eleven unaccounted for.

In any case, Richard Brown's research reveals that #141 was one of 50 machines shipped to London in September 1894. Surviving iron fittings would seem to indicate that it was one of the ten machines installed in the first Kinetoscope parlour in London, at 70 Oxford Street. When this parlour was closed, the machine apparently was purchased by Mr C E Berrington and preserved by his family until auctioned. It is the first Kinetoscope to have surfaced in many years, perhaps since the two that Charles Clarke found in the 1930s.

The three surviving Kinetophones have been described already: the almost complete one in Sydney; the barely recognisable one at Bradford; and the one at the Cinémathèque Française. A brief description of the restoration of the latter machine might be of interest. When I first saw the machine, it was missing a pair of wheels used to guide the drive belt down to the phonograph, the phonograph itself, and the repeating mechanism for it, the belts to drive the phonograph, and the rubber tubes used to carry the sound to the ears of the patron.

By great good fortune, I had most of the missing pieces and knew how to replicate those I did not have. Several years ago, a fellow phonograph collector in England found part of a phonograph in a pile of scrap iron and bought it. Since it had no motor or cabinet, he lost interest in it and asked another collector who might be interested in it. He did not realise that it was the phonograph for a Kinetophone. Fortunately, this collector suggested me, and I bought it.

Another friend, Steve Oliphant, found a repeating mechanism in a pile of phonograph parts belonging to a dealer in Northern California, recognised it, bought it and gave it to me. I knew how to make the wheel mechanism and assemble the belt and rubber eartubes from seeing them on a machine in Australia. Thus, it took assistance from England, Australia and the United States to restore a Kinetophone in France. Vital to the whole project, of course, was the realisation by the Cinémathèque Française of the importance of its machine.

Until the restoration described above, the only almost-complete Kinetophone in the world (missing only the repeat mechanism and nameplate) was the one in Sydney, Australia. Its custodian has been kind enough to allow me to inspect it twice.

The Edison National Historic Site does not have a Kinetoscope. Most of what Edison saved burned in a tragic fire in 1914. I offered to build excellent working replicas for the site of the invention of the Kinetoscope. Instead, they chose to use plywood boxes containing miniature Japanese television sets showing videotapes of Edison Kinetoscope films!

There are two fine machines, not quite originals but certainly not replicas. The first, belonging to the author, has quite a history. Several years ago, after advertising for a Kinetoscope for two years, I was offered a cabinet from which everything was missing except the spoolbank. The antique dealer in Idaho Falls, ID, had bought it at an auction several years before. It would appear that someone had taken it apart, perhaps as part of a restoration project, and it had remained that way. The dealer said that a box of miscellaneous metal parts had sold separately at the auction and that, looking back on it, the box must have contained the missing works. He did not know enough about such machines at the time to buy the box, and too long a time had passed to try to trace it.

Fortunately, I had been helpful to the library of the Motion Picture Academy, and the Director, Linda Harris Mehr, graciously (albeit nervously) permitted me to measure and photograph the Library's machine. As I had already examined and measured the machines at the Science Museum, Eastman House and others, I was able to produce replicas more complete than any single surviving machine, as all were incomplete in one way or another, but not all in the *same* way!

Through mutual friends, I found that Glenn Grabinsky of Montville, NJ, had also found an empty cabinet. Fortunately, his still had its original nameplate, with the serial number (#457) intact. This number enabled the owner to trace the original ownership back to a resort hotel on the New Jersey coast. In order to help defray the anticipated substantial expense of restoring my machine, I restored Glenn's and built my first complete replica for a private collector. This replica has recently been sold to the International Cinema Museum, 319 West Erie Street, Chicago, IL. Since then, the museum has closed, hopefully to reopen at a new location.

However, I was not the first to make replicas. The Cinematheque Yugoslavie, Belgrade, has a replica Kinetoscope made in Yugoslavia in 1952. The Cinémathèque Royale de Belgique, Brussels, has a replica of the Kinetoscope in Denmark. At the American History building of the Smithsonian Institution, Washington, DC, is a good replica, made some years ago as a copy of the one at Eastman House, even to the serial number. In 1990 I did not see it on display. Paul Potash, an engineer in Philadelphia, PA, has made at least one replica and was gracious enough to help me with mine.

The Deutsches Filmmuseum, Schaumainkai 41, Frankfurt, Germany, has a replica made in Germany several years ago and modelled on the Kinetoscope formerly in the Science Museum, London. Part of an interesting display in a lovely new museum, it is meant to operate but does not, as it apparently "tears the film".

The Museum of the Moving Image, 34-12 36th Street, Astoria, NY, has an excellent working replica which I made for them. If it is not on display, it can probably be seen by request. At the Museum of the Moving Image, London, one may view films on two of my operating replicas (illustration 63). The museum has

Illustration 63 · Two of the author's replicas
Stephen Herbert, formerly Deputy Technical Manager of the Museum of the Moving Image, London, with the author (right). The recently opened museum has already had its millionth visitor, and many have used the 10p slots to view the Kinetoscopes – Stephen estimates several hundred thousand.

added coin-boxes: for 10p one may watch Annabelle's *Serpentine Dance* or *The Fire Scene*, or one of several additional films I sent it recently. The Museum has had two additional replicas made locally, so one may be able to see four films. The staff of the Museum seemed a little reluctant to tell me about their locally-made replicas, thinking perhaps that I might be angry. I reminded them that 100 years ago Paul was able to make replicas of Edison machines because Edison had not patented them in England, and now history was repeating itself! I jokingly suggested that they use Paul-made films in their two replicas. They saw the humour in that and agreed that that might be a good idea!

One of my recent replicas went to a collector in Spain. Three machines originally sold to collectors have been resold to museums. One has already been mentioned above. Another was just sold to the Museo Nazionale del Cinema, Piazza San Giovanni 2, Turin, Italy. In November 1994, the enormous photographic collection of Thurman Naylor, Chestnut Hill, MA, was sold to the Japanese Government. Among the 31 000 items was one of my early replicas. It will be part of an enormous museum being built in Yokohama, which was due to be completed by the end of 1995. Most recently, replicas have been sent to collectors in the United States and Germany, an original but empty cabinet restored for a collector in London by adding the missing Kinetoscope mechanism, and a complete replica sent to Oslo to be part of Norway's new film museum.

If any reader knows of any Kinetoscope which I have missed – original or replica – I hope that he/she will write to me. I would like to make more operating replicas to supplement those already being shown to the public. These primitive machines and quaint films fascinate me: with the scarcity of original machines, replicas are the only way in which the public can experience Edison's invention of over a century ago. London's Museum of the Moving Image tells me that several hundred thousand visitors have viewed Edison films through the replicas which I made for it. This tells me that the general public greatly enjoys the experience once given the opportunity.

Considering the enormous industry that motion-pictures has become in the last 100 years, it is gratifying to realise that Edison's Kinetoscope and its films are still honoured and appreciated.

Several years ago I first saw a modern reprint of Dickson's 1895 *History of the Kinetograph, Kinetoscope & Kinetophonograph.* Used as an illustration in it were sixteen consecutive frames of *Buffalo Bill.* The subject was Buffalo Bill kneeling and firing a lever-action repeating rifle. Later I found that no copy of the film had survived; all that remained was this single illustration. I thought this regrettable, as the film was not only an early one (24 September 1894), but also of a man whose fame survives to this day.

I had seen a film in which a number of sets of Muybridge's prints had been "animated" by copying each print of a set onto film and then repeating the set several times, as each set by itself would be only perhaps two seconds long. For example: a woman walked up the stairs/up the stairs/up the stairs. Each time she "magically" reappeared at the bottom of the stairs. With no "continuity", the project was interesting, but showed Muybridge's limitations as well as his accomplishments.

Later I saw *Annie Oakley* at the French SAF. The film begins with Annie standing and firing a lever-action repeating rifle several times. Then she kneels and continues firing until the end of the film. She fires, moves the rifle's lever down to eject the spent cartridge casing, then moves the lever back up, which inserts a new cartridge and cocks the trigger. She fires again and repeats the sequence until the end of the film, never moving from her kneeling position.

What if the sixteen frames could be returned to film and repeated several times? Perhaps a portion of *Buffalo Bill* could be recreated?

Since I knew that UCLA had restored to film many of the Library of Congress Paper Print Collection, I thought that they might be able to assist. In 1992 Blaine Bartell helped me by copying the sixteen frames onto film. This showed that the sixteen frames included part of a sequence. Bill fired, then moved the lever down, and the frames stopped there. Frames that would show him raising the lever back to firing position were missing. I was afraid that I could only duplicate Muybridge's incomplete results. Then I realised that by reversing the last seven frames and adding them to the sequence, Bill would lift the lever back into firing position and a sequence would be completed. Then, by repeating this sequence several times, at least the known portion of *Buffalo Bill* would be replicated – or at least simulated. Before any further work could be done, Blaine became too busy and the project stopped.

In spring 1995, Phil Condax, recently retired Chief Curator of Technology at Eastman House, introduced me to International Creative Effects (ICE), its President, Larry Benson, and his Director of Computer Graphics, Dean Sadamune, and they agreed to help. At Dean's work-station was a Silicon Graphics computer, an "Extreme" model equal in power to a "supercomputer". It was like magic! Within a few minutes the computer had scanned a copy of the sixteen-frame illustration in Dickson's *History.* A few minutes later and the computer had placed each frame in order and was showing them to us repeatedly! It was wonderful – but still incomplete. Bill's hand and the rifle's lever moved down and then jumped back to firing position.

Then, with some moves of the computer's "mouse", Dean added to the sequence frames, 15, 14, 13, 12, 11, 10 and 9, and started the sequences again... Bill worked the lever just as he had done on the Black Maria's stage. The action was smooth and convincing. There was still a problem, but its solution had to wait a little while.

In May 1995 I went to ICE to interview Dean for this chapter. That completed, I asked him if he could take *Buffalo Bill* a little further towards perfection. To me, the most noticeable problem was that on the seven reversed frames the cloud of smoke, which had come from the rifle when it was fired and billowed away from the end of the barrel, started to blow back towards the rifle! Dean brought up a programme on the computer that had a grey scale from which he could pick the shade of grey he wanted. On each of the seven reversed frames, Dean used the computer's mouse and erased the offending cloud of smoke, replacing each with the exact shade of grey of the background. Another problem, one which I recognised as being common not only to this film, but also to several other early films, was that the image "floated" – a wonderfully descriptive word for a very unsteady image. Dean felt that it was because the film was not held *perfectly* steady in these earliest of motion-picture cameras. "Floating" is not a problem when the films are viewed in the Kinetoscope, but when enlarged or projected it can be distracting. Dean and a colleague steadied Bill dramatically and improved the image by smoothing it out and removing minor blemishes, all on the computer. Then they put the result on "8mm Exabite" tape, and the result was ready for the next step.

They attached this short tape to a much longer project, in order to avoid

Illustration 64 · Sixteen frames
from *Buffalo Bill*
An illustration in W K-L Dickson's 1895 *History of the Kinetograph, Kinetoscope and Kinetophonograph*

the necessity of a new set-up, with its consequent (impressive!) fee, and turned the tape over to a post-production facility. At this facility the film was displayed on a very special "monitor". This monitor closely resembles the screen on a television set. The difference is that the television has only a few hundred lines, whereas this monitor has thousands. The image was photographed frame-by-frame by an Oxberry 35mm camera with pin registration. Two pins held each frame in perfect registration – to avoid "float". The result was 23 frames of 35mm film.

Michael Friend, Director of the Film Archive of the Academy of Motion Picture Arts and Sciences, generously offered to have the 23 frames copied a dozen times, and the copies spliced together into a short film. This has been accomplished, and now Buffalo Bill demonstrates his skill at rapid firing just as he did almost 103 years ago.

In one way, my ambition of some five years has been accomplished. A portion of the lost 1894 film, *Buffalo Bill*, has been recreated – and Buffalo Bill has been "resurrected"! But I would like to see at least two results come from the successful completion of this film. One would be to combine the several films that Edison took of Buffalo Bill *and* of members of his troupe in the summer and autumn of 1894 into a short film. I have assembled, I believe, all the known films and will soon have *Buffalo Bill* to add to the collection. I think it would make an attractive short film. My other ambition is to have about ten groups of frames, similar to the sixteen frames of *Buffalo Bill* and representing other lost films, returned to film. One consists of 65 frames, which should produce an excellent result; several others were published in October 1892. If recreated, they would be the earliest "surviving" films in a vertical 35mm format. Each and every one of these would add to the earliest history of motion-pictures. It would be gratifying indeed if publication of this book interested a reader into adapting one or both of these projects.

Illustration 65 · Dean Sadamune at his work place

The main reason for compiling this index is that one simply cannot refer to a comprehensive existing catalogue. A very few brief lists exist from this early period, some dated, some not, some fragmentary. Films were made that appear on no known list. A few experimental films have survived to this day, such as *Dickson Violin* and what I call *Fred Ott Holding a Bird*. Many films appeared on one list, but were dropped from all subsequent lists. In the early catalogues there were usually a few titles that included a sentence describing the action, but most were listed by title alone. A tremendous advantage in using over 30 sources is that among them I was able to find titles *with* accompanying descriptions for an amazingly large percentage of the films listed. This should make this index much more helpful and certainly more interesting.

I have attempted to include films from the very earliest period in which films were made on 35mm film in a vertical format, as early as 1892. For the next few years, Edison made films for several different organisations, primarily Raff & Gammon (The Kinetoscope Company), Maguire & Baucus, and the Continental Commerce Company. To distinguish the films produced for each company, a card was placed on the stage so that it usually, but not always, appears in the lower right-hand corner of the frame. Raff & Gammon used an "R", Maguire & Baucus "MB", and the Continental Commerce Company a "C". Edison did not make or distribute films under the Edison name until a date much later than this index covers.

Each distributor put out its own series of lists, adding new films and dropping those that did not sell well. Maguire & Baucus numbered their films, very approximately in order of their taking. Film number 183 seems to have been the last one made in 1896, and therefore – other than for a few exceptions – I have stopped with that number.

I have used the end of 1896 as a cut-off date because the active "peep-show" Kinetoscope period had come to an end, with the growing popularity of projection, and with it the increased use of the longer (so called 150') film, which was transparent rather than translucent. The manufacture of "peep-show" Kinetoscopes (that term was used not necessarily to criticise these machines, but because Edison, causing much confusion, continued to use the term "Kinetoscope", and he simply called his projectors "Projecting Kinetoscopes") virtually ceased, and the demand for new "50'" films declined rapidly.

In addition, because of unauthorised (and unpaid for) duplication of his films by the International Film Company and others, Edison started copyrighting his films on 23 October 1896. After that date, titles and paper print copies of films became part of official copyright office records, making 31 December 1896 an appropriate date to end this index.

Even though they were not always carefully handled, many of the early paper print copies of Edison films and other early films survived in the files of the Library of Congress until recently. For many years, Kemp Niver worked to preserve, document and copy back onto film the surviving paper prints, and the University of California at Los Angeles (UCLA) continued this work in cooperation with the Library of Congress. However, since there were no paper prints made until late 1896, destruction and deterioration of the nitrate films have caused the loss of all but a relatively few of Edison's films taken between 1892 and 1896, the period covered by this book.

While there are collections of Kinetoscope films, as noted herein, they are few, widely scattered and often disorganised. The Library of Congress has some examples. One that is rather amusing is a 35mm film of four Kinetoscope subjects. The first two subjects are fine, but the second two are spliced in backwards! To see them, one needs to fast-forward the film to the end, and play the second two backwards. Hopefully, it has now been corrected.

I have contacted all the major film collections in this country and approximately 90 film archives in other countries all over the world, but relatively few collectors. If you know of any Kinetoscope films I have missed, whether old or modern copies, please let me know; if this book goes into a second edition, they will be included. You are welcome to write to the author at 12337 Landale Street, Studio City, CA 91604, USA (fax +1 818 508 7717); for those who require an answer, please include a self-addressed, stamped envelope (stamps requested only in the USA).

For those who wish to obtain copies of Kinetoscope films, let me offer my services or recommend George C Hall.

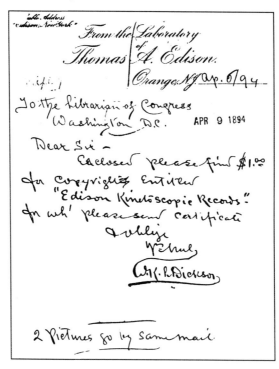

Illustration 66 · Copyright application for "Edison Kinetoscopic Records"
(From the collection of the Library of Congress)

Key to style and abbreviations

- Film title in upper and lower case letters: film is known to have been taken, but is not in any presently known catalogue. Possibly experimental; no formal title.

- Film title in capital letters: film is listed in a catalogue, list, book, magazine article or the like, from the 1892-97 period. Wording in capital letters following the title is part of the original film listing.

- Film title underlined: a copy of the film survives.

Number or numbers in parentheses after the film title: source of the film title (see *Key to sources of film titles*).

Letters following "Copy:/Copies:" are abbreviations of the name of the film's location (see *Key to film locations*)

Maguire & Baucus numbered its films. If a number precedes the title, the film was either produced or later purchased by Maguire & Baucus.

Key to sources of film titles

1	Author's personal observations.
2	Kemp R Niver, *Motion Pictures from the Library of Congress Paper Print Collection 1894-1912* (Berkeley: University of California Press, 1967).
3	*The Phonogram* October 1892.
4	Charles Musser (ed), *Thomas A Edison Papers: A Guide to Motion Picture Catalogs by American Producers and Distributors, 1894-1908: A Microfilm Edition* (Frederick, MD: University Publications of America, 1985).
4aa	Fragment of "The Kinetoscope Co. (Raff & Gammon) Bulletin #1, December 1894".
4a	Fragment of "The Kinetoscope Co. (Raff & Gammon) Bulletin #2, January 1895".
4b	Maguire & Baucus Catalog, April 1897.
4c	Maguire & Baucus Catalog, autumn 1897.
	(Other motion-picture catalogues advertising Kinetoscope films appear in the six-reel microfilm edition.)
5	"Edison Films for Projecting Machines and Kinetoscopes" sold by the Chicago Talking Machine Company, Chicago. Supplementary catalogue issued 20 January 1897. Originals in the Canadian Film Museum and New York Public Library.
6	"Edison's Invention of the Kineto-Phonograph" *Century Magazine*, June 1894.
7	Museum of Modern Art, New York, NY.
8	Museum of the Moving Image, Astoria, NY.
9	Eastman House, Rochester, NY.
10	Library of Congress, Motion Picture, Broadcasting, and Recorded Sound Division, Washington, DC.
11	Letter from Gordon Hendricks to the author, 1 January 1959, and advertising card from Tally's Kinetoscope Parlor of late autumn 1896.
12	Raff & Gammon film list c.May 1895, from collection in Baker Library, Harvard University, Boston, MA.
13	W K-L Dickson and Antonia Dickson, *The Life & Inventions of Thomas Alva Edison* (London: Chatto & Windus, 1894).
14	Late 1895 catalogue of the Continental Phonograph Kinetoscope Company of Milan, Italy, with a January 1896 supplement. Collection of Allen Koenigsberg, Brooklyn, NY.
15	The Edison Kinetoscope Price List, August 1895, of the Ohio Phonograph Company. From the Collection of Lawrence A Schlick, Wawatosa, WI.
16	Films listed in a column entitled "New Films for Screen Machines", published in *The Phonoscope* in issues between November 1896 and April 1897, after which 1896 films became scarce. The lists seem to

have been supplied by The International Film Company, which "duped" Edison films and soon began making films of its own and "duping" Lumière and other films. From microfilms in the Margaret Herrick Library, AMPAS.

16a   November 1896 issue.

16b   December 1896 issue.

16c   January/February 1897 issue.

16d   April 1897 issue.

17   Em Gee Film Library, Reseda, CA.

18   Gordon Hendricks, *The Kinetoscope: America's First Commercially Successful Motion Picture Exhibitor* (New York, 1966) [self-published].

19   Raff & Gammon, statement of 18 April 1895, Baker Library, Harvard University, Boston, MA.

20   "Catalog of Photographic Films for use in the Moto-Photoscope, or other Projecting Machines", published in London, England, c.December 1896. Collection of David Francis.

21   Jay Leyda and Charles Musser, *Before Hollywood* (New York: American Federation of the Arts, 1979).

22   John Fell, *A History of Films* (New York: Holt, Rinehart and Winston, 1979).

23   National Film and Television Archive, London, England.

24   *Edison Phonographic News*, November/December 1894.

25   Gordon Hendricks, *Origins of the American Film* (New York: Arno Press and The New York Times, 1972).

26   Hendricks Collection, Archives of the National Museum of American History, Smithsonian Institution, Washington DC.

27   Charles Musser, "American Vitagraph: 1897-1901", *Cinema Journal* 22: 3 (spring 1983): 4-46.

28   Earl Theisen Collection, Seaver Center for Western History Research, Natural History Museum of Los Angeles County, CA.

29   Edison Film Catalog of 1 November 1905, Collection of Lawrence A Schlick, Wawatosa, WI.

30   Charles Musser, *Before the Nickelodeon: Edwin S. Porter and the Edison Manufacturing Company* (Berkeley; Los Angeles; Oxford: University of California Press, 1991).

31   Chris Long and Clive Sowry, "Australia's First Films: Facts and Fables", *Cinema Papers* 100 (August 1994) and issues in 1995.

32   *Edison Films*, complete catalogue, October 1900.

33   W K-L Dickson and Antonia Dickson. *History of the Kinetograph, Kinetoscope & Kinetophonograph* (New York: Arno Press & The New York Times, 1970).

34   Terry Ramsaye, *A Million and One Nights: A History of the Motion Picture*, volume I (New York: Simon and Schuster, 1926)

35   Irving Deutelbaum, *Image: On the Art and Evolution of the Film* (New York: Dover Publications, 1979). This is a reprint of the article published in *Image* in 1959.

AMMI	American Museum of the Moving Image, Astoria, NY.
AMPAS	Academy of Motion Picture Arts and Sciences, Beverly Hills, CA.
EH	Eastman House, Rochester, NY.
ENHS	Edison National Historic Site, West Orange, NJ.
FPA	Film Preservation Association, Box 71, Hat Creek, Sun Valley, CA 96040.
GCH	George C Hall, PO Box 64246, Tucson, AZ 85728-4246, is expecting to have prints of these films for sale.
GH	Gordon Hendricks film collection; now at the Library of Congress, Division of Motion Picture, Broadcasting, and Recorded Sound, Washington, DC.
H	Charles Hummel, Wayne, NJ.
HFM	Henry Ford Museum, Dearborn, MI.
LOC	Library of Congress, Division of Motion Picture, Broadcasting and Recorded Sound, Washington, DC.
MCL	Musée du Cinéma, Lyon, France
MG	Em Gee Film Library, Reseda, CA.
MOMA	Museum of Modern Art, New York, NY.
MOMI	Museum of the Moving Image, London, England.
NA	National Archives, Washington, DC.
NAC	David Flaherty Collection, National Archives of Canada, Ottawa, Canada.
NFTVA	National Film and Television Archive, London, England.
P	Ray Phillips, Studio City, CA.
SAF	Service des Archives du Film, Bois d'Arcy, France.
UCLA	UCLA Film and Television Archive, University of California at Los Angeles, CA.

In addition, John E Allen, Inc, of Park Ridge, NJ, may have some Kinetoscope films, but their nature is undetermined.

Acrobatic Dance **see** Leigh Sisters

Amateur Gymnast **see** Calisthenics

161. AMERICAN FALLS (FROM ABOVE, AMERICAN SIDE). SHOWS
GLITTERING ICE BACKGROUND AND A GROUP OF PHOTOGRAPHERS
PREPARING TO TAKE PICTURES. **(2, 4b, 4c, 5)**
Filmed: 11 December 1896. Date may be a little late, as it was copyrighted on 12
December 1896. Also called "American Falls from top of American shore" in a late
spring 1897 Edison "Supplemental List". **See** NEW NIAGARA FALLS SERIES.
No known copy.

163. AMERICAN FALLS (FROM CANADA SHORE, BELOW). THIS IS
PROBABLY THE BEST GENERAL VIEW OF NIAGARA, AND IS SO CLEAR
THAT THE MIST CAN BE SEEN ARISING AND GRADUALLY SETTLING OVER
THE FALLS. **(2, 4b, 4c, 5, 11, 16c)**
Filmed: 11-13 December 1896.
Also called "American Falls from Bottom of Canadian Shore" in a late spring 1897
Edison "Supplemental List", and copyrighted under that name on 24 December 1896.
See NEW NIAGARA FALLS SERIES.
No known copy.

162. AMERICAN FALLS (FROM INCLINE RAILROAD) **(2, 4b, 4c, 5)**
Filmed: 11-13 December 1896. Copyrighted on 24 December 1896.
See NEW NIAGARA FALLS SERIES.
No known copy.

101. AMERICAN LINE PIER. SHOWING THE CROWDS AWAITING THE
ARRIVAL OF LI HUNG CHANG **(4b, 4c)**
Filmed: 24 February 1896.
Li Hung Chang was a Chinese Viceroy. He toured the United States between 24
February and 26 May 1896.
See 61. LI HUNG CHANG. THE GREAT VICEROY LEAVING THE HOTEL
WALDORF
No known copy.

AMERICAN WRESTLING: LEONARD VS. STEPHENS **(31)**
Filmed: unknown. **31** lists it as being shown in Sydney, Australia, beginning 6
December 1894.
No known copy. No other information.

1. AMY MULLER. A BEAUTIFUL FANTASTIC TOE DANCE. A GOOD SUBJECT

IF COLORED. (**4b, 4c, 5, 20**)

Filmed: between 24 March and 8 April 1896, according to Hendricks writing in *Image* in 1959.

It is interesting to see Maguire & Baucus' film number one. The subject first appeared in a Raff & Gammon catalogue c.8 April 1896, according to Hendricks, but Raff & Gammon did not number their films; Maguire & Baucus did, but mostly in approximately date order.

However, when Maguire & Baucus bought Raff & Gammon's library and numbered its films along with theirs, they apparently applied some random unused numbers that were scattered among their numbers, so that a 1896 film appears among 1894 films in this case. At present, this is a conjecture! In **4b** is a 150' film of this subject, #28.

A still appears in **35**: ill. **11**.

Copies: EH; GCH.

Amy Muller (courtesy of G Hall & R Martinique)

2. ANNABELLE – BUTTERFLY DANCE (**4b, 4c, 5, 14, 15, 20, 18: 82**)

Filmed: autumn 1894.

Butterfly Dance

15 describes it and the Serpentine and Sun dances as "By the famous 'Annabelle.' These dances are among the finest for the effects of costume, light and shade, and are very popular. Each, $12.50." **20** describes the same three dances as "Three of the most popular dances ever presented. Beautiful costumes and light effects. Extra fine colored. Price £3 10s. 0d. Extra". The listing in **15** would almost certainly indicate a Raff & Gammon film, while **4b** is a Maguire & Baucus list and may describe a different "take" of this subject. **14** gives the title in Italian as "Anna Bell, la Farfalla" (English: "Butterfly") and suggests "Tobasco, Valse Mio Sogno" (English: "Tobasco, My Dream Waltz"). In the Edison record catalogue was a cylinder by the Edison Symphony Orchestra, "Tobasco Waltz", #626.

Copies: AMPAS; GCH; HFM; LOC (#Feb 4707) 32' long; MOMA; P.

Note: examine the costume in the illustration. It seems clear that these are butterfly wings and antennae, and therefore that this is Annabelle's "Butterfly Dance". The lack of titles on these early films leads to much confusion, and I have seen films which to me are obviously the SERPENTINE, called "Butterfly", most likely by someone who had not the opportunity to see this film. I doubt if I could identify the "Sun" and "Fire" dances, as I have never seen a film that would clearly fit either of these titles. The stage has the Continental Commerce Company's "C" logo on the right side. At least one "take" of *Butterfly* was available from Edison until at least November 1905, as #5030, a 35' film.

ANNABELLE – FIRE DANCE. (29)

Filmed: unknown.

Not in any known catalogue of the 1894-96 period, nor in 2. However, it does appear in an Edison film catalogue of 1 November 1905 as #5183, a 50' film. LOC may have a copy of this film. On a typed sheet received from LOC, at the bottom is the following: "5. Title referred to in un-numbered 9/12/73 memo as 'Annabelle and Her Firedance'. 6. Probable prod. co. per notation on film. 7.0201 15/17 18 cbh."
Filmed: unknown; film included here for information.
Copy: possibly at LOC.

ANNABELLE – SERPENTINE DANCE (2 [1897 version], 4b, 4c, 5, 15, 29)

One of the most popular Kinetoscope subjects, this dance was filmed by Edison at least three times, once before 21 July 1894, 13 May 1895 and spring 1897, copyrighted on 8 May 1897. Several hand-tinted copies survive. The earliest version can be identified by the newel posts on the railings at each side of the stage. The newel posts and railings were replaced when the "Black Maria" was enlarged in winter 1894. The new railings had no newel posts. The last film can be identified by the "Copyright 1897" that appears on one frame. The LOC copy contains this copyright notice. An *Annabelle Serpentine Dance* appeared in Edison catalogues when he began to distribute films under his own name, at least until 1 November 1905, and perhaps later. Annabelle also danced for the Mutoscope Company and perhaps others. To describe one film: Annabelle, in a very full costume, floor-length and of a light material, holds a wand in each hand. To the wands are attached ends of the outer layer of her multi-layered skirt. By waving the wands, Annabelle causes the material to flutter in a wave-like manner. Several tinted copies survive.

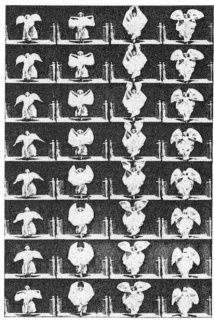

Annabelle – Serpentine Dance
Note the ball finial on the newel post at the right of the stage. This indicates that these frames are of the earliest, or one of the earliest, of Annabelle's Serpentine Dances. (Photograph by W K-L Dickson, from his *The Life & Inventions of Thomas Alva Edison* [1894])

Tinting was most appropriate. 34: 117 states: "Annabelle's Serpentine Dance was one of the most popular dances on the variety theatre stage. The dancer was illuminated with changing shafts of colored light thrown by tint slides in a stereopticon...Many of the prints of the Annabelle picture were tinted with slide colours by hand, a frame at a time, a most tedious process." In the Kinetoscope, where these films were meant to be seen, the effect of colouring is delightful, but when these films are projected, the defects in the quite crude hand-tinting become quite obvious.

Annabelle performed three, perhaps four, dances for Edison, and repeated one or more. In addition, other artists performed "skirt dances" for Edison. I confess to being unable to distinguish a "Serpentine" from a "Sun" from a "Fire", and probably Annabelle from another "skirt dancer". (Identifying "Butterfly" is simple, because of the costume.)

Copies: AMPAS (b/w and coloured); LOC; MOMA (two versions); NAC (beautifully coloured, but listed as "Butterfly Dance"); NFTVA (two versions); P (b/w and coloured). Of the NFTVA versions, one, a 42' film, 603081A, has a "C" on a board on the right and is an exceptionally nice film. The other, 44' (60134A[g]), has frames with "Copyright 1897 by T A Edison" at three different places in the film! The stage is carpeted with a carpet that goes at least two feet up the background (there are two other films in this *Index* carpeted in this way), there are barricades on the sides of the stage, but no "R" or any further identification. This is the film that AMPAS and P have in colour.

Annabelle in one of her dances.
From the costume, it would appear to be a "Serpentine". The stage appears to be carpeted, with the carpet extending up the side of a board placed at the back of the stage. This unusual feature also can be seen in the illustrations for *Annabelle – Sun Dance* and *Parisian Dance*. A filming date can be approximated from the copyright date of *Parisian Dance*: 15 January 1897. The original film is tinted and gives Annabelle reddish-auburn hair, as do one or two others. Her dress appears in various colours, as it would have appeared on the stage of a theatre, illuminated by changing coloured spotlights.

Note: Annabelle was still in her teens when she became a popular dancer. Later she married a rich New Yorker. He lost his money, died, and Annabelle lived to an advanced age, and died in extreme poverty. **34: 338ff** relates more about her.

Soon after the period covered by this *Index*, the "Serpentine" and other similar dances were filmed with other dancers by Edison competitors, so every "Serpentine" is not necessarily being danced by Annabelle.

A still of the earliest version appears in **18: ill. 13**, and a portrait in **34: opp. 340**.

ANNABELLE – SUN DANCE. BY THE FAMOUS "ANNABELLE". THESE DANCES, (SERPENTINE, BUTTERFLY AND SUN) ARE AMONG THE FINEST FOR THE EFFECTS OF COSTUME, LIGHT, AND SHADE, AND ARE VERY POPULAR. (2, 4b, 4c, 5, 15, 20, 29)
Filmed: autumn 1894, and several versions made later. There was one made for Raff & Gammon, one in the Maguire & Baucus catalogue, selection #4. The one listed in **2** was copyrighted on 8 May 1897. In **20**, it was described as "extra fine colored".
For all its popularity, there are no identified copies extant. Because of the 8 May 1897 copyright date and "extra fine colored", this might be the film described under "Serpentine" as being carpeted.

ANNIE OAKLEY, THE "LITTLE SURE SHOT" OF THE "WILD WEST". EXHIBITION OF RIFLE: SHOOTING AT GLASS BALLS, ETC. $15.00. (4, 4b as

#32; **4c**, **12**, **15** also mentions "FINE SMOKE EFFECTS")
Filmed: 1 November 1894 (**18: 7**).
This is the famous Annie Oakley, heroine of the musical and film, *Annie Get Your Gun*.
The illustration shows the action occurring in the first half of the film. The film begins
with Annie standing at the left of the scene, with a man standing behind her. Annie is
holding a mirror over her shoulder. (Note: this is puzzling since, while shooting over
her shoulder by means of a mirror was part of the act, it is not done here.) Annie drops
the mirror and begins firing at the target, as shown in the illustration. When she finishes
she kneels, laying down the rifle she has been using, and picking up one of two lying at
the front of the stage. While she is doing this, the man who was standing behind her
runs over to the right-hand side of the stage, carrying several ball-shaped targets. He
kneels and throws the targets into the air
one at a time, while Annie fires at them
from a kneeling position. Has Raff &
Gammon's "R" logo at lower right. A
delightful film!

Copies: AMPAS; EH; GCH; GH; MG's –
their "The Archaeology of the Cinema"
includes about five seconds of the film; P;
SAF under the title *Annie Oakley*
(PMU12915.22862, also the same film
under the title "Femme tirant un fusil"
("Woman firing a rifle"), PMU 9181.

Annie Oakley (Photo courtesy SAF)

Arab "Sword Combat" (**18: 83**). Also known as "Salem Nassar and Najid – Sword
Combat". (**18: 126**)
Filmed: autumn 1894 (**18: 126**).
18: 126 states: "negative bad, so deleted from Raff & Gammon list 8 January 1895", and
also quotes the comment: "thrown out owing to faulty punches & as they are so good
they should be taken again". However, apparently they never were.
No known copy.

ARMAND 'ARY. FRENCH DANCEUSE AND CHANTEUSE. PANTOMIME,
SONG, ETC. (**24**); **See also 16** and **18: 82**.
Filmed: autumn 1894 (**18: 82**).
Also known as "Madame Armand Ary". The Sydney (Australia) *Morning Herald* of 17
January 1895 describes the film as: "A Parisian danseuse, the famous Armande (sic)
Ary, gives us a rehearsal of one of her dances with all the wealth of gesture
characteristic of her nation". (**31**)
No known copy.
A still appears in **33: 33**. It is hard to tell, but she is sitting with an early Edison
phonograph!

ARRIVAL OF THE LOCAL EXPRESS (**12**)
Also known as *Chicago and Buffalo Express*, which was copyrighted on 12 December
1896.
Filmed: late November 1896 (**11**).
Under 169. CHICAGO AND BUFFALO EXPRESS, Maguire & Baucus gives this

description: "This scene shows the arrival at a station, and the passengers alighting from and boarding the train, together with the usual bustling activity of the baggage men, etc. It is an interesting and impressive subject of its kind" (**4**). In a letter to the author dated 1 January 1959, Hendricks states that "'Arrival of the Local Express' is apparently the subject described in the Maguire & Baucus catalogue of April 1897 (**4b**) as showing 'The arrival at a station, and passengers alighting and boarding the train'. It was apparently shot in Buffalo on the visit which resulted in the Niagara Falls group from which the above subject was selected for this Los Angeles Kinetoscope showing." He was referring to the Tally broadside (see illustration 42).

From the above, it is clear that more than one scene of this type has been taken. EH has a film of this type called "Railway Station Scene", but Hendricks states it was taken by the International Film Company in February 1897.
No known copy.

144. ARTILLERY PRACTICE (**4b**, **4c**, **5**; "dupe" listed in **16a** as "Firing of Cannon")
Filmed: the listing in **16a** would indicate autumn 1896.
No known copy.

Aunt Dinah's First Sleigh Ride (**18: 7**)
Filmed: 24 (?) December 1896 (**18: 7**).
The LOC has recently transferred Hendricks' collection of Kinetoscope films on 16mm film back to 35mm. Among them is a very brief fragment that must be this film. The scene is a snow-covered road. A horse-drawn sleigh faces the camera. The river is on the left. Seated on the right is a large black woman who falls out of the sleigh into a snowbank. The fragment is about 20' long.
Copy: GH.

84. BABY PARADE. SHOWING HUNDREDS OF BABIES IN THE ANNUAL PARADE AT ASBURY PARK, N.J. A 150' film, $45. (**4b**, **4c**, **5**)
Filmed: probably summer 1896.
No known copy.

112. BAG PUNCHING, AN EXHIBITION BY MIKE LEONARD, THE FAMOUS TRAINER (**4b**, **4c**, **20**)
No known copy. No other information.

102. BAGGAGE WAGONS. LI HUNG CHANG'S BAGGAGE WAGONS LEAVING AMERICAN LINE PIER. (**4b**, **4c**)
Filmed: 24 February 1896.
No known copy.

BAND DRILL, FROM HOYT'S "MILK WHITE FLAG." REPRESENTS THE MARCH OF THE BAND, WITH LEADER AT THEIR HEAD PLAYING POPULAR AIRS. $15.00. (**4b**, **4c**, **12**, **14**, **15**, see below). Note that an "R" is posted on the stage at the lower left corner.
Filmed: autumn 1894 (**18: 83**).
In **4b**, #64 is listed as "Milk White Flag", but is almost certainly the finale of the first act, for which **15** uses the title of the whole play, "Milk White Flag". **14** lists this film as "Band Drill", and suggests cylinders "Marcia del Centenario" (English: "Centennial

March") and "Marcia Liberty Bell" (English: "Liberty Bell March"), both by "Banda di Gilmore". Gilmore recorded for Edison from at least 1892 to 1894, but by 1896 was recording for Columbia. These cylinders are not on the Columbia list, but the surviving Edison lists from this period are so incomplete that these might have been Edison cylinders still in stock. A third cylinder, "Marcia Tommy Atkins" (English: "Tommy Atkins March"), appears on no surviving list, but most likely was an Edison cylinder.
Copies: AMPAS; EH; GCH; GH; P.
Stills appear in **18: ill. 23**; **30: 51**; **33: 50**; **35: ill. 8**.

Band Drill (courtesy G Hall/R Martinique)

BARBER SHOP. INTERIOR OF A BARBER SHOP. MAN COMES IN, TAKES OFF HIS COAT, SITS DOWN, SMOKES, IS HANDED A PAPER BY ATTENDANT, WHO POINTS OUT A JOKE, BOTH LAUGH. MEANTIME THE MAN IN THE CHAIR IS SHAVED AND HAS HIS HAIR CUT. VERY FUNNY. **(4: 24)**
Filmed: early March 1894 **(18: 74)**.
One of the ten films shown on 14 April 1894, the first commercial showing of the Kinetoscope. As this is one of the earliest films of an "event", as distinguished from a dancer or an acrobat, the description given in the *Northern Queensland Herald*, Townsville, Australia, 4 September 1895, is worth quoting:

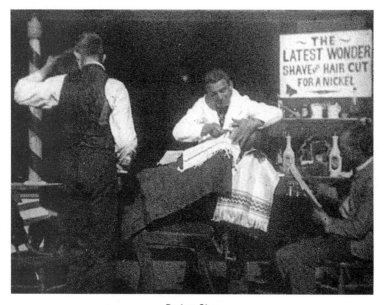

Barber Shop

Among many subjects secured thus far for the kinetoscope is the interior of a barber's shop. The beholder, who is looking down through the window of the kinetoscope cabinet, sees the actual interior of the barber's shop. A man is reclining upon a barber's chair about to be shaved. The barber goes to his case, secures his cup, makes a lather with which he proceeds to lather the man's face. Meanwhile a colored gentleman, who is probably following the occupation of porter, boot-black and jack-of-all-trades, is moving about the room. He picks up a newspaper, and sits down to read it. Another customer comes in, pulls off his hat and coat, takes a cigar from his waistcoat pocket, lights it, picks up a paper and sits down to smoke, read and await his turn. The colored gentleman aforesaid finds something very funny in the newspaper he is reading, and therefore crosses the room and points out the amusing article to the waiting customer. They both laugh heartily, and show every sign of merriment. Meanwhile the barber has been shaving his man, and both the saver and the shavee have been going through many motions--the one plainly evincing his desire to hurry through his work of shaving and be ready for the "next", the other plainly showing the results of this immoderate haste on the part of his torturer by sundry grimaces and winces when the razor takes off sections of his cuticle. On the wall is seen the appropriate legend "with or without chloroform," which is eloquent of appropriateness after we have witnessed with our own eyes the torture the victim has been subjected to. It should be understood that this is not an imaginary scene emanating from the pencil or brush of an artist, or the imagination of the romancer or humorist, but it is an actual living moving reproduction of a scene which has actually taken place, and that quite recently in a real barber's shop, fitted up in Mr. Edison's Kinetographic Theatre, at Orange, New Jersey. Every movement, from the walking of the man across the floor, to the sweep of the razor and even the very wink of an eyelash (so marvelously distinct and true to nature is the reproduction) is recorded and is witnessed by the beholder through the window of the Kinetoscope. Even the smoke of the cigar which the man is smoking is blown across the face of the scene and slowly disperses in the air – a most startling evidence of the fidelity to nature of the Kinetoscopic reproductions.

The fact that the reporter had to remind his readers that the scene was not drawn or painted, and his fascination with every detail of the scene demonstrate the astonishment that greeted the Kinetoscope wherever it was shown. Another Australian newspaper reports: "Mr. Edison himself is said to consider the scene in the barber's shop one of the best, and the way in which the man with the razor gets through his work and hoists the next customer into the chair is certainly droll".

Note the photograph of the "Black Maria" (illustration 24). Hendricks must have had a lighter print than mine, as he said that the sign in this film – "The Latest Wonder/ Shave and Haircut for a Nickel" – was visible through the open door on the side of the "Black Maria"! The *Herald* reporter used a bit of imagination in saying that a sign on the barbershop wall said anything about chloroform. There was no such sign! (**31**) Copies: AMMI; AMPAS; ENHS (as part of E156 283, which may be 16mm); GCH; MOMA; P.

BARROOM SCENE. PRESENTS A BARROOM WITH ALL THE ACCESSORIES, INCLUDING A BARMAID, WHO SERVES A POLICEMAN WITH A GLASS OF

BEER AT THE SIDE ENTRANCE. TWO MEN ARE SMOKING AND HAVING A QUIET GAME OF "DRAW", WHEN A COUPLE OF "TOUGHS" LOUNGE IN AND A QUARREL ARISES, IN WHICH THE POLICEMAN TAKES A HAND AND FORCIBLY EXPELS THE CROWD. A VERY POPULAR AND REALISTIC SUBJECT OF THIS KIND. $12.50. (**15, 24**) Filmed: by June 1894 (**18: 82**).

Barroom Scene

Copies: AMPAS; P: original film purchased with Kinetoscope #141 by the author on 2 October 1992 (see page 100). The film is complete, but in poor condition. The heavily damaged sprocket-holes were repaired by NFTVA when they copied it in 1963. The author also has a print of the NFTVA copy. NFTVA (London) #60134 A(f). The copy is somewhat scratched and quite unsteady, due to the damaged sprocket-holes. The author's original is now in the film archives of AMPAS, where a better copy may be attempted. Note that the description of *New Bar Room* is so similar that the existing film could possibly be this subject.
A still appears in **30: 43**.

35. <u>BATHING SCENE AT ROCKAWAY</u>. SURF BATHING AT ROCKAWAY BEACH. (**4b, 4c, 5**) A 50' version. There was also a 150' version, #85.
Filmed: early July 1896 (**30: 67**).
30 calls this *Bathing Scene at Coney Island.*
Copy: EH.

BEFORE THE KINETOGRAPH **see** <u>CORBETT AND COURTNEY BEFORE THE KINETOGRAPH</u>

Belly Dance, Princess Ali **see** <u>PRINCESS ALI ORIENTAL DANCER</u>

BERTHOLDI. THE MARVELOUS LADY CONTORTIONIST AND ACROBAT, IN ONE OF HER INIMITABLE PERFORMANCES. (TABLE CONTORTION). (**4b, 4c, 15**)
Filmed: both films taken before 14 April 1894 (**19**).
Also listed in **4b, 4c, 12, 20** as #120, and in **14** as "Bertoldi, Contorsionista", with cylinders "Cav. Rusticana", "Padrone Feming Valse" and "Danza Agile" suggested as accompaniment. In Edison's cylinder record catalogue, #551 was "Cavalleria Rusticana Intermezzo" played by the Edison Symphony Orchestra. The last two would translate something like "Master Feming (Fleming?) Waltz" and "Agile (or Nimble) Dance", but neither Edison nor Columbia catalogues yield any titles similar to these. In **33: 13** is a still that may be from this film. It shows Bertoldi (a woman) face down, resting on her forearms with her body bent so far up in the air and over her back that her feet are above and in front of her head.
No known copies.

BERTHOLDI, THE MARVELOUS LADY CONTORTIONIST (MOUTH SUPPORT)

see BERTHOLDI. THE MARVELOUS LADY CONTORTIONIST AND ACROBAT, IN ONE OF HER INIMITABLE PERFORMANCES. (TABLE CONTORTION).

38. BICYCLE PARADE. ON THE BOULEVARD, NEW YORK CITY. (4b, 4c, 5)
This is the 50' version. A 150' version was available under #86, at $45
Filmed: 27 June 1896 (30: 67).
No known copy.

87. BICYCLE RIDING. BY RICHARDSON, CHAMPION TRICK RIDER. (4b)
A 150' film, cost $45.
Filmed: copyrighted on 15 January 1897, so might have been filmed in 1896.
No known copy.

BILLY EDWARDS AND THE UNKNOWN. A SPIRITED FIVE ROUND SPARRING CONTEST BETWEEN THIS WELL-KNOWN PUGILIST AND A SKILLFUL ANTAGONIST (EACH FILM) $15.00. NOTE: EACH FILM OF THE ABOVE FIGHT CONTAINS ONE ROUND (15).
12 states: "BILLY EDWARDS AND THE UNKNOWN, BOXING BOUT IN 5 ROUNDS. (THIS WELL-KNOWN AND PROMINENT PUGILIST, WITH AN ANTAGONIST SCIENCED AND SKILLFUL, GIVES ONE OF THE MOST, IF NOT THE MOST, SPIRITED AND EXCITING EXHIBITIONS OF SPARRING EVER TAKEN FOR THE KINETOSCOPE.) PRICE FOR EACH ROUND $25.00.
See 113. BILLY EDWARDS BOXING.

113. BILLY EDWARDS BOXING (4a)
(4b, 4c, 20) give #113 as BILLY EDWARDS AND WARWICK. A SCIENTIFIC BOXING BOUT IN FIVE ROUNDS. EACH FILM CONTAINS ONE ROUND.
Filmed: 18: 136 states that in January or February 1895 two subjects of the boxer Billy Edwards were made. 18: 116 states that "MB" (sic) was set on the stage for this subject. That would indicate that the films were made for Maguire & Baucus, and so would the number "113", as Maguire & Baucus numbered their films in this way.
Copy: EH has a film entitled *Billy Edwards Boxing*, but I suspect that it would be very difficult to differentiate the two films.
A still appears in 35: ill. 6.

168. BLACK DIAMOND EXPRESS. THIS SCENE PRESENTS THE FAMOUS LEHIGH VALLEY "FLYER" EMERGING FROM A WOOD IN THE DISTANCE AND APPROACHING THE CAMERA UNDER FULL HEAD OF STEAM. A SECTION GANG IN THE FOREGROUND, ENGAGED IN REPAIRING TRACK, WAVE THEIR HATS TO THE ENGINEER, WHO IS LEANING OUT OF THE CAB WINDOW. THE SNOWY LINEN WHICH THE PORTERS WAVE FROM THE PLATFORM OF THE DINING CAR ADDS TO THE EFFECT PRODUCED. THE "BLACK DIAMOND" IS UNDOUBTEDLY THE HANDSOMEST AND ONE OF THE FASTEST TRAINS IN AMERICA, AND THE SUBJECT IS THE ONLY ONE IN EXISTENCE SHOWING THE EXPRESS TRAIN MAKING SEVENTY MILES AN HOUR. (2, 4b, 4c)
Filmed: 3 December 1896 and copyrighted on 12 December.
2 lists a Black Diamond Express in both 1896 and 1897 without calling the second film "new", as was the custom. The first film was a "50'" film, the second a "150'" film.

Black Diamond Express
(From the Flaherty Brothers Collection in the National Archives of Canada)

The illustration is a frame enlargement from a film in the Flaherty Brothers collection at NAC. The sign at the right reads "BLACK DIAMOND EXPRESS, LEHIGH VALLEY RAILROAD". Note that there are only two men standing on the bank.

In the 1902 Edison film, *Uncle Josh at the Moving Picture Show*, "Uncle Josh" is sitting in a moving-picture theatre watching a film. It is either the *Black Diamond Express* or the *New Black Diamond Express*. At the time I viewed *Uncle Josh* at the LOC, I did not realise that there were the two films, so I cannot now state which was used, as the films are so similar. The same applies to MG and MOMA below.
Copy: GH; MG #9997; MOMA, part of its "Films of the 1890s"; NAC.

BLACKSMITH SHOP. The negative of this film was worn out and destroyed by the end of 1894, so the film appears in no known catalogue.
Filmed: before 9 May 1893 (18).
The scene is a blacksmith shop. Three blacksmiths pound on an object which the centre blacksmith is holding on the anvil with a pair of tongs in one hand. Amusingly, at the very beginning of the scene, an onlooker's back partially obscures the blacksmith on the left. The onlooker promptly disappears from the scene; undoubtedly after being yelled at, or even pulled out of the way! Midway through the scene, the blacksmiths pause to pass around a bottle, from which each drinks, then they resume their work.
That is a description of the film as viewed by the author. A reporter for the Sydney (Australia) *Morning Herald*, 17 January 1895 gives a more vivid description:

> ...in the blacksmith's shop, one can see the three sturdy smiths hammer out the red iron, even the sparks fly before your eyes, and the smoke from the forge ascends in a clearly visible cloud. Then, when the men, exhausted by their rapid labour, grow thirsty, they hand the bottle round from one to another like

a flash of lightning, and the picture ends. All this passes before the eye in the brief space of 35 seconds, and though the little picture is but an inch and a half square, it is as clear and distinct as any stage performance.

This was used as a demonstration film at the Brooklyn Institute, 9 May 1893, according to an article entitled "Enter the Inventors". It was one of the ten films shown on 14 April 1894, in the first commercial showing of the Kinetoscope (18: 56, 126). The latter reference states: negative "destroyed" by 29 December 1894, as "worn out". The scene was sufficiently popular that a similar scene was taken; see 39. NEW BLACKSMITH SHOP.

Copies: HFM; MOMA. In the summer of 1988, I found an original copy of this film in its original film can, lying on the shelf of a damaged Kinetoscope in storage since at least 1929 at HFM. It was sent to the MOMA for copying, so MOMA has a copy on "Edison Kinetoscope Loops" #2, #19064. HFM has the original and a copy.

A still appears in 18: ill. 18.

BLACKTON SKETCHES. THE NEW YORK "WORLD'S" CARICATURE ARTIST DRAWING SKETCHES ON A SCREEN.
NO. 1 REPRESENTS HIM AS DRAWING A LARGE PICTURE OF MR THOMAS A EDISON.
NO. 2 SHOWING THE ARTIST DRAWING PICTURES OF MCKINLEY AND PRESIDENT CLEVELAND.
NO. 3 IS A HUMOROUS SELECTION SHOWING THE ARTIST DRAWING A LIFE SIZE PICTURE, IN WHICH THE EXPRESSIONS OF THE COUNTENANCE ARE RAPIDLY CHANGED. (16a)
These are "dupes" of *Sketching Mr. Edison* and others.

Sketching Mr. Edison (Photo courtesy of Charles Musser)

88. BOAT RESCUE. THREE SMALL BOYS, CHASED FROM A DOCK, JUMP INTO THE RIVER AND ARE RESCUED BY A PASSING ROWBOAT. A 150' film. $45 (4b, 4c)
Filmed: almost certainly summer-autumn 1896.
No known copy.

Bob Brough, The Champion Club Swinger.
Copy: possibly at GH. No other information.

103. BOWLING GREEN (STREET SCENE) (4b, 4c, 5)
No known copy. No other information.

BOXING (3)
Filmed: before October 1892.
In *The Phonogram* magazine for October 1892 appeared an article called "The Kinetograph, a New Industry Heralded". On page 217 appear 24 frames of two men boxing in front of a white picket fence. This and the other illustrations, of "Fencing", "Wrestling" and "A Hand-shake" are the earliest published frames of vertical-feed Kinetoscope films.
No known copy.

BOXING. (Newark Turnverein)
Filmed: before 18 March 1894.
The World, a New York newspaper, had a long article entitled "Wizard Edison's Kinetograph" in its Sunday, 18 March 1894 edition. It illustrates 76 frames of a "somersault", one of the sequences described herein under *Calisthenics*. However, the last sentence in the article ends "...and still another shows a boxing match between members of the Newark Turnverein".
No known copy.

BOXING CATS (PROFESSOR WELTON'S). AN INTERESTING AND SCIENTIFIC BOUT BETWEEN TWO TRAINED THOMAS CATS. (15, 20, 12, 4b, 4c, 5, as #114)
Filmed: c.July 1894 (18: 76).
Two cats on a table paw at each other. A man's face, presumably Professor Welton's, appears in the background. (1)
Copies: AMPAS; EH; GCH; GH; MG; P; SAF. An excellent copy under the title of "Chat Boxeurs", #PMU 12913. This film, along with a number of others, was transferred from the Conservatoire des Arts et Métiers, Paris.
A still appears in 18: ill. 16.

BREAKDOWN (DANCE) **see** GRUNDY AND FRINT. BREAKDOWN FROM "SOUTH BEFORE THE WAR"

BROADSWORD COMBAT. BETWEEN THE FAR FAMED CAPT. DUNCAN ROSS, CHAMPION OF THE WORLD, AND LIEUT. MARTIN. AN EXCITING CONTEST IN FULL ARMOR. (15)
Also listed in 20 as "116. GLADIATORIAL COMBAT. BY CAPT. DUNCAN ROSS AND LIEUT. HARTUNG (sic) WITH BROADSWORDS". In 14 as "Lotta di Gladiatori", it goes on to say that there are five films and that each shows two men

fighting in armour and on horseback.
Filmed: 21 January 1895 (**18: 135**).

This reference states that *Broadsword Combat* was the same subject later called
Gladiatorial Combat in a Maguire & Baucus catalogue of April 1897 (**4b**). No
explanation is given for the different names of Captain Ross' opponent.
No known copy.

111. "BROADSWORDS". BY TWO FAMOUS LADY FENCERS. (**15, 4b, 4c**)
Filmed: probably 26 September 1894, as their "with foils", was shot that day. These
were the "Englehart Sisters".
See LADY FENCERS. (WITH FOILS) **and** LADY FENCERS. EXHIBITING THE
ENGLEHART SISTERS IN AN EXCITING BROADSWORD CONTEST
18: 80n8 states that these ladies were called "the Englehardt sisters", although there was
only one Englehart; the other was named Blanchard. **18: 80** states: "On September 26
[1894] the Englehardt Sisters, lady fencers, were shot in two subjects". As **12** states
"with foils", and **15** states "broadsword", it would appear that these are the two films.
Both these films were made by Raff & Gammon (The Kinetoscope Company), while
111. *Broadswords* is a Maguire & Baucus film. With too high a number for a 1894
film, this almost certainly was a purchase by Maguire & Baucus.
No known copy.

105. BROADWAY AND 14TH ST. STREET SCENE. A SCENE AT "DEATH
CURVE" (**4b, 4c, 5**)
See 109. DEAD MAN'S CURVE. BROADWAY AND FOURTEENTH STREET.
Filmed: possibly summer 1896.
No known copy; MOMA has several New York street scenes.

104. BROADWAY AT POST OFFICE. (STREET SCENE) ONE OF OUR BEST
STREET SCENES. (**4b, 4c, 5**)
Filmed: possibly summer 1896.
No known copy; MOMA has several New York street scenes.

221. <u>BRUSH IN THE PARK</u>. THIS IS THE FIRST OF OUR WINTER SCENES,
AND SHOWS A SPIRITED RACE IN PROSPECT PARK, BROOKLYN, N.Y. FULL
OF LIFE AND SURE TO PLEASE ALL. EXCELLENT SNOW EFFECTS.
Filmed: unknown. The serial number, 221, seems late for 1896. The fact that the listing
does not appear in Maguire & Baucus' January 1897 catalog, but first in its April 1897
catalogue, is also suspicious, but the above does say "first of our winter scenes", and
179. "First Sleigh Ride" states it was taken "after the recent first fall of snow", and was
filmed on 24-26 December 1896, albeit in Harrisburg, PA. *Brush in the Park* might
therefore have made it onto the end of 1896!
Copy: FPA.

99. BRYAN TRAIN SCENE AT ORANGE. 150', $45 (**4c**)
See 99. TRAIN SCENE AT ORANGE. SHOWING MR. BRYAN ADDRESSING A
CROWD OF PEOPLE FROM THE REAR PLATFORM OF A MOVING TRAIN.

BUCK AND WING DANCE (**4b, 4c**)
See JAMES GRUNDY. BUCK AND WING DANCE, FROM "SOUTH BEFORE THE
WAR".

[Buffalo Bill and his Wild West Show had a long run in Brooklyn, New York during the summer and autumn of 1894. During and just after their run, Buffalo Bill and several members of his troupe made films for the Kinetoscope. See, in alphabetical order: *Annie Oakley, Bucking Broncho, Buffalo Bill, Buffalo Dance, Hadji Cheriff, Indian War Council, Lasso Thrower, Mexican Knife Duel, Sheik Hadji Tahar,* and *Sioux Ghost Dance.*]

Bucking Broncho (Photo courtesy R Martinique)

BUCKING BRONCHO. AN OUT OF DOOR SCENE FROM "BUFFALO BILL'S WILD WEST", SHOWING AN INTERESTING BOUT BETWEEN A COW PUNCHER AND AN UNRULY BRONCHO. $15.00 (**15**; **4b**, **4c**; **5** as #33; **12**). Filmed: 16 October 1894 (**18**: **82**).
This reference states that four broncos busting subjects were taken. **18**: **ill. 25** states of this frame enlargement: "Lee Martin, of Colorado is riding Sunfish, while Frank Hammitt stands on the fence and fires a pistol. In the background, press agent Madden waves his stick. The riders were paid $35 – including transportation for the horses – for their work."
Copies: AMPAS; EH; GCH; GH; P.
Stills appear in **18**: **ill. 25**, **35**: **ill. 7**.

Buffalo Bill

40. BUFFALO BILL. THE NOTED PROPRIETOR OF THE "THE WILD WEST" IN AN EXHIBITION OF RIFLE SHOOTING. $12.50. (**4b**, **4c**, **12**, **15**, **16**) Filmed: 24 September 1894 (**18**: **80**).

A Melbourne, Australia, newspaper said about this film: "Buffalo Bill moves a living personality before you, and will move a hundred years hence when he has grown up into daisies and grass". Little did the writer realise that, while several films of Buffalo Bill survive, this one, the first, seems not to have.
Copy: until recently I would have stated "No known copy". However, after the work described on pages 104-106, I am happy to state: AMPAS and (copyrighted by) P.
Stills appear in **30: 51**; **33: 20**.

Buffalo Dance
Filmed: 24 September 1894 (**18: 7, 80**)
The latter reference states: "On September 24 the Maria's stage was host to Buffalo Bill and an aggregation from his Wild West Show, which had just closed a long run at Ambrose Park in Brooklyn...and the Indians from his company were shot in subjects later called 'Sioux Indian Ghost Dance', 'Indian War Council' and 'Buffalo Dance'." I have found no catalogue listing for *Buffalo Dance*, although a number of copies survive. In the film, three Indians in costume dance in a circle, accompanied by two drummers seated cross-legged in the background. On six feet of film, Maguire & Baucus' logo, "MB", has been handwritten at the very top left of each frame.
Copies: AMPAS; GCH; GH; MCL; MG, as part of "Archaeology of the Cinema", a 16mm rental; MOMA; NAC; P; SAF, under title "Peaux-Rouges", PMU.12914.22858.

BUFFALO HORSE MARKET (2)
See 174. HORSE MARKET, BUFFALO, N.Y.

115. BURLESQUE BOXING (**4b, 4c, 5**)
See GLENROY BROS. BOXING BOUT (BURLESQUE) and WALTON & MAYON-BURLESQUE BOXING
18: 83 states "a boxing match". It may have been this one.

Burning Stable

136. BURNING STABLE. SHOWS A BARN ACTUALLY IN FLAMES, FROM WHICH FOUR HORSES AND A BURNING WAGON ARE RESCUED BY FIREMEN AND STABLE HANDS. THE SCENE IS EXCITING, FULL OF ACTION FROM BEGINNING TO END, AND ALL ITS DETAILS ARE SHARPLY DEFINED. THICK VOLUMES OF SMOKE POURING FROM THE DOORS AND WINDOWS OF THE STABLE ADD GREATLY TO THE REALISTIC EFFECT. (**4b, 4c, 5, 16b**) "147. BURNING STABLE" is a 150' film. (**4b**).
Filmed: 31 October 1896, shortly before it was copyrighted.
Copies: AMPAS; EH; GCH; GH; MG #9997; MOMA, in its "Films of the 1890s"; NFTVA #9155; P.

BUTTERFLY DANCE – ANNABELLE **see** 2. ANNABELLE - BUTTERFLY DANCE

Cadets' Charge (Theisen Collection, AMPAS)

143. CADETS' CHARGE. SHOWING A SQUADRON OF CAVALRY (AT THE U.S. MILITARY ACADEMY, WEST POINT, N.Y.) CHARGING TOWARDS THE CAMERA AT HEADLONG SPEED. THE FLASHING OF THEIR SABRES IN THE SUNLIGHT AS THEY ARE BRANDISHED ALOFT ADDS VIM TO THE PICTURE. (**4b, 4c, 5, 16c**)
Copyrighted as *Charge of the West Point Cadets* on 27 November 1896, so probably filmed within the previous week or ten days (2).
No known copy.
The illustration is from a few frames in the Earl Theisen Collection at the Margaret Herrick Library, AMPAS.

CAICEDO, THE "KING OF THE WIRE" IN HIS MARVELOUS SLACK WIRE PERFORMANCE, IN WHICH CAICEDO TURNS SOMERSAULTS IN THE AIR

CAICEDO, KING OF THE WIRE.
THE WONDER OF THE 19th CENTURY.

No other Performer attempts the Feats performed by CAICEDO.

CAICEDO, THE SENSATION OF ENGLAND. | CAICEDO, THE SENSATION OF AUSTRALIA.
CAICEDO, THE SENSATION OF AMERICA. | CAICEDO, THE SENSATION OF THE WORLD.

Read what the English Press says of CAICEDO'S Marvellous Performance :—

"A great attraction at the Alhambra is Don Juan Caicedo, whose exploits on the wire are really extraordinary. How lightly he springs aloft from a sitting position on the thin thread of steel ! With what marvellous adroitness and accuracy he revolves in air, always to return to the same altitude with complete security ! And with what skill, what grace, what ease his surprising feats are performed ! He is certainly an artist of rare capability." — THE ERA, Dec. 19, 1896.

" Don Juan Caicedo is quite justified in assuming the title of 'king of the wire.' He performs apparently impossible feats on a slack wire with the greatest ease and finish." — LLOYD'S, Dec. 6.

"The new 'turn' is only comparatively new. It is the return of Don Juan Caicedo, the king of the wire, who created a sensation here a few years ago. No other performer ever attempts Caicedo's feats. At running, leaping, pirouetting, and somersaults on the wire, the famous Columbian is unequalled. He performs in heavy spurred riding boots as easily as in slippers."—WEEKLY TIMES AND ECHO, Dec. 6, 1896.

" In the variety programme the chief performance is probably that of Don Juan Caicedo, rightly described as the 'king of the wire.' Without seeing it, it is difficult to believe in the possibility of such a skilful and daring exhibition as that given by Don Juan Caicedo on the wire."—AFRICAN REVIEW, Dec. 5, 1896.

"Don Juan Caicedo has once again come to show Londoners his extraordinary ability as a funambulist. The accomplishment as a dancer and acrobat that Juan exhibits on his narrow causeway are more than are possessed by a good many specialists in these lines. It is a marvellous show."—LICENSED VICTUALLERS' MIRROR.

" The new turns on Monday were Don Juan Caicedo, king of the wire, who made a sensation here a few

years ago by his marvellous feats on a wire stretched lengthwise of the stage. On this slender line he walks and runs with apparent ease, throws somersaults, pirouettes, and performs a variety of acrobatic feats which would be deemed astonishing if executed on a wider pathway. Caicedo's reception was enthusiastic in the extreme."—MORNING ADVERTISER, Dec. 2, 1896.

Read the Opinions of the Australian Press on CAICEDO'S Marvellous Performance :—

" Princess Theatre. The astonishing acrobatic business of the king of the wire, Don Juan Caicedo, fairly thrilled the house, and it was several minutes before the vast audience threw off the spell sufficiently, and broke out into a prolonged storm of cheers and applause." — EVENING STANDARD, Melbourne, Dec. 27, 1893.

"The interruption to the cable in no way affected Caicedo. His nonchalance, to say nothing of his *sang froid*, increases in virulence, so to speak, at each performance, and the same crowds who sit under him in the theatre are beginning to hang affectionately around his photograph in the city shops. Rumour says that his balance in the theatre is nothing to his balance in the bank."—THE AUSTRALASIAN, Jan. 1894.

" Caicedo, the marvellous wire performer made his appearance. We shall not attempt to describe what this gentleman does, but we shall say that during his act the house simply gasped in wonderment until it was ended, and then the roof started skywards. Astounding as Caicedo's feats are, it is in the perfect grace with which they are accomplished that the main charm lies. Anything cleverer or more finished in this branch of entertainment it would be impossible to conceive, and the four recalls to which he responded were thoroughly merited. Caicedo will boom."—THE AUSTRALIAN STAR, Sydney, February 12, 1894.

The entire Press of France, Russia, Germany, and Austria—in fact, throughout the World— are equally enthusiastic in their remarks concerning CAICEDO'S Marvellous Performances.

Just concluded a most successful engagement at the ALHAMBRA, LONDON.

The Era Annual 1897-98 (Theatre Museum, Covent Garden, London)

WHILE BALANCING ON THE WIRE. $10.00 (**15**, **4b**, **4c**; **20** as #121)
Filmed: 25 July 1894 (**18: 76**). Actually, two films were taken, commonly called
Caicedo No. 1 and *Caicedo No. 2*. The first was with a balancing pole, the second
without. The still shows a pole, but the existing film shows no pole. **18: 76** states that
this was the first open-air film; that the "Black Maria's" camera was turned around to
shoot through an open door. W K-L Dickson states that it was filmed through the small
window in the darkroom where the film was changed. "First open-air film" would seem
to be an overstatement. More appropriate perhaps would be "first open-air film in
commercial production".

The Brisbane (Australia) *Courier* of 12 August 1895 states: "Caicedo (the wire
walker) as he appeared in Melbourne at the Princess's Theatre, Melbourne". In the 13
August edition is: "Next, Caicedo, the wire-rope walker is seen. This artist turns a
double somersault, besides executing many other wonderful feats on the slack wire
rope." (**31**)
Copies: AMPAS; GCH; GH; MOMA; P; SAF, under the title of "Saute à la perche",
#PMU.28859.12909.
A still appears in **18: ill. 14**.

CAKE WALK see JAMES GRUNDY, CAKE WALK

Calisthenics
Filmed: before 18 March 1894, possibly 13 February 1894.
Four subjects of athletes doing calisthenics, here grouped together, as there is no listing
in any known catalogue. **25: 178** lists them as:
Calisthenics #1, with Wand
Calisthenics #2, Successful Somersault
Calisthenics #3, Unsuccessful Somersault
Calisthenics #4, Parallel Bars
No known copies, except possibly #1. A film at SAF shows a man in a light coloured
T-shirt and trousers exercising with a wand. The stage is otherwise bare, except for a
dog lying in the right foreground. Finding this film in France suggests caution, as
Lumière did film gymnasts, and the French do take their dogs everywhere! Suggesting
Edison is the fact that only he listed "Calisthenics, with wand", which this appears to
be. The print is too dark to show any signs of the "Black Maria" stage, if there are any.
The film is listed under the title "La Leçon de Baton", #22861; AMPAS; EH; GCH;
GH; P; SAF.
Stills appear in **30: 40**.

41. CAMEL PARADE. A NUMBER OF CHILDREN RIDING ON THE "SHIPS OF
THE DESERT". (**4b**, **4c**, **5**, **16a**)
Filmed: before November 1896.
No known copy.

CARMENCITA (**14**)
Filmed: c.11 March 1894 (**18: 7**).
Carmencita is a good example of the high-quality performers that Edison's persona was
able to attract for the Kinetoscope; other examples are Buffalo Bill and Caicedo. All
were world-class performers. Although making only this film, Carmencita was the first
of several delightful dancers to perform for the Kinetoscope.

A reporter for the *Brisbane Courier* of 13 August 1895 writes: "One sees the world-famous Spanish danceuse, Carmencita, now appearing nightly at the Palace of Varieties in London at a salary exceeding that of the Chancellor of the Exchequer. She has revived the glories of a lost art, and is undisputed queen of the ballet. As the spectator sees every motion of that graceful, agile form he recognizes that Carmencita is now the queen of the ballet; she embodies the poetry of motion. No need to travel round the globe to see her; in the Kinetoscope you can see every movement of the celebrated danceuse as well as if seated in the dress circle of the London theatre." Also: "Thus, by means of this wonderful machine, Carmencita will dance for the amusement of generations, born centuries after she herself is dust and ashes" (31).

"Carmencita" was a favourite for use in the Kinetophone. **14** lists her as "Carmensite", and suggests the following cylinders "Valse Santiago" (English: "Santiago Waltz"), which is Edison cylinder #64 by the Edison Grand Concert Band, also #607 by the Edison Symphony Orchestra. "La Paloma", Edison cylinder #565 by the Edison Symphony Orchestra, also "Alma-Danza Spagnuola" (English: "Spanish Soul-Dance"), which might be Edison cylinder #91, "Spanish Fandango" by the Edison Grand Concert Band. **18: 77** states this was the first film to have censorship difficulties, because of the amount of "limb" shown.

Copies: GH; US National Archives; the first 38' of 200195A. Excellent copy, but unfortunately has distracting spots in the background of each frame; probably water spots caused by improper drying of some negative or print in the distant past. It is the first subject of a very long reel of Asiatic scenes of the early 1900s!

Stills appear in **18: ill. 12; 30: 42**.

6. THE CARNIVAL DANCE, BY 3 DANCERS FROM THE "GAIETY GIRL" COMPANY OF LONDON. SAID TO BE AMONG THE BEST DANCERS IN THE WORLD IN THIS LINE. (**4, 4a, 4b, 4c, 5, 12, 15**). **20** as #6 describes the film as "SKIRT DANCE BY 3 YOUNG LADIES OF THE "LONDON GAIETY GIRL COMPANY. $15.00".

Filmed: 1 November 1894 (**18: 82**).

18: 125 states that this dance was a Kinetophone "favorite". **14** lists it as "Danza Carnevalesca (3 Danzatori)". It suggests cylinders "Duetto Banjo" (English: "Banjo Duet") or "Danza del Ventaglio" (English: "Fan Dance"). These names are not sufficiently specific to locate in the Edison or Columbia record catalogues.

No known copy.

42. <u>CARPENTER SHOP</u>. A REALISTIC REPRESENTATION. THREE MEN AT WORK. (**4b, 4c, 5, 16a**).

Filmed: unknown, but probably summer 1896.

A good clear film of three men, one hammering, one planing and one sawing. The setting is that of a carpenter shop, almost certainly on the stage of the "Black Maria". This is a strange one, as all the other "shop" scenes – *Barber Shop, Blacksmith Shop, Barroom Scene* – were taken in 1893 or early 1894. By summer 1896 all, or almost all, films were exteriors taken "on location". Yet here comes *Carpenter Shop*! One is tempted to wonder whether this was not taken earlier, but not issued until later. After all, Hollywood does this all the time. Sometimes events such as the thawing of the Cold War or the brief battle with Iraq, "Desert Storm", will cause the release of a film to be untimely or, as is the case with some films deemed unworthy of release, they may never be released at all.

Copy: NAC.

211. CAVALRY CHARGE. SHOWING THE CHARGE OF THE WEST POINT CADETS AT WEST POINT, N.Y. THE CHARGE, SALUTE AND RETREAT MAKE THIS ONE OF THE MOST ANIMATED PICTURES EVER MADE. THE GLISTENING OF THE SABRES IS PLAINLY VISIBLE. (4b, 16b)

The description is almost identical to 143. CADETS' CHARGE. However, the words "and retreat" being added would seem to indicate that 211 may be a 150' version of *Cadet's Charge*, although the catalogue does not make this clear. The number 211 does not fit in with my theory that the numbers around 187 end the year of 1896! Filmed: almost certainly on the occasion of the filming of *Cadet's Charge* shortly before the copyright date of 27 November 1896.
No known copy.

212. CAVALRY DRILL. SHOWING THE MANUAL OR DRILL OF THE CADETS OF WEST POINT, N.Y. (4b, 16b)
Unlike 143. CADETS' CHARGE, there seems to be no 50' version of this film, which was certainly taken on the same occasion as the films described above. I might hazard a guess that the asterisk is used to identify a 150' film, but nowhere in the catalogue is this explained, and a list of 150' films is given at the end of the catalogue.
Filmed: see previous entry.
No known copy.

CENTRAL PARK see 51. FOUNTAIN IN CENTRAL PARK

CHANG, LI HUNG see 61. LI HUNG CHANG. THE GREAT VICEROY LEAVING THE HOTEL WALDORF

CHARGE OF THE WEST POINT CADETS (2) see 143. CADETS' CHARGE.

169. CHICAGO AND BUFFALO EXPRESS (4b, 4c, 5, 16c)
See ARRIVAL OF THE LOCAL EXPRESS

THE CHICKEN FIGHT. MOST POPULAR OF ALL. SHOWS TWO COCKS FIGHTING, AND SPECTATORS BETTING. PERFECTLY TRUE TO LIFE. (24)
Filmed: before 14 April 1894.
Under the title "ROOSTERS", one of the ten films shown at the first commercial showing of the Kinetoscope on 14 April 1894 (18: 56).
See the several listings under *Cock Fight*.

From all the evidence, it would seem that Edison for some reason did not make extra copies of his negatives for use in printing. Either he did not anticipate the demand, or there was something about the film, but he made no copy negatives. When his sole negative of a film wore out, and *The Chicken Fight* is an example, he simply dropped the film or, in a few cases where the subject was quite popular, refilmed the subject. While in some cases, such as the *Barber Shop* and *Blacksmith Shop*, the second film differed in some details, all descriptions of the three films, of which *The Chicken Fight* was the first, are described as showing two cocks fighting and spectators, betting in the background.

This description would seem to rule out as an Edison product a cockfighting film at the SAF, #5774. Lumière film #1026 was called "Fighting Cocks", and may well be the one at SAF. See 175. <u>COCK FIGHT.</u>

43. CHILDREN'S PARADE. GERMAN PICNIC GROUNDS, SHOWING OVER 200 CHILDREN IN LINE. (**4b, 4c; 16a** as GERMAN CHILDREN).
Filmed, probably summer 1896, since, besides this 50' version, there is #89, 1 150' version priced at $45.
No known copy.

<u>CHINESE LAUNDRY SCENE.</u> REPRESENTS THE PURSUIT OF HOP LEE BY POLICEMAN O'FLANNIGAN, IN, OUT, AND AROUND HOP'S LAUNDRY CABIN. $12.50. (**15; 4b, 4c; 5** as #44)
Filmed: 1894.
Also known as CHINESE LAUNDRY, WITH ROBETTA AND DORETTO.
Copies: GH; MG, excerpt in their film #9997; MOMA "Films of the 1890s".
A still appears in **18: ill. 20.**

Chinese Laundry Scene

CHINESE OPIUM DEN POLICE RAID – A COMIC **see** ROBETTA AND DORETTO. CHINESE OPIUM DEN.

8. CISSY FITZGERALD. SKIRT DANCE BY THE QUEEN OF THE ENGLISH VARIETY STAGE. (**4b, 4c, 5, 20**)
Filmed: unknown.
34 adds this description: "A new dance by this celebrated English artist. Her famous wink adds to the interest of the picture."
No known copy.

CLARK'S THREAD MILL (**2**) **see** 129. <u>EMPLOYEES LEAVING FACTORY</u> (**4**)

Cock Fight (**see** THE CHICKEN FIGHT. MOST POPULAR OF ALL. SHOWS TWO COCKS FIGHTING, AND SPECTATORS BETTING. PERFECTLY TRUE TO LIFE; **see also** Roosters)
Filmed: before 14 April 1894.
Although this film was one of the first ten shown at the 14 April 1894 introduction of the Kinetoscope under the title "Roosters", it never appeared in a catalogue under this name. The cage in which the cocks fought appears in a March 1894 photograph (illustration 23) of the Black Maria. Australian researcher Chris Long found this description in a 30 November 1894 Australian newspaper: "Marvelously exact is the scene of the cock fight, with the whir of wings and rapid stroke of the spurs, whilst a stout man sitting nearby smiles confidently upon his champion, and evidently offers to bet upon his bird to any extent."
No known copy.

Cock Fight

175. <u>COCK FIGHT.</u> A LIVELY AND EXCITING ENCOUNTER BETWEEN TWO GENUINE GAME BIRDS, IN WHICH THEIR RESPECTIVE OWNERS ARE SEEN IN THE BACKGROUND EXCHANGING BETS ON THE PROBABLE FINISH. WHEN PROJECTED ON CANVAS THE BIRDS APPEAR MUCH LARGER THAN LIFE, AND EVERY FEATHER (INCLUDING THOSE WHICH ARE SHED IN THE FRAY) IS DISTINCTLY SHOWN. NOTE: THIS SUBJECT WAS PHOTOGRAPHED ON 21 DECEMBER 1896, AND IS NOT THE OLD NEGATIVE WHICH WAS FAR INFERIOR IN EVERY PARTICULAR. (2, 4b, 4c, 5)

This film was copyrighted on 24 December 1896. Cock-fight films were immensely popular; this is the only subject to have been filmed three times.

Copies: AMPAS; EH (this copy is most likely the January/February 1895 fight. Two men appear in the scene, which rules out the first film, but there are no copyright frames in the film, which makes the third film unlikely); GCH; MOMA; P; SAF have a film which they call "an Edison cock fight", but I think it looks French. The background appears to be a sheet; it is heavily wrinkled and several men peer over the top of it. Although only portions of their heads can be seen, to me they appear decidedly French!

COCK FIGHT. AN EXCITING CONTEST BETWEEN LIVELY GAME BIRDS, IN WHICH THE FEATHERS FLY FREELY. THE OWNERS OF THE BIRDS ARE SEEN IN THE BACKGROUND EXCHANGING BETS. $12.50 (12, 15)

Filmed: January or February 1895 (18: 136).

Copy: see previous entry.

COL. CODY AND HIS SIOUX INDIANS **see** INDIAN WAR COUNCIL, SHOWING SEVENTEEN DIFFERENT PERSONS-INDIAN WARRIORS AND WHITE MEN-IN COUNCIL.

CORBETT AND COURTNEY BEFORE THE KINETOGRAPH

Filmed: noon, 7 September 1894 (**11**) or 8 September (**18: 136**).

This famous film appears in no known 1894 or 1895 catalogue because it was taken, not for Raff & Gammon or Maguire & Baucus, but for the Latham Kinetoscope Exhibition Company (**18: 75**). It was also known as *Before the Kinetograph* (**10**). *The Edison Phonographic News* of November/December 1894 describes the scene as follows:

KNOCKED OUT.

CORBETT PUTS A MAN TO SLEEP FOR THE KINETOSCOPE.

James J. Corbett celebrated the second anniversary of the winning of the championship to-day by an exhibition fight before an Edison kinetoscope, in which he knocked out Peter Courtney, of Trenton, a local pugilist of some note, who stood before Fitzsimmons for four rounds.

The bout took place at the Edison laboratory, in Orange, N.J. It was arranged by the proprietors of the kinetoscope, and the preliminaries were conducted with the utmost secrecy, being known only to the principals and their managers.

There were ten spectators, including the referee – John P. Eckhardt – and Corbett pocketed a big check for his efforts.

Corbett was seconded by J. McVey, the heavy-weight wrestler, who has been with him for several seasons, and William A. Brady, his manager. Delaney was not present. Neither was Mr. Edison.

The gloves used were hard mitts, weighing a shade over two ounces.

Courtney weighed in at 195 pounds. He stands 5 feet 10 inches. Corbett weighed his average weight, of about 195 pounds. He stands 6 feet 1½ inches.

It has been arranged that if Courtney stayed six rounds he was to receive $500. The Trenton pugilist put up such a game fight and took his punishment so well that, although he did not last the entire six rounds, he received the stated amount.

Corbett and Courtney, stripped to fighting costume, stepped into a fourteen foot ring and immediately began operations. The rounds were of one minute each, with one minute and a half between.

The first and second rounds were pretty to look at, but uneventful. In the third round Corbett knocked Courtney down with a straight right-hand blow from the shoulder.

In the fourth round Courtney made a play for Corbett's ribs and succeeded in getting two right-hand blows which made Corbett wince. Courtney repeated the dose with his left in the fifth round, and as Corbett left an opening reached Jim's ear with his right.

In the sixth round Corbett, evidently bent on finishing Courtney, started in to show what he could do. He feinted with his left and then shot out his right, striking Courtney back of the ear, knocking him down and out.

When Courtney fell the referee began counting the final 10 seconds. When he said "five" Courtney seemed to realize what was going on, and made a painful effort to arise. He struggled to his knees, but was too weak to do more, and sank back thoroughly exhausted. It was a straight, clean knock-out.

Courtney remained "out" for 20 seconds.

The fighting throughout had been in earnest, the blows coming swift and hard. Corbett was handed the check by the referee, and left with a pleasant smile on his face.

Several extra-long Kinetoscope cabinets were built to accommodate the longer films required by one-minute rounds, of which there were six. Several were used in Tally's Kinetoscope Parlor in Los Angeles, CA (see illustration 26).

By 1897, apparently having been bought by Maguire & Baucus, the film was #188 in their April and autumn 1897 catalogues (4b, 4c). The listing in the April 1897 catalogue is reprinted below to show how fast the industry was changing. Maguire & Baucus had bought the film, Edison had started producing "clear" stock for projection (16c):

SPECIAL PRIZE-FIGHT SUBJECTS.

188. CORBETT-COURTNEY FIGHT.

Corbett

189. LEONARD-CUSHING FIGHT.

Cushing

Each of the above spirited boxing contests consists of SIX lively rounds with "knock-out" in the last. Both fights made great hits when exhibited in connection with the Kinetoscope and proved exceedingly popular and productive of large returns to their exhibitors.

Special arrangements having been made by the Edison Manufacturing Company to reproduce these upon CLEAR stock, for Projecting Machine Exhibition work, we are pleased to announce that we are now prepared to sell them for this purpose without restrictions.

They are photographed upon *150 foot length films only:* each film contains *one full round* and gives an exhibition of about one minute and a half.

Price per film, $45.00.

Copies: GH; LOC #FLA 2928 (44'). These would seem to be excerpts. No known copy of all six rounds of 150' films seems to have survived.

Stills appear in **18: ill. 54**; **30: 49**.

Corbett-Fitzsimmons Fight

Filmed: 31 October 1895 in Dallas, TX.

18: 141 states that Edison made cameras for this fight for "Rector".

Copies: possibly NFTVA and P. One of the films that came with Kinetoscope #141 was labelled "Fitzsimmons Fight", but I cannot confirm it.

Couchee Dance. Other possible names are "Fatima's Danse du Ventre" and "Fatima's Coochee Coochee Dance".

Filmed: June-July 1896.

On a stage with a painted background, Fatima does a most enthusiastic belly dance. A censored version also exists and is on the same MOMA reel. If this film is listed in a catalogue, I have not seen it.

Copy: MOMA – Early Edison Shorts (7096).

CUPID DANCE. THREE BEAUTIFUL LITTLE GIRLS – LA REGALONCITA, LA GRACIOSA AND LA PRECIOSA – IN A CHARMING DANCE. (24)
Filmed: autumn 1894.
18: 125 states that phonograph cylinders were sent to Little Rock, AR, on 6 May 1895 to accompany a film called "Fairies Dance" on the Kinetophone. There is no known listing under either name or under "Children Dancing", a name which Hendricks gives as a possible alternative title. However, *Cupid Dance* is listed in 24 as "now being exhibited to the public".
No known surviving copy.

7. CYCLONE DANCE. SPANISH DANCE BY SENORITA LOLA YBERRI (4b, 4c).
Filmed: c.September 1895.
No known copy. No other information.

DANCE. FRANK LAWTON AND MISSES WILLIAMSON AND FRANCE. "HOYT'S MILK WHITE FLAG." $15.00. (12) See TRIO. A LIVELY ECCENTRIC DANCE BY FRANK LAWTON AND MISSES WILLIAMSON AND FRANCE, OF HOYT'S MILK WHITE FLAG. ATTRACTIVE COSTUMES.
Filmed: before May 1895.
No known copy.

9. DANCE OF REJOICING.
Listed in 15 as PADDLE DANCE, DANCE OF REJOICING. NATIVE DANCES BY SAMOAN ISLANDERS, AS PRODUCED AT THE FAMOUS "MIDWAY PLAISANCE". Each $12.50.
12 lists it as DANCE OF REJOICING, BY SAMOAN ISLANDERS, WITH BARNUM AND BAILEY'S "GREATEST SHOW ON EARTH. $15.00. See PADDLE DANCE, BY FIJI ISLANDERS WITH BARNUM AND BAILEY'S "GREATEST SHOW ON EARTH".
Filmed: 27 April 1895 (18: 137).
Also listed (4b, 4c, 20) as "9. Dance of rejoicing, by natives of the Fiji Islands". Also listed in 4b. (The Samoan Islands and Fiji are only about 400 miles apart!)
No known copy.

10. DANCING DOG. SKIRT DANCE BY A TRAINED DOG, A FILM FOR CHILDREN (4b, 20)
Found, so far, only on 20 under this title, but it would seem likely that it is the same film as *Skirt Dance Dog*.

109. DEAD MAN'S CURVE. BROADWAY AND FOURTEENTH STREET. See 105. BROADWAY AND 14TH ST. STREET SCENE. A SCENE AT "DEATH CURVE" (4b, 4c)
Filmed: summer 1896.
No known copy, although MOMA and others do have unidentified New York street scenes.

45. DEATH SCENE (COMIC) (4b, 4c, 5).
See also TRILBY'S DEATH SCENE.

46. THE DENTIST'S CHAIR. REPRESENTS DR. COLTON, THE FAMOUS INVENTOR OF "LAUGHING GAS," IN THE ACT OF ADMINISTERING SAME. ALSO SHOWS METHOD OF EXTRACTING TEETH. $10.00. (15).
Also listed in 12 as IN THE DENTIST'S CHAIR, – ADMINISTERING GAS AND EXTRACTING A TOOTH. DR. COLTON, WHO FIRST USED GAS FOR EXTRACTING TEETH, IS SHOWN ADMINISTERING THE GAS IN THIS FILM. $15.00. Also in 4b and 4c as 46. DENTAL SCENE.
Filmed: 18: 81 states "possibly before January 1, 1895". 18: 135 states more likely "shortly before January 21" 1895.
No known copy.
A still appears in 18: ill. 26.

Dickson Violin (also sometimes called *Dickson Experimental Sound Film*)
Filmed: between autumn 1894 and 2 April 1895, when Dickson left Edison (18: 122).
See illustration 45. Since this was an experimental film, even though it has an "R" in the lower right-hand corner of the stage, it is not listed in any known catalogue. From observation, the film consists of the following: on the left is an enormous metal recording horn hung from a cord. The recording phonograph is out of the scene to the left. See illustration 46 of a phonograph, which may well be the one used for this film. In the centre is W K-L Dickson playing his violin into the horn. On the right, two Edison workmen in shirtsleeves dance together to supply "motion". Towards the end, a man in a dark suit wearing a derby walks into the rear of the scene from the left. His face is never seen, as the film stops when his face is still behind the recording horn.

Carl Malkames informs me that he discovered this film in Edison's desk at the Edison National Historic Site in the 1950s, while preparing a film for Pathé.
Copies: AMPAS; ENHS #156-104 (16mm?); LOC #FLA374 (43'); MG "Films of the 1890s" #9997 (16mm rental); UCLA (#1 on "The Operator Cranked-The Picture Moved" on ½" videocassette Loc. P-VA3093M and 400' 16mm print Loc. R-A1-149-4, Inv. #M14872).
A still appears in 18: ill. 45.

Dog Fight
Filmed: by March 1895.
No known copy.

170. DOLORITA'S PASSION DANCE. A CHARACTERISTIC MIDWAY DANCER.
(4b, 4c, 12) (Also spelled as "Dolarita" in one catalogue)
Filmed: before 5 May 1896 (12).
34 gives the best description of this dance: musicians are seated, playing, while the graceful Dolorita dances. It is the Danse-du-Ventre, the famous Oriental muscle dance.

A letter from The Kinetoscope Company (?) or from Raff & Gammon (?) – there is no signature – to Edison Manufacturing Company of 5 April 1897 mentions: "Also a pair of Portiers, which are in Mr. Heise's office and which we took over there at the time Dolorita was taken" (Heise was the Black Maria's cameraman). 12 quotes a letter of 6 May 1896 to W D Standifer of Butte, MT, a Kinetoscope peep-show exhibitor who was looking for something arranged for the taste of the copper town: "We are confident that the Dolorita 'Passion Dance' would be as exciting as you desire. In fact, we will not show it in our parlor. You speak of the class of trade which want something of this character. We think this will certainly answer your purposes. A man in Buffalo has one of these films and informs us that he frequently has forty or fifty men waiting in line to see it. We do not send out films for inspection."

Dolorita's dance consisted of an Americanised version of the "Ouled Nail" girl's dance from North Africa, done in charming synchronism to the tom-tom and flute imported with such decided success in 'The Streets of Cairo' on the Midway of the Chicago World's Fair of 1893. This picture held the box office record of the slot-machines of the Kinetoscope parlour on the boardwalk at an Atlantic City.

Then one day an uplifter, giving the boardwalk a careful sociological examination, observed the line at the "Dolores" machine. He waited his turn and had a long and nourishing look at the "Passion Dance". Two days later, H R Kiefaber, owning the Kinetoscope parlour on the boardwalk, wrote to Frank R Gammon as follows: 'The authorities request us not to show the Houchi Kouchi, so please cancel order for new Dolorita, and also order for Amy Muller, colored. The emulsion on the Rope Dance is coming off in large pieces.'" **See also** 1. AMY MULLER. A BEAUTIFUL FANTASTIC TOE DANCE. A GOOD SUBJECT IF COLORED.
Filmed: between 24 March and 8 April 1896, according to Hendricks.
Copy: LOC.

Duel between two historical characters
Filmed: 30 September 1895 (**18: 140**).
Described as "taken in a forest", but not found in any catalogue, nor is any copy known, so there is no description available.

EAST SIDE DRIVE (PARK SCENE). (**2**, **4b**, **4c**, **5** as #130). Also listed in **20**, **16b** as "130. EAST SIDE DRIVE, A SCENE ON THE FASHIONABLE DRIVE, CENTRAL PARK, NEW YORK, SHOWING MANY STYLISH EQUIPAGES DRAWN BY SPIRITED THOROUGHBRED HORSES." There is also an EAST SIDE DRIVE #2.
Filmed: both films were copyrighted on 31 October 1896, which would normally put the filming date just a few days prior. There seem to be several scenes of this description extant, but not specifically identified. MOMA has several.

MR. EDISON AT WORK IN HIS CHEMICAL LABORATORY (**2**)
Filmed: exact date unknown, but almost certainly only a few days before the copyright date of 5 June 1897. Technically, this film is too late for this *Index*. In a list of films published by F M Prescott, Edison Building, 44 Broad Street, New York, NY, in about June 1897 is the following:

LATEST EDISON FILMS FOR PROJECTING MACHINES.
(Copyright by Thomas A. Edison)

Mr. EDISON AT WORK IN HIS CHEMICAL LABORATORY. This film is remarkable in several respects. In the first place, it is full life-size. Secondly, it is the only accurate recent portrait of the great inventor. The scene is an actual one, showing Mr. Edison in working dress engaged in an interesting chemical experiment in his great Laboratory. There is sufficient movement to lead the spectator through the several processes of mixing, pouring, testing, etc, as if he were side by side with the principal. The lights and shadows are vivid, and the apparatus and other accessories complete a startling picture that will appeal to every beholder. 50 feet only. Price, $15.00.

Mr. Edison At Work in His Chemical Laboratory
(Library of Congress)

It would seem logical for this film to appear in the autumn 1897 Maguire & Baucus catalogue (**4c**), but only #47 appears again. Hendricks believes that this film was not made in Edison's actual laboratory, but on a "set" in the "Black Maria"!

Long points out his clipping from the *Sydney Morning Herald* of 31 July 1897. Below is quoted part of an advertisement of the Edison Electric Parlour:

> NEW PICTURES! TO-DAY!! TO-DAY !!!
> Just arrived a Life-size Picture of
> "MR. EDISON AT WORK IN HIS CHEMICAL
> LABORATORY."
> This film was made specially to our order, and shows Mr.
> Edison in working dress engaged in an interesting
> chemical experiment. The scene is an actual one, and is
> the only accurate recent portrait of the great inventor.

It is always possible that the Edison Electric Parlour, whose advertisement this was, was referring to the print, and not the negative, but Long believes that it was not unusual for an exhibitor to request that a particular subject be taken, particularly through Maguire & Baucus, who were responsible for Australia. Certainly the timing is persuasive. The film was made about 1 June 1897, and was delivered in Sydney just two months later.

Copies: AMPAS; EH in Smithsonian Collection No. 4 1897-98 USA, #7 under title of "Mr. Edison at Work in His Chemical Laboratory (1897) Copyrighted June 5, 1897"; MG, a sequence in "American Primitives" #2-9995-S 16mm; MOMA; P. Also in New

Zealand Film Archive, PO Box 9544, Wellington, NZ, and in National Archives, Washington, DC.

In **4b** is the following entry:
47. Edison Laboratory. Front view, boys playing, trolley cars passing and porters sprinkling street. (**4b, 4c, 5**)
Filmed: unknown.
No known copy.
There are several copies extant of a film usually called *Edison Laboratory*, and I expect most people have assumed that it is the one listed above, as some catalogue listings merely give the two-word title with no description. However, the film that they have is really *Mr. Edison at Work in His Chemical Laboratory*.

11. EGYPTIAN DANCE. (**4b, 4c, 5**). Also EGYPTIAN DANCE BY "PRINCESS ALI", THE STAR OF THE MIDWAY PLAISANCE" (**20**).

48. ELEVATED RAILROAD. SHOWING TRAINS APPROACHING THE STATION. (**4b**)
Filmed: within a week of 11 May 1896 (**30: 66**).
Shows the 23rd Street "L" station, with the train running at top speed.
Copy: MG, a sequence on "American Primitives" #2-9995-S, 16mm, shows a steam-operated elevated railroad; MOMA; John E Allen – Primitives, Roll #4, item #6.

ELSIE JONES, NO. 1, "THE LITTLE MAGNET". BUCK DANCE. $15.00. (**12; 15** – $12.50; **20, 4b, 4c, 5** as **12**).
18: 82 says "two Elsie Jones dance subjects" "taken Fall 1894". Perhaps the second one is the next entry.
No known copy.

ELSIE JONES SPAGNUOLA (English: "Elsie Jones, Spanish") (**14**)
This is almost surely the second of the two Elsie Jones dance subjects taken in autumn 1894, although it does not appear in a Maguire & Baucus catalogue (see preceding entry). **14** recommends a cylinder titled "Faudanze Spagnuolo" (English: "Spanish Fandango"), almost surely Edison cylinder #91 of that name, by the Edison Grand Concert Band.
No known copy.

129. <u>EMPLOYEES LEAVING FACTORY</u>. A SCENE AT THE GREAT CLARK THREAD MILLS, SHOWING HUNDREDS OF EMPLOYEES COMING OUT OF THE FACTORY. (**4b, 4c, 5, 20**).
Title also given as CLARK'S THREAD MILL (**2**), and EMPLOYEES LEAVING THE GREAT CLARK THREAD MILLS (TAKEN BY JAMES H. WHITE) (**11**).
Filmed: October 1896 (**11**) and listed on Tally's "flyer" (see illustration 42). A 150' version is #146.
Filmed: copyrighted on 31 October 1896 as *Clark's Thread Mill*, therefore undoubtedly filmed only a few days before. Hendricks believed that this film was made as a result of the popularity of the French Lumière film #1091, *Sortie d'un usine* (*Leaving the Factory*).
16b gives an expanded description of the action: CLARK'S THREAD MILLS –

Employees Leaving Factory (Library of Congress)

SHOWING ABOUT 500 EMPLOYEES, MEN WOMEN AND CHILDREN LEAVING THIS GREAT FACTORY AT THE END OF THEIR WEEK'S TOIL, THEIR FACES LIGHTED UP WITH HAPPINESS IN ANTICIPATION OF THE DAY OF REST AT HAND. THE FACIAL EXPRESSION OF EACH OF THIS VAST ARMY OF TOILERS IS CLEARLY DEFINED.

Edison's copyrighting of this film did not seem to deter International Film Company from very promptly "duping" it.

Copy: NAC.

(Edison) Employees Picnic (**18: 55**)
Filmed: before 14 April 1894.
33: 49 describes the scene as follows:

> On another occasion, an impromptu picnic was rigged up just outside the stately grounds of the 'Black Maria.' The actors fell readily into position, being possessed of a good deal of unsuspected histrionic talent, and the scene was soon animated in the extreme. A fire was lit, a gipsy kettle hung, and some one commenced energetically to blow the embers; crockery and comestibles were unpacked and set out invitingly by several deft-handed maidens, while a *mauvais sujet*, oblivious of the presence of these charmers, vaulted upon the table, drew a beaker of foaming ale and started a general frolic.

No known copy.
A still appears in **18: ill. 29.**

49. <u>EXECUTION.</u> REPRESENTING THE BEHEADING OF MARY, QUEEN OF

SCOTS – A REALISTIC REPRODUCTION OF AN HISTORIC SCENE. (**4b**, **4c**).
Filmed: 28 August 1895.

Execution of Mary, Queen of Scots
Note her head lying on the ground, left.
(Photo gift of Richard Bueschell)

This film is famous for being the first to use "stop motion", the very earliest of the special effects so popular today. In fact, it has a competitor for that title. 57. *Joan of Arc* also used "stop motion", and was filmed on the same day. There appears to be no record as to which was filmed first. The films were directed by Alfred Clark. R L Thomae, secretary-treasurer of the Kinetoscope Company, played "Mary". Thomae placed his head on the block, the camera was stopped, a dummy was substituted for Thomae, the camera started again, and the head of the dummy chopped off. It rolls away, the headsman picks it up and holds it towards the camera.

Hendricks found a fascinating letter, reprinted here, that shows us preparations made for both *Execution* and *Joan of Arc*.

August 24, 1895

Voegeler
222 E. Houston St. City

Dear Sir

As per your estimate given me on the 21st int you will please have sent to me-addressed as follows

Alfred C. Clark
c/o Edison Laboratory
Orange, N.J.

the Costumes as below

Mary Queen of Scots
Headsman and assistant
2 Noblemen of that period
6 Jackets & Armours & shoes and 12 Helmets
2 Joan of Arc (white) one to be burned up
3 Peasants costumes 2 women &
2 priests and 1 Bishop
You are to send a man with them to dress the people.
You are to furnish also 2 dummies (straw) without heads-one of which will be returned to you and the other destroyed.
A large axe
and the Cross you showed me.
The things are to be used on Wednesday morning Aug. 28th and will have to leave your store Tuesday morning early. Your man will go out Wednesday morning on the 8.10 train from the foot of Barclay St. He gets off at <u>Orange</u> Station and takes the trolley car to the laboratory. Any one out there will tell him the way.

As I understand it you will pack the costumes and properties in trunks so they will arrive safely and on their arrival will be placed in care of your man.

As we also agreed – if Wednesday morning is a cloudy or stormy day you will let the costumes stay until the next <u>clear</u> morning, and do not send your man over if it is cloudy Wednesday, but wait until the next clear day as we will have no use for him.

Yours truly
Alfred E. [sic] Clark

In the 1960s, Hendricks believed that no copy of *Joan of Arc* had survived. Another noted author, as recently as 1991, wrote that it had not. One of the gratifying things about compiling this *Index* is bringing the knowledge of the existence of these early films and their location to a wider audience.

Copies: EH; GH; MG, #9997, "Films of the 1890s" (16mm for rent); MOMA "Films of the 1890s".

A still appears in **18: ill. 31.**

13. FAN DANCE. A CHARACTERISTIC SPANISH DANCE BY LOLA YBERRI. **(4b, 4c, 20)**
Filmed: autumn 1894 (?)
18: 82 says "a fan dance" was taken at this time, but does not specify an artist. **25** lists two dances by Miss Yberri, FAN DANCE and CYCLONE DANCE, A SPANISH DANCE BY LOLA YBERRI.
No known copy.

178. FARMER'S TROUBLE. A RATHER DILAPIDATED FARM WAGON LOADED WITH CABBAGES IS BEING DRIVEN ALONG THE MARKET PLACE, WHEN A DARK MISCREANT TRUNDLING A WHEELBARROW SUCCEEDS IN COLLIDING WITH ONE OF THE REAR WHEELS. THE WHEEL PARTS COMPANY WITH THE VEHICLE, AND WRECKING IT, SCATTERS THE CONTENTS IN ALL DIRECTIONS. THE FARMER, CONVINCED THAT THE DARKEY WAS RESPONSIBLE FOR THE BREAKDOWN, JUMPS FROM HIS WAGON AND A PUGILISTIC ENCOUNTER TAKES PLACE, IN WHICH THE BYSTANDERS INTERFERE. A CLEAR PICTURE OF A LUDICROUS SUBJECT. **(4b, 4c, 5)**
Filmed: Christmas time, 1896 at Harrisburg, PA, and copyrighted on 8 January 1897. Several other films were taken on this trip.
No known copy.

90. FAST TRAIN. AN EXPRESS TRAIN OF THE HUDSON RIVER AND NEW YORK CENTRAL RAILROAD PASSING AROUND A CURVE IN THE PICTURESQUE MOHAWK VALLEY AT VERY FAST SPEED. **(4b, 4c)**
Filmed: October 1896.
No known copy.

100. FAST TRAINS. EXPRESS TRAINS PASSING ON THE NEW YORK CENTRAL RAILROAD. 150', $45.00. **(4b, 4c)**
Filmed: late October 1896.
Copies: Hendricks identified a 15.66' fragment of film at EH as probably being from this film. A still appears in **35: ill. 19.**

Feeding the Doves (Library of Congress)

Fatima's Danse du Ventre (7)
Filmed: June-July 1896.
A belly-dancer appears from the left and dances across towards the centre. The background seems to be in Coney Island, NY. No known catalogue listing. Alternative titles are *Couchee Dance*, or possibly *Fatima's Couchee Couche Dance*.
Copy: MOMA.

131. FEEDING THE DOVES. A FARM YARD SCENE SHOWING A YOUNG GIRL AND HER BABY SISTER SCATTERING GRAIN TO THE DOVES AND CHICKENS. THE FLUTTERING BIRDS AND EXCITED FOWLS GIVE AN ABUNDANCE OF ACTION TO THE SCENE, WHICH IS ONE OF THE PRETTIEST, CLEAREST AND MOST ATTRACTIVE EVER TAKEN. (2, 4b, 4c, 5, 16b, 20)
Filmed: c.13 October 1896 and copyrighted 23 October 1896, one of the first group of films copyrighted by Edison.
Copies: AMPAS; EH; GCH; GH; LC #FEB4689; MG #9997, "Films of the 1890s", a 16mm film rental; MOMA "Films of the 1890s"; NAC; P.
A still appears in 35: ill. 16.

Fencing
Filmed: 1892.
Two men in white, with masks and foils; white picket fence in background. Hendricks states that the scene was filmed against the interior east wall of the 1889 building, before October 1892. A series of frames is used as illustrations in 3 as early as 1892, also 6 and 13 in 1894. The film would appear to have been experimental, since no catalogue listing or existing copy of the film is known.

FERRIS WHEEL (30: 67)
Filmed: summer 1896.
30: 67 states that "[t]he Ferris wheel, almost 200 feet high, was a local landmark that provided visitors with a magnificent view of Jamaica Bay".
No known copy.

FIGHTING COCKS see Cock Fight

176. FIGHTING THE FIRE. REPRESENTING A FIRE ENGINE IN ACTION. THE BLACK SMOKE RISING FROM THE ENGINE STACK AND THE FIREMEN PLACING LADDERS AND DIRECTING STREAMS OF WATER AGAINST A BURNING BUILDING SERVE TO MAKE A VERY INTERESTING SCENE. (2, 4b, 4c, 5)
Viewing the film makes one pity the firemen! In the foreground is a classic steam engine belching enormous quantities of black smoke. To the right is a tall building, of which only the first three storeys are visible. (It shows no signs of being on fire!) On a very tall ladder which leans against the building, several firemen climb with hoses that begin spraying large streams of water. At this moment, the wind changes and the firemen are enveloped in a blinding cloud of black smoke.
Filmed: shortly before the copyright date of 27 November 1896.
Copies: EH; NFTVA, #9156, 45'.

FINALE OF 1ST ACT, HOYT'S "MILK WHITE FLAG", SHOWING 34 PERSONS
IN COSTUME. THE LARGEST NUMBER EVER SHOWN AS ONE SUBJECT IN
THE KINETOSCOPE. $15.00 (12, 15, 14, 4c as #64)
Filmed: autumn 1894 (18: 83).
15 lists it as MILK WHITE FLAG. THIS SCENE REPRESENTS THE GRAND
ASSEMBLY MARCH FROM THE FINALE OF THE FIRST ACT IN HOYT'S
'MILK WHITE FLAG' AND CONTAINS THIRTY-FOUR FIGURES IN FULL
COSTUME, INCLUDING BANDS, VIVIANDIERES, DRUM CORPS, MESSENGER
BOYS, ETC., ETC. A VERY FINE SUBJECT. $15.00.
14 lists it as 1. ATTO DEL MILK WHITE ILAG (English: "First Act of Milk White
Flag"), and suggests cylinders "Marcia della luna di miele" (English: "Honeymoon
March"). Edison cylinder #34 carries that name, played by the Edison Grand Concert
Band, and "Marcia del Centenario" (English: "Centennial March") described as being
played by "Banda di Gilmore" (English: "Gilmore's Band"). Gilmore recorded for
Edison from 1892 to 1894. Records are too fragmentary to have a listing for this
cylinder, but it was undoubtedly Edison. A third cylinder, "Marcia Arcadica" (English:
"Arcadian March"), finds no matching name in either Edison or Columbia catalogues.
14 merely indicates that it is played by an orchestra.
No known copy.

Fire Rescue Scene

FIRE RESCUE SCENE. SHOWING FINE SMOKE EFFECTS AND UNIFORMED
FIRE-MEN IN ACTION. $15.00 (12, 15).
4b lists 50. FIRE RESCUE. FIREMEN RESCUING PEOPLE FROM A BURNING
BUILDING. 4c and 5 give just 50. FIRE RESCUE.
At least two versions filmed. The first was used in a press showing in 1893 (9), the

second taken between 1 October 1894 and 21 December 1894 (21). **18: 82** states "Fall 1894". The "R" in the lower left would indicate that the film was taken for Raff & Gammon. Its later listing in Maguire & Baucus catalogues as "50" would indicate that it was almost certainly part of a sale of Raff & Gammon's film library to Maguire & Baucus in early 1897.

The above description does not do justice to a beautiful, dramatic film. Seeing it shows smoke billowing up from the rear. At lower left, a fireman holds a ladder which extends out of the scene at the upper right. A fireman on the ladder at about the centre of the scene receives a little girl, handed down to him from out of the scene above. He hands the girl to a fireman below him, and receives a small boy, whom he then hands down to the fireman below.

Copies: AMPAS; EH; GH; GCH; P. (AMPAS, EH and P are almost certainly of the second filming, as would be the illustration.)

First Sleigh Ride

---

179. FIRST SLEIGH RIDE. THIS SUBJECT TAKEN AFTER THE RECENT FIRST FALL OF SNOW SHOWS TWO ENTHUSIASTIC HORSEMEN INDULGING IN A "BRUSH" WITH THEIR RESPECTIVE HORSES AND CUTTERS. (**2, 4b, 4c, 5**)
Filmed: 24-26 December 1896 in Harrisburg, PA, and copyrighted on 7 January 1897. In a 1959 article in Eastman House's *Image*, Hendricks states that the camera was about in the middle of Market Street, between Front and Second, that Edison's camera crew arrived on 23 December, and that seven subjects were copyrighted from that visit.
Copies: EH; GH; GCH.
A still appears in **35: ill. 18.**

51. FOUNTAIN IN CENTRAL PARK. (4b, 4c)
Filmed: 11 May 1896 (**30: 66**). No known copy.

108. FOURTEENTH AND BROADWAY. LOOKING DOWN BROADWAY FROM UNION SQUARE. (**4b, 4c**)
No other information.
Copy: MG, a sequence on "American Primitives" #2-9995-S, 16mm. MOMA has several unidentified street scenes.

Fred Ott Holding a Bird

Fred Ott Holding a Bird
Filmed: unknown, but seems quite early and primitive.
As seen, this film is a close-up (upper torso) of Fred Ott wearing a hat and standing outside one of the West Orange buildings. He holds a bird in his left hand, and with his right hand teases the bird to make it flutter its wings (**1**). This must be a very early experimental film. I have never seen it, or any reference to it, elsewhere.

Copy: UCLA (sequence #2 of "The Operator Cranked-The Picture Moved", a 1" videocassette, Loc. P-VA3093M); also a 16mm print, 400', Loc. R-A1-149-4, Inv. #M14872.

French Ballet
An exhibitor's title for an Edison film, although it has not been determined which film this was. <u>187. PARISIAN DANCE</u> would seem a likely candidate.

A Frontier Scene **see** 63. LYNCHING SCENE. LYNCHING OF A HORSE THIEF BY A BAND OF COWBOYS.

"The Gaiety Girls," a Broadway Musical.
See separate listings for the three dances filmed from this musical: 6. THE CARNIVAL DANCE, BY 3 DANCERS FROM THE "GAIETY GIRL" COMPANY OF LONDON. SAID TO BE AMONG THE BEST DANCERS IN THE WORLD IN THIS LINE, PAS SEUL NO. 1 (DANCE) BY MISS MURRAY OF THE "GAIETY GIRL" COMPANY, and PAS SEUL NO. 2 (DANCE) BY MISS LUCAS OF THE "GAIETY GIRL" COMPANY.
34: 86 describes the circumstances as follows: "Mr. Edison came to a performance of the Gaiety Girls at Daly's in September, says Mrs. Rhodes [Mrs. Rhodes was the May Lucas of 1894]. He saw a performance, came back stage, and requested that the 'Carnival Dancers,' Maggie Crosland, Lucy Murray – both since dead – and I dance for him before his Kinetoscope. He stated that he had been able to produce pictures of people walking about and had reached the stage where he would like to attempt the picture in rapid motion."
The dancers consulted their travelling manager, J A E Maloney, about this weighty matter, and he in turn cabled George Edwards, the London manager of the show. The great name of Edison won, and the following Sunday he sent carriages in which the dancing girls were driven to Orange to pose at the Black Maria. This was 1 November 1894 (**18: 82**).
The Gaiety Girls were sufficiently popular for the Columbia Phonograph Company to

list in its 1896 catalogue, "#5040, 'One of the Gaiety Girls,' sung by Dan Quinn".
See photograph in **34: opp. 85**. Stills appear in **33: 18**.

52. <u>GARDEN SCENE.</u> A LADY WATERING FLOWERS WITH A HOSE: MISCHIEVOUS BOY STOPS THE FLOW OF WATER: SHE LOOKS FOR CAUSE, WHEN HE PERMITS WATER TO FLOW AGAIN. RESULT: AN UNEXPECTED BATH FOR THE LADY AND A THRASHING FOR THE YOUTH. (**4b, 4c, 5**)
Filmed: c.July 1896.
Writing in Eastman House's *Image* in 1959, Hendricks states that this film was inspired by Lumière's *L'arroseur arrose* (English: *The Sprinkler Sprinkled*). This was a 50' film. **4b** lists a 150' film, from which the 50' film was almost surely excerpted, as #91, and refers to the catalogue description of the 50' film.
Copy: NAC.

GERMAN CHILDREN. SHOWING A PROCESSION OF CHILDREN AND ADULTS, WITH A GERMAN BAND (**16a**)
Edison's film, *Children's Parade* was "duped" by International Film Company and issued as *German Children*.
See 43. CHILDREN'S PARADE. GERMAN PICNIC GROUNDS, SHOWING OVER 200 CHILDREN IN LINE.

14. GHOST. A DANCE BY GENUINE SIOUX INDIANS IN WAR PAINT AND COSTUME. (**20, 4b, 4c, 5**)
See <u>SIOUX GHOST DANCE.</u> (A VERY INTERESTING SUBJECT, FULL OF ACTION AND TRUE TO LIFE)

Glenroy Bros. Boxing Bout (Burlesque)
(Still courtesy of G Hall and R Martinique)

116. GLADIATORIAL COMBAT. (**4b, 4c**)
See BROADSWORD COMBAT. BETWEEN THE FAR FAMED CAPT. DUNCAN ROSS, CHAMPION OF THE WORLD, AND LIEUT. MARTIN. AN EXCITING CONTEST IN FULL ARMOR.

GLENROY BROS, BOXING BOUT (BURLESQUE). $15.00. (**12**)
BURLESQUE BOXING, BY GLENROY BROTHERS. (**15, 4a, 4b, 4c, 20** as #115)
The Glenroy Brothers appeared before the Kinetograph three times: 13 September 1894 (**18: 79**), 22 September 1894 (**18: 80**) and 6 October 1894 (**18: 79-80**). However, only two titles appear in existing catalogues, this and the next listing. The only difference seems to be that the next listing mentions "costume", and the several titles may well be describing a single film.
Copy: AMPAS; EH; GCH; GH, although this is dubious, as at one time Hendricks confused *Glenroy Bros.* with *Billy Edwards Boxing*; P.

GLENROY BROS. FARCICAL PUGILISTS IN COSTUME. $15.00. (**12**)
See previous entry.

135. GOING TO THE FIRE. THIS SCENE SHOWS ALMOST THE ENTIRE FIRE DEPARTMENT LED BY THE CHIEF, RESPONDING TO AN ALARM. THE HORSES, SAID TO BE THE FINEST OF THEIR KIND IN THE COUNTRY, PRESENT A THRILLING SPECTACLE AS THEY DASH RAPIDLY BY, FLECKED WITH FOAM AND PANTING FROM THE EXERTION OF THEIR LONG GALLOP. (**2, 4B, 5**) **20** uses #135, and for a description has ENGINE COMING DOWN STREET WITH HORSES AT FULL GALLOP (**16c**).
Filmed: 14 November 1896 (see below).
This film is an excellent example of how titles become confused. Hendricks says that the original film can bears the title *Starting for the Fire*, a subject copyrighted on 16 November 1896. He says that this title is improbable, there not being sufficient time for the film to have been taken on Saturday, 14 November, and copyrighted in Washington on the following Monday. Therefore, he gives it the title of *Going to the Fire* and a filming date of 14 November. The NFTVA has an excellent copy which it calls *New York Fire Brigade*. Hendricks says that there were three films shot at this time, but in Newark, NJ!
  It is an excellent film. Hendricks says that it was filmed on Broad Street, Newark, NJ, at noon on 14 November 1896, and that the camera was near the old city hall "in a wagon with a blanket wrapped around it", to quote a contemporary newspaper. It was apparently a hand-cranked camera, perhaps even one of the two illustrated here (illustration 10) in the description of the Kinetograph. As I saw the film, there was a long line of streetcars at the far right of the scene. One can be seen in the illustration. In front of them is a long line of spectators. From the left rear comes a series of ten pieces of horse-drawn fire-fighting equipment at top speed, led by the fire chief's wagon. As the descriptive words following the title say, it was "almost the entire fire department"! A lot happened in 44' of film!
See 134. STARTING FOR THE FIRE. SHOWS ENGINE LEAVING HOUSE and
134. MORNING FIRE ALARM. THIS SHOWS THE FIRE DEPARTMENT LEAVING HEADQUARTERS FOR AN EARLY MORNING FIRE. THE SCENE IS REMARKABLE FOR ITS NATURAL EFFECT. THE OPENING OF THE ENGINE HOUSE DOORS. THE PRANCING OF THE HORSES, AND EVEN THE

STARTLED EXPRESSION UPON THE FACES OF THE SPECTATORS ARE ALL
CLEARLY DEPICTED.
Copies: AMPAS; EH; GCH; NAC; NFTVA, under the title, *New York Fire Brigade*,
#606035A – this copy has a frame stating "Copyright 1896 by T. A. Edison".
A still appears in **35: ill. 17.**

Going to the Fire

**181. GOVERNOR'S GUARD. THIS SUBJECT, TAKEN AT HARRISBURG, PA.
SHOWS THE GOVERNOR'S GUARD EN ROUTE FOR THE CAPITOL GROUNDS.
VARIOUS MANOEUVRES WERE EXECUTED WHILE THE PICTURES WERE
BEING TAKEN, ALL OF WHICH ARE DISTINCTLY SHOWN. THE SCENE IS
INTERESTING, CLEAR AND SHARP (4b, 5)**
Filmed: c.Christmas 1896.
Six other films were made in Harrisburg at the Christmas season, 1896. It is likely that
this film was made at that time; *Ambulance Call* may have been another.
No known copy.

**152. GRAND BOULEVARD, PARIS. THIS SCENE SHOWS THE STYLISH
EQUIPAGES AND PROMENADERS ON ONE OF THE FINEST AVENUES OF
THE GAY METROPOLIS. (4b, 4c, 16c)**
Filmed: from the late number, 152, it would appear to be late 1896. However, if all the
known Maguire & Baucus films are listed in numerical order – which is also
approximately date order – a strange circumstance appears. Number 150 is a 150' film
of the *Wine Garden Scene*. There is no 151, this *Grand Boulevard, Paris* is 152, and
then there are no numbers used until 161, which starts the NIAGARA FALLS series.
152 is the only European view in the series of numbers up to about 183, which is
approximately where filming in 1896 ends, and 1897, which is beyond the period

covered in this work, begins. Two possibilities come to mind. Maguire & Baucus might have "duped" a Lumière film such as 1152# *Carriages on the Champs-Elysées*, or could there have been a catastrophe? Could a team have been sent over for Parisian scenes, only to take no more than one successful film out of perhaps ten? Charles Musser feels that it is simply a Lumière film. By autumn 1897, Maguire & Baucus was importing Lumière films, and its autumn catalogue had a long list of them; however, their numbers were all over 1000.
No known copy.

92. GRAND REPUBLIC. SHOWING EXCURSION STEAMER UNLOADING PASSENGERS AT ROCKAWAY BEACH. 150' $45.00 (**4b**, **4c**)
No known copy. No other information.

124. GROTESQUE TUMBLING, BY GUYER, THE FAMOUS CLOWN (**4b**, **4c**)
See GUYER. THE FAMOUS CLOWN, IN AN EXHIBITION OF GROTESQUE TUMBLING.

GRUNDY AND FRINT. BREAKDOWN FROM "SOUTH BEFORE THE WAR". $15.00 (**12**, **15**). $10.00
Filmed: before April 1895 – perhaps 12 February 1895. **18: 136-137** states that James Grundy did "three dances" for the Kinetograph, "a buck and wing, a cake walk and a breakdown". Hendricks does not mention Frint's participation.
No known copy.

Gun Spinner **see** Kessel. Whirlwind Gun Spinning.

GUYER. THE FAMOUS CLOWN, IN AN EXHIBITION OF GROTESQUE TUMBLING. $12.50. (**15**; **20** as #124)
Filmed: between 25 January 1895 and 18 April 1895 (**19**), before 12 February 1895 (**18: 136**).
No known copy.

Gymnastics **see** Calisthenics

Hadji Cheriff (**18: 80**)
Filmed: 6 October 1894 (**18: 80**).
Hendricks states: "from the Wild West Show and Cleveland's minstrel show". No listing in any catalogue and no existing copy. Long after saying the above, a listing turns up in **32** under the title *Arabian Gun Twirler*. It gives this description: "Twirls his rifle over shoulder, behind back, under leg, both hands and one hand".
No known copy.

A Hand Shake (**13**)
Filmed: before October 1892.
William Heise shakes hands with W K-L Dickson. One of the earliest 35mm films in a vertical format. Used as an illustration in the October 1892 *Phonogram*, and later in **13**. This was almost certainly an early experiment and was not issued commercially.
No known copy.

53. HAYMAKERS. MAKING HAY WITH SCYTHE, SICKLE AND HAND RAKE.
(4b, 4c, 5, 16a)
Filmed: summer 1896 (30: 67)
No known copy.

Hear Me, Norma (6)
Filmed: before June 1894 (18: 10).
18: 10n5 quotes Dickson's booklet: "The organ-grinder's monkey jumps up on his shoulder to the accompaniment of a strain of Norma". Dickson says that the first filming of this scene was done in the 1889 studio, then it was repeated later in the Black Maria because of the improved stage and lighting. Used in 6 and elsewhere as an illustration, but appears in no known catalogue. 18: 10n5 says that the film may not have even been issued by Raff & Gammon, or that it must have been unpopular, as he could find only two references to its having been shown. It is in his file at the National Archives (26) as "Organ Grinder".
No known copy.
A still appears in 33: 15.

106. HERALD SQUARE. SHOWING "HERALD" BUILDING AND ELEVATED RAILROAD. (4b, 4c)
Filmed: 11 May 1896 (30: 66).
30: 66 quotes *The New York Herald* as saying that the film was taken when the square was "crowded with cable cars, carriages and vehicles of all sorts, while now and then an 'L' train would thunder by", and that the scene included the *Herald* building and an area around Broadway and Sixth Avenue. As street scenes are difficult to identify, let me add this description from 32: 50: "Formed by the function of Broadway, Sixth Avenue and 35th Street. The picturesque low roofed Herald building is plainly shown, also the passing crowds and group of idlers."
Copy: GH includes several New York street scenes, of which this might be one.

High Kicking.
This title appears in illustration 20, and I have come across it in several other places. It is apparently an exhibitor's title for an Edison film, as this title does not appear in any Edison material, and I do not know which film it was used for. *Ruth Dennis* and *Amy Muller* are possibilities.

HIGHLAND DANCE (in 14 as "Danza Highland")
One of the ten films shown on 14 April 1894 at the first commercial showing of the Kinetoscope, this is the only catalogue listing found under this name. The film is more usually called *Scotch Reel*, and more detailed information may be found under this entry.

HINDOUSTAN FAKIR AND COTTA DWARF, FROM BARNUM AND BAILEY'S "GREATEST SHOW ON EARTH." $15.00 (12, $10.00)
Filmed: 27 April 1895 (18: 137), although Hendricks' notes say "May 14" 1895.
No known copy.

117. HORNBACKER AND MURPHY, FIVE ROUND GLOVE CONTEST TO A FINISH. PRICE PER SET OF FIVE FILMS, EACH SHOWING ONE ROUND,

$100., OR SINGLE ROUNDS, EACH $20. (**12**, **4b**, **4c**; **20** as #117).
15 describes it as follows: HORNBACKER AND MURPHY, A FIVE ROUND
GLOVE CONTEST, SHOWING KNOCKOUTS IN THE THIRD AND FIFTH
ROUNDS. LIVELY SPARRING THROUGHOUT. EACH FILM $15.00. NOTE:
EACH FILM OF THE ABOVE FIGHT CONTAINS ONE ROUND.
Filmed: 29 September 1894 (**18**: 80, 136).
As fight films are difficult to distinguish one from another, I will describe the scene.
The round finial on the newel post on the far left shows that the film was taken before
the building was remodelled in winter 1894. At the rear of the ring are captains' chairs
– one on the left and one on the right. On the left one is a towel. A man kneels by the
one on the right. Except for him, only the boxers and the referee are readily visible.
One boxer wears black knee breeches, the other extremely brief light-coloured trunks.
The umpire wears black trousers, a black vest and a long-sleeved white shirt.
Copy: MOMA, Kinetoscope Loops #1 (15375), apparently the only one of the five
films to have survived. MOMA gives a date of 2 October 1894.

174. <u>HORSE MARKET, BUFFALO, N.Y.</u> PHOTOGRAPHED AT THE MOST
FAMOUS STOCK YARDS IN AMERICA, FROM WHICH AS MANY AS 5,000
HORSES ARE FREQUENTLY SHIPPED IN ONE DAY. THE SPIRITED ANIMALS
ARE SEEN BEING LED TO THE CARS AND THE PASSING OF A PAIR OF
HIGH-STEPPING COACHERS HITCHED TO A LIGHT RUNABOUT LENDS
ADDITIONAL ACTIVITY TO AN ALREADY LIVELY SCENE. (**4b**, **4c**, **5**)
Filmed: probably December 1896, on the way to film *Niagara Falls*. Copyrighted on 24
December 1896 (**26**) as *Buffalo Horse Market* (**10**).
The camera was stationed just outside the gate and to the right, rather close in. Pairs of
horses are led by men running, first a group go out, then a number of pairs are led in.
Towards the end a cart (the "light runabout"), driven by a man standing, enters and the
film ends shortly afterwards. This is the 150' version. The 42' version is the last 42', as
it includes the "light runabout".
Copy: NAC, although presently under the title *Blacksmith Shop*.

164. HORSE SHOE FALLS (FROM LUNA ISLAND). SHOWING TOP OF FALLS,
A PORTION OF THE RAPIDS ABOVE THEM AND THE CATHOLIC CONVENT
(ON CANADA SIDE) IN BACKGROUND (**2**, **4b**, **4c**, **5**).
Filmed: 11-13 December 1896, and copyrighted on 24 December 1896.
See NEW NIAGARA FALLS SERIES.
No known copy.

165. HORSE SHOE FALLS (FROM TABLE ROCK). THIS IS THE BEST GENERAL
VIEW OF THE HORSE SHOE FALLS, AND SHOWS NEARLY A MILE OF THE
SEETHING RAPIDS ABOVE THIS POINT. THE PICTURE IS SHARP AND
CLEAR.
Filmed: 11-13 December 1896, and copyrighted on 24 December 1896.
See NEW NIAGARA FALLS SERIES.
No known copy.

Horse Shoeing (**18**: 56)
Filmed: before 14 April 1894 (**18**: 56).
Although it was one of the ten films shown on 14 April 1894 at the first commercial

showing of the Kinetoscope, it does not seem to appear in any catalogue. However, the film not only was shown in Australia, but also Australian researcher Chris Long found this description in an Australian newspaper of 30 November 1894: "A blacksmith at work shoeing a horse, with a man at its head patiently flapping away the flies with a cloth, and the owner demonstrating its docility by jumping on its back". Note the illustration below from **18: ill. 19.** Hendricks says that W K-L Dickson identified the man on the left as himself.

No known copy.

Horse Shoeing (Photo courtesy Natural History Museum of Los Angeles County)

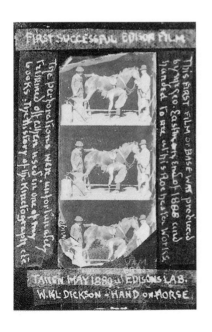

One of several film clips produced by W K-L Dickson. The top says "FIRST SUCCESSFUL EDISON FILM"; the bottom says "TAKEN MAY 1889 AT EDISON'S LAB. W.K.L. DICKSON – HAND ON HORSE". On the left: "The perforations were unfortunately trimmed off when used in one of my books; The History of the Kinetograph etc". The right side reads: "This FIRST FILM or BASE was produced by Mr Geo. Eastman end of 1888 and handed to me at his Rochester works". Hendricks' *The Edison Motion Picture Myth* states that the first vertical-feed camera was not made until the summer of 1892. So the date above seems highly unlikely. (Photo courtesy Natural History Museum of Los Angeles County)

HUMAN PYRAMID. MARVELOUS ACROBATIC PERFORMANCE BY SEVEN MEMBERS OF "BENI ZOUG'S FAMOUS ARAB TROUPE." $12.50. **(15)**
Filmed: autumn 1894 **(18: 83)**.
26 lists this as "Salim Nassar and Arab Troupe, Human Pyramid".
No known copy.

93. HUMOROUS CARTOON. BLACKMAN (sic), THE "WORLD" ARTIST, SKETCHING A CARTOON. **(4b, 4c)**
See BLACKTON SKETCHES. THE NEW YORK "WORLD'S" CARICATURE ARTIST DRAWING SKETCHES ON A SCREEN. **(16a)**
Filmed: July 1896.
The name was *not* "Blackman", but J Stuart Blackton (1875-1941), who later became famous in the motion-picture industry. Taken for Maguire & Baucus as a 150' film. Promptly "duped" by the International Film Company, which described its "dupe" as "a humorous selection, showing the artist drawing a life-size picture of a female figure, in which the expressions of the countenance are rapidly changing".
No known copy.

171. <u>HURDLE RACE.</u> THIS SCENE, PHOTOGRAPHED AT THE BUFFALO "COUNTRY CLUB," SHOWS A NUMBER OF THOROUGHBRED HORSES (PRIZE WINNERS AT THE RECENT HORSE SHOW IN NEW YORK) TAKING AN EXTREMELY HIGH HURDLE, WHICH WAS SO PLACED THAT THE RACERS ARE SEEN COMING STRAIGHT AT THE AUDIENCE. A SUBJECT FULL OF ACTION AND VERY INTERESTING. **(2, 4b, 4c, 5)**
Filmed: copyrighted on 24 December 1896 as HURDLE RACE-HIGH JUMPERS, so filmed only shortly before that date.
Copies: AMPAS; EH; GCH; H; P.

Hurdle Race (courtesy of G Hall and R Martinique)

66. HYPNOTIC SCENE (BURLESQUE). (4b, 4c, 5)
See also TRILBY HYPNOTIC SCENE. SVENGALI HYPNOTIZES EVERY ONE IN
SIGHT, AND CAUSES THEM TO GO THROUGH SUNDRY BURLESQUE
PERFORMANCES. VERY POPULAR. (15), for illustration.

IMPERIAL JAPANESE DANCE. THREE JAPANESE LADIES IN THE COSTUMES
OF THEIR COUNTRY. $15.00. (12, 15 – $12.50, 16)
Filmed: autumn 1894 (9, 18: 82).
Note Raff & Gammon's "R" at lower right. A charming scene. Hendricks was
commissioned to study some Edison Kinetoscope films in the Eastman House collection,
and wrote an article for the September 1959 issue of *Image*. He says that Huber's
Theater booked "Japanese dancing girls" for the week beginning 15 October 1894, and
that it was likely that the troupe journeyed to West Orange after this engagement to
make this film, and that Dickson identified them as the Sarashe Sisters. Listed in the
April 1896 Maguire & Baucus catalogue as 16. JAPANESE DANCE. BY THREE
IMPERIAL JAPANESE LADY DANCERS.
Copies: AMPAS; EH; GCH; GH; LOC #FLA 8439; P.
A still appears in **35: ill. 10** and **33: 46.**

Imperial Japanese Dance

IN THE DENTIST'S CHAIR **see** 46. THE DENTIST'S CHAIR. REPRESENTS DR.
COLTON, THE FAMOUS INVENTOR OF "LAUGHING GAS," IN THE ACT OF
ADMINISTERING SAME. ALSO SHOWS METHOD OF EXTRACTING TEETH.

Indian Club Swinger **see** John R Abell Fancy (Indian) Club Swinger

Indian Scalping Scene **see** 74. SCALPING SCENE. A SETTLER PURSUED,
OVERTAKEN AND SCALPED BY INDIANS.

Indian War Council

INDIAN WAR COUNCIL, SHOWING SEVENTEEN DIFFERENT PERSONS-
INDIAN WARRIORS AND WHITE MEN-IN COUNCIL. $15.00 (**12**)
Filmed: 24 September 1894 (**18: 80**).
From Buffalo Bill's "Wild West Show". **4b** and **4c** give it as 54. INDIAN WAR
COUNCIL. BUFFALO BILL ADDRESSING SIOUX INDIANS IN WAR COUNCIL.
Although the film is terribly dark, a canvas at the lower right reads "Buffalo Bill's Wild
West Sw". The last letters are not visible, but must read "Show".
Copies: GCH.
A still appears in **33: 21**.

182. INFANTRY MANOEUVRES. THIS SCENE WAS ALSO TAKEN AT
HARRISBURG, PA, AND SHOWS THE STATE MILITIA EXECUTING ORDERS
ON "DOUBLE-QUICK" TIME. THE BEST SUBJECT OF ITS KIND YET
PRODUCED. (**4b, 5, 16c**)
Filmed: c.Christmas 1896
See 181. GOVERNOR'S GUARD. THIS SUBJECT, TAKEN AT HARRISBURG, PA.
SHOWS THE GOVERNOR'S GUARD EN ROUTE FOR THE CAPITOL GROUNDS.
VARIOUS MANOEUVRES WERE EXECUTED WHILE THE PICTURES WERE
BEING TAKEN, ALL OF WHICH ARE DISTINCTLY SHOWN. THE SCENE IS
INTERESTING, CLEAR AND SHARP
No known copy.

55. INTERRUPTED LOVERS. ANOTHER INSTANCE WHERE "THE COURSE OF
TRUE LOVE NEVER RUNS SMOOTH".
Aka: INTERRUPTED LOVE AFFAIR. *Aka (in Boston):* LOVERS AND ANGRY
FATHER (**4b, 4c, 5**)
In a wooded setting under a tree, a couple sits on a park bench hugging and kissing. A
man lurks behind the tree. A farmer appears, assaults the man and kicks the woman,
presumably his daughter. The woman appears to be a man in woman's costume.

Filmed: c.7 July 1896.
Hendricks states: "taken in the same locale as GARDEN SCENE".
Copies: AMPAS; EH; GCH; GH; P.
A still appears in **35: ill. 13.**

80. THE INTERRUPTED SUPPER. SECOND FILM – THE GAY YOUNG MAN,
THE PRETTY TYPEWRITER AND THE IRATE WIFE.
Filmed: unknown.
This is the second of two films. The first is 79. TELEPHONE APPOINTMENT. Note
that in the 1890s a "typewriter" was not the machine, but the young lady that operated
it.
No known copy.

56. IRISH POLITICS (**5**), also given as 56. IRISH WAY OF DISCUSSING POLITICS.
A CAN OF BEER, CLAY PIPES AND TWO SONS OF ERIN FOR THE
PRINCIPALS. COMIC. (**4b, 4c**)
Almost surely the same film as *Irish Political Discussion. Showing two Irishmen
Discussing Politics over a Glass of Whiskey*, the title given by the International Film
Company to its "dupe" of the Edison film (**16a**).
Filmed: before October 1896.
No known copy.

Interrupted Lovers (courtesy R Martinique)

Jack Cushing vs. Mike Leonard **see** <u>MICHAEL LEONARD vs. JACK CUSHING</u>

JAMES GRUNDY. BUCK AND WING DANCE, FROM "SOUTH BEFORE THE WAR"

$12.50. (**4b, 15, 20 see** BUCK AND WING DANCE; **14** see below, **12**)

Filmed: 12 February 1895 (**18**).

This appears in **14** as "Danio e ventaglio" (English: "Buck and Fan"), and suggests cylinders "Parkies [sic] Tukle" (English: "Darky Tickle"), in the Columbia Phonograph Company catalogue of 1896 as #2503, played by Issler's Orchestra, and "Danza del Ventaglio" (English: "Fan Dance"). No cylinder matching this name has been found. No known copy.

JAMES GRUNDY, CAKE WALK. $15.00. FROM "SOUTH BEFORE THE WAR." THESE [referring to this subject and also *Buck and Wing Dance*] ARE THE BEST NEGRO SUBJECTS YET TAKEN, AND ARE AMUSING AND ENTERTAINING (**12, 15**) $12.50

Filmed: 12 February 1895.

See GRUNDY AND FRINT. BREAKDOWN FROM "SOUTH BEFORE THE WAR".

No known copy.

15. JAMIES. A BURLESQUE SCOTCH DANCE, IN FULL HIGHLAND COSTUME, BY RICHARD CARROLL AND THE JAMIES, FROM THE WHITNEY OPERA COMPANY'S "ROB ROY". $12.50. (**15, 4b, 4c, 5** as #15; **25, 14** – see below)

Filmed: January or February 1895 (**18: 136**).

Listed in **12** as "ROB ROY". $15.00.

Do not confuse this with *Highland Dance*, listed in **14** as "Rob Roy, danza Scozzese" (English: "Rob Roy, Scottish Dance") with cylinder "Nullo troppo buono per l'Irlandese" recommended (English: "Nothing's Too Good for the Irish"), Edison cylinder #7359. This film is most likely the one described in **18: 137** as having a "C" in the corner, indicating that it was shot for the Continental Commerce Company, the overseas branch of Maguire & Baucus. It is likely that there was some relationship between it and the Continental Phonograph Kinetoscope Company that issued this January 1896 list of films with their appropriate cylinders (**14**).

No known copy.

16. JAPANESE DANCERS (**4b, 4c, 16**) **see** IMPERIAL JAPANESE DANCE. THREE JAPANESE LADIES IN THE COSTUMES OF THEIR COUNTRY.

57. JOAN OF ARC. REPRESENTING THE BURNING OF THE MAID OF ORLEANS. (**4b, 4c**)

"Joan of Arc" is tied to the stake

Filmed: most likely 28 August 1895 (**18: 139**).

Strangely, although Maguire & Baucus commissioned Edison to make this film "before August 1895", and it did get made in August, it did not appear in a catalogue until April 1897. Perhaps the scene was too gory? The scene opens with the stake, surrounded with a pile of wood in the foreground. In the background are soldiers in armour; to the right are church officials. "Joan of Arc", in a flowing white robe, is led to the stake and tied to it. A cross is shown to her. Then the film is stopped, and a straw-stuffed figure with a dark cloth over its head is substituted. The wood is lighted, and a man throws another log on the fire! The figure is quickly surrounded by black smoke, and burns to a cinder. This film and 49. EXECUTION. REPRESENTING THE BEHEADING OF MARY, QUEEN OF SCOTS were the first two films to use "stop motion", and apparently were filmed on the same day.

Copy: NAC, under the title "Death Scene", although a change has been suggested.

John R Abell Fancy (Indian) Club Swinger
Filmed: late autumn 1894 (**18: 83**).
Negative removed from Raff & Gammon list 8 January 1895 due to bad negative (**18: 126**), so it would appear unlikely that any prints were ever sold.
No known copy, except perhaps a brief segment in GH.

JOHN W. WILSON AND BERTHA WARING–"LITTLE CHRISTOPHER COLUMBUS", ECCENTRIC DANCERS. $15.00. **12** and **15** describe the scene as AN ECCENTRIC DANCE FROM "LITTLE CHRISTOPHER COLUMBUS" BY JOHN WILSON, THE FAMOUS "TRAMP" AND MISS BERTHA WARING.
See also 14; **4b** and **4c** as #27.
Filmed: autumn 1894 (**18: 83**).
14 lists them as "Warring e Vilson", and suggests a cylinder entitled "Soirée al Club Lione Kiln" (English: "Evening at the Lion's Club"). There is no Edison or Columbia cylinder listing of that description. The programme is from **26**.
No known copy.

Kessel. Whirlwind Gun Spinning. (**25: 179, 18: 126**)
Filmed: apparently autumn 1894.
Unfortunately for Mr. Kessel, this negative was among those defective because of bad hole-punching, and was deleted from Raff & Gammon's list on 8 January 1894.
No known copy.

58. <u>THE KISS.</u> FROM THE PLAY "THE WIDOW JONES", WITH MAY ERWIN AND JOHN C. RICE.
Sometimes called "The Kiss Scene" (**4b, 4c, 5, 18: 7**)
Filmed: 16-18 April 1896.
12: 257 takes five pages to describe the kiss as "persisting, adhesive osculations, doubtless made more delightful by the sweeping model of the hero's mustache", and quotes a critic as saying that "the spectacle of their prolonged pasturing on each other's lips was hard to bear...it was beastly...it is absolutely disgusting... degrading". This kiss certainly made waves! (I am sure it also made lots of money!) It not only survived for projection, but was probably made for projection, as **12** describes.

Copies: AMPAS; EH; GCH; GH; MG – Edison films (collection #1, #897); MG, as MOMA, #9997, 16mm copy for rent; MOMA "Films of the 1890s"; P.
A still appears in **30: 65**.

The Kiss

L. Bloom – the Tramp (**18: 83**)
Filmed: autumn 1894.
One of the five scenes taken from the play *The Milk White Flag*. **18: 127** notes that this film was taken off Raff & Gammon's list of negatives because of "faulty" punchings on 8 January 1895, so it is unlikely that copies were sold; certainly none appears in known catalogues.

LADY FENCERS. (WITH FOILS) $12.50. (**12, 14**)
Filmed: 26 September 1894 (**18: 80**).
See 111. "BROADSWORDS". BY TWO FAMOUS LADY FENCERS for information about the Englehart Sisters.
No known copy.

LADY FENCERS. EXHIBITING THE ENGLEHART SISTERS IN AN EXCITING BROADSWORD CONTEST. $12.50 (**4, 15**).
See previous entry.
Filmed: probably 26 September 1894.
No known copy.

LASSO THROWER. VINCENTE ORO PASSO. THE CHAMPION LASSO THROWER, GIVES AN INTERESTING EXHIBITION OF LASSO TWIRLING AND THROWING, FROM "BUFFALO BILL'S WILD WEST." $12.50 (**15**). (**12** lists it under the heading VINCENTE ORO PASSO, etc.) (**16**).
In **4b** and **4c** as 59. LASSO THROWER. Also **14**.
Filmed: 6 October 1894 (**18**).
Possibly also listed as "Texas Cowboy Throwing Lasso". According to **25: 179**, two other films of this subject were taken: one of a man named "Hammitt", the other named "Martin". Hendricks names these two as also appearing riding bucking broncos. No catalogue listing of lasso-throwing by Hammitt or Martin appears.
No known copy, but sixteen frames in **33: 25**, as is the case with <u>BUFFALO BILL</u>. As has been done with that film, I am attempting to find a source to have LASSO THROWER returned to 35mm film. A newly-found cousin and amateur roper, John Cloud, has provided the correct spelling of Vicente Oropeza's name, and identified what he is doing as "The Reverse Ocean Wave" (contra del oro), a difficult "reverse".
Oropeza was with Buffalo Bill for sixteen years. Later in the 1890s, he and Will Rogers

Lasso Thrower. Vincente Oro Passo

were in the same Wild West show. Rogers began his illustrious career as a roper in New York vaudeville, but soon became America's favourite humorist. His newspaper column of gentle humour was carried in over 300 American newspapers until his tragic death cut short his life. He was on an aeroplane trip with the famous flyer, Wiley Post, when their plane crashed in Alaska. It is said that his mentor in roping was Vicente Oropeza. The illustration is one of the frames.

LAYMAN, THE MAN OF 1000 FACES. $12.50 (**4b, 4c, 12, 14**)
Filmed: 21 September 1894 (**18: 79**).
Viewing the film shows a close-up (head and shoulders) of a man, apparently in his sixties, wearing a wing collar, coat and tie, talking and making expressive faces. He pretends to shoot himself in the head; he drinks from a bottle and pretends to be tipsy, etc. (**1**). The film had a frame inserted claiming an 1897 copyright, but **2** does not list this film as being copyright 1897. Listings in **4b** and **4c** as 60. THE MAN OF 1000 FACES PORTRAYING THE VARIOUS EMOTIONS are surely this film. Amusingly, **14** lists him, but only gives him credit for 100 faces!

Layman, The Man of 1000 Faces

Copies: FPA; UCLA Sequence #3 of The Operator Cranked-The Picture Moved, a ½" videocassette, Loc. P-VA3093M, also a 16mm print 400', Loc. R-A1-149-4, Inv. #M14872.

La Leçon de Baton **see** Calisthenics

LEE RICHARDSON AND HIS TRICK BICYCLE RIDING (**26**). **See** 87. BICYCLE RIDING. BY RICHARDSON, CHAMPION TRICK RIDER.

Leigh Sisters **see** 25. UMBRELLA DANCE. BY LEIGH SISTERS **and** Acrobatic Dance (**25**)

Leonard **see** 112. BAG PUNCHING, AN EXHIBITION BY MIKE LEONARD, THE FAMOUS TRAINER

61. LI HUNG CHANG. THE GREAT VICEROY LEAVING THE HOTEL WALDORF (**4b, 4c, 16a**).
Filmed: Li Hung Chang arrived in New York on 24 February 1896.
See also 101. AMERICAN LINE PIER. SHOWING THE CROWDS AWAITING THE ARRIVAL OF LI HUNG CHANG.
16a gives an expanded description: "SHOWS LI HUNG CHANG ENTERING HIS CARRIAGE AT THE DOOR OF THE WALDORF HOTEL, WITH A FILE OF THE SIXTH U. S. CAVALRY, WITH DRAWN SABRES, STANDING NEARBY."
No known copy.

29. LITTLE JAKE AND THE BIG DUTCH GIRL. A BURLESQUE DANCE. 150', $45.00. (**4b, 4c**)
No known copy. No other information.

LOLA YBERRI – FAN DANCE **see** 13. FAN DANCE. A CHARACTERISTIC SPANISH DANCE BY LOLA YBERRI.

62. LONE FISHERMAN. ILLUSTRATING "FISHERMAN'S LUCK". Also issued as

#94, a 150' film, which listing adds: "THIS IS A MUCH MORE COMPLETE SUBJECT" (**4b, 4c, 5**).
Filmed: late August 1896.
30: 68 states: "a man casts for fish from a plank cantilevered off a bridge. His friends come and upend the plank, sending him into the water." In addition, he then tries to splash water up onto his tormentors. The 150' film, which the Eastman House film is, contains action before and after the 50' version.
Copies: AMPAS; NAC (50'); 150' versions (now actually 109' long) at EH, GCH, GH and P.
A still appears in **35: ill. 15**.

123. LOTILDE ANTONIO, THE LADY ACROBAT. (**20, 4b, 4c**)
Filmed: unknown.
The subject's name is almost certainly "Clotilde", as it is spelled elsewhere in **20**. This subject is almost certainly Maguire & Baucus, as they numbered their films. Also listed in **20** is a 150' film, "#127. Clotilde Antonio, Hand dancing, Head balancing, etc."
No known copy.

Love in a Sleigh. (**7**)
Filmed: by mid-July 1896.
Copy: MOMA (14313), but no known contemporary listing.

18. LUCILLE STURGIS. A SKIRT DANCE. (**4b, 4c, 5**)
Filmed: 1896 (?).
Poor Lucille must not have made much of an impression – not even a complimentary adjective in the description!
No known copy. No other information.

Luis Martinetti (courtesy of G Hall and R Martinique)

17. LUCY MURRAY. SKIRT DANCE BY A MEMBER OF THE GAIETY GIRLS.
(4b, 4c)
Probably either PAS SEUL NO. 1 (DANCE) BY MISS MURRAY OF THE "GAIETY GIRL" COMPANY or PAS SEUL NO. 2 (DANCE) BY MISS LUCAS OF THE "GAIETY GIRL" COMPANY.

LUIS MARTINETTI, GYMNAST AND CONTORTIONIST PERFORMING ON THE FLYING RINGS. $12.50. (4b, 4c, 12, 15, 20 as #125)
Filmed: 11 October 1894 (18: 82).
18: 82 gives the last name as "Martinelli", but 12, 15 and 20 all indicate "Martinetti".
Copy: AMPAS; EH; GCH; GH; P.

63. LYNCHING SCENE. LYNCHING OF A HORSE THIEF BY A BAND OF COWBOYS. (4b, 4c)
Filmed: 30 September 1895 (18: 140).
18: 140 says "taken in a forest"; however it was taken in front of a high fence, not in a forest. It is described under the name of *A Frontier Scene*, but seems never to have been catalogued under that title, or catalogued at all until autumn 1897. This brief description hints that there might have been more than one victim.
No known copy.

Madam Rita, Dancer
Filmed: 1 October 1894 (18: 80).
No known copy. No other information.

177. MARKET SQUARE (HARRISBURG, PA.). A TYPICAL HOLIDAY SEASON STREET SCENE SHOWING MANY SHOPPERS LUGGING HOME THEIR HOLIDAY PURCHASES. TROLLEY CARS AND VEHICLES ARE PASSING BACK AND FORTH, AND THE WELL-KNOWN COMMONWEALTH HOTEL LOOMS UP IN THE BACKGROUND.
(4b, 4c, 5)
Filmed: 24-26 December 1896 (21). Copyrighted on 8 January 1897.
Copy: NAC, under the name "Allison Hill Street Car", although a change has been suggested.

MAY LUCAS. ECCENTRIC SKIRT DANCER, OF "THE LONDON GAIETY GIRL COMPANY", $12.50. (15)
See PAS SEUL NO. 2 (DANCE) BY MISS LUCAS OF THE "GAIETY GIRL" COMPANY.
No further information; no known copy.

133. MCKINLEY PARADE, A NEW YORK STREET SCENE TAKEN DURING THE GREAT POLITICAL PARADE OF OCTOBER 31. (20, 4b, 4c, 16b)
16b gives this additional description: THE GREAT MCKINLEY PARADE. THOUSANDS OF MEN IN LINE AND SPECTATORS, WITH BANNERS FLYING AND FLAGS WAVING. An enthusiastic description of a film "duped" from Edison's! The fact that Edison's film was copyrighted did not seem to deter the International Film Company.
Filmed: 31 October 1896 and copyrighted on 7 November 1896. There were several

McKinley Parade

McKinley films – at least four – all listed in **2** as copyright 1897. However, the other three were taken at McKinley's inauguration in 1897, and so are not listed here. In **4b**, a 150' film is listed as #148.
Copies: AMPAS; EH; GCH; P.

145. <u>MESS CALL.</u> TROOPERS GOING TO DINNER AT THE NEW YORK STATE CAMP. (**4b**, **4c**)
Filmed: unknown.
Viewing the film, one sees soldiers carrying mess kits and mugs milling around a mess tent. Towards the end, several recognise the camera and "mug" for it.
Copy: MOMA, #14314 – Miscellaneous Edison Shots.

<u>MEXICAN KNIFE DUEL.</u> BETWEEN PEDRO ESQUIREL AND DIONESCO GONZALES. FULL OF ACTION. $15.00 (**4b**, **4c**, **15**).
Filmed: 6 October 1894 (**18: 80**).
12 lists this film as PEDRO ESQUIREL AND DIONESCO GONZALES-MEXICAN DUEL. (FULL OF ACTION, EXCITING AND INTERESTING). $15.00. **20** lists it as 118. MEXICAN KNIFE DUEL, A FIGHT WITH MACHETES.
This is about as good an example as can be found of the fact that no specific titles were given to these films, sometimes leading to confusion, particularly at this late date. The *Brisbane Courier* of 13 August 1895 describes the scene: "...a Mexican duel fought with knives. Each thrust and parry is distinctly seen, until the knife is hurled from the hand of the weaker combatant" (**31**).
On viewing the copy of this film obtained from SAF (an identical copy is at MCL), an amusing circumstance can be seen. It would appear that either someone put the wrong sign on the stage, or the ownership to the film was changed before it was

printed. The signboard in the lower right-hand corner of the stage with an "R" on it has been blanked out (or almost so), and a handwritten "MB" added on every frame!
Copies: AMPAS; GCH; MCL (each under the title of "Combat de Mexicains"); P; SAF.
Stills appear in **33: 32**.

MICHAEL LEONARD vs. JACK CUSHING
Not in a catalogue until Maguire & Baucus apparently bought the film. It first appeared in their 1897 catalogue (**4b, 4c**).
See <u>CORBETT AND COURTNEY BEFORE THE KINETOGRAPH</u> (**16c**). Listed in **31** as being shown in Sydney, Australia, beginning 29 February 1896.
Filmed: 14 June 1894 (**18: 75**).

Michael Leonard vs. Jack Cushing (MOMA)

34: 109 describes the fight: "the world's first prize fight pictures were staged at the Black Maria in West Orange. Michael Leonard, then known as 'the Beau Brummel of the prize ring,' met Jack Cushing, a likely contender for the lightweight title. They fought in a ten-foot ring. They went about ten of the snappy short rounds, of which the Kinetograph recorded six. At the finish Cushing was trapped by a feint and fell under a chop to the jaw. Nearly a thousand feet of film had been made. It was by far the longest motion picture that had yet been attempted." **34: 108** also says that the film was made for the Kinetoscope Exhibition Company, and that the size of special Kinetoscopes was enlarged so that they could show rounds of 150'. The films were shown at a special parlour of the Kinetoscope Exhibition Company at 83 Nassau, New York, in six especially large Kinetoscopes; on opening day, throngs packed the place. By the second day, long lines of waiting patrons trailed back into the street.
Copy: AMPAS; NFTVA #9153; P.
A still appears in **18: ill. 56**.

"Microscopic Subjects"
In **13: 316-318**, W K-L Dickson writes: "We have yet to speak of the microscopic subjects, a class of especial interest, as lying outside of the unaided vision of man. In the treatment of these infinitesimal types, much difficulty was experienced in obtaining a perfect adjustment so as to reproduce the breathing of insects, the circulation of blood in a frog's leg and other attenuated processes of nature. The enlargement of animalculæ in a drop of stagnant water proved a most exacting task, but by the aid of a powerful lime-light, concentrated on the water, by the interposition of alum cells for the interception of most of the heat-rays, and by the use of a quick shutter and kindred contrivances, the obstacles were overcome, and the final results were such as fully to compensate for the expenditure of time and trouble.
We will suppose that the operator has at last been successful in imprisoning the tricksy water-goblins on the sensitive film, in developing the positive strip, and placing it in the projector. A series of inch-large shapes then springs into view, magnified

stereoptically to nearly three feet each, gruesome beyond power of expression, and exhibiting an indescribable celerity and rage. Monsters close upon one another in a blind and indiscriminate attack, limbs are dismembered, gory globules are tapped, whole battalions disappear from view. Before the ruthless completeness of these martial tactics the Kilkenny cats fade into insignificance. A curious feature of the performance is the passing of these creatures in and out of focus, appearing sometimes as huge and distorted shadows, then springing into the reality of their own size and proportions."

These films apparently were experimental only, as none appears in any existing catalogues or descriptions of Kinetoscope films or filming such as **18**, and none is known to have survived.

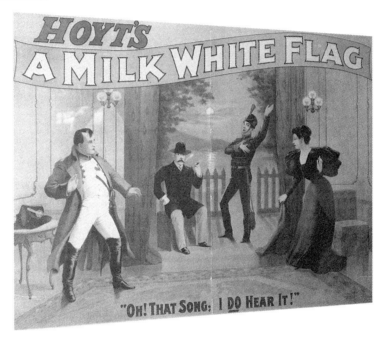

A poster for Hoyt's very popular musical, *A Milk White Flag*
The original of this photograph graces the wall of a bar and gambling house in Gardnerville, NV.
The picture tapers because the photograph had to be taken at an angle.

---

64. MILK WHITE FLAG, ASSEMBLY MARCH. (**4b, 4c, 5**)
Filmed: autumn 1894.
[*Milk White Flag* was a musical comedy about two rival groups of volunteer soldiers so feckless that the only flag they could be depended to follow in battle was the flag of surrender, the Milk White Flag! It opened in Hoyt's Theater, New York, in October 1894. Five excerpts were filmed at the Black Maria. Two were spoiled by "bad punching", and three released: *Band Drill, Finale of 1st Act* and *Trio*.]
This film is another example of a subject being given a different name. It is most likely
BAND DRILL, FROM HOYT'S "MILK WHITE FLAG". REPRESENTS THE MARCH OF THE BAND, WITH LEADER AT THEIR HEAD PLAYING POPULAR AIRS.
No known copy under this name. **See** BAND DRILL.

Miss Isabelle Coe as "The Widder"
Filmed: late autumn 1894 (**18: 83**).
This was one of the five subjects from the musical, *The Milk White Flag*. **18: 126** states
that a note from Dickson to Raff & Gammon on 8 January 1895 listed this film as one
that had to be deleted because of faulty punching of the perforations, so it would appear
that it was never sold.
No known copy.

Miss Rosa-Oriental Dancer (**18: 126**)
Filmed: apparently late 1894, as it was deleted from Raff & Gammon's negative list on
8 January 1895 because of bad negative, presumably as a result of faulty punches.
Noted in **18: 126** as "so good [it] should be taken again", but there is no evidence that
this was ever done.
No known copy. Not catalogued.

MLLE. CAPITAINE. "THE PERFECT
WOMAN" EXHIBITING IN A
GRACEFUL TRAPEZE
PERFORMANCE. $12.50. (**4, 4a, 4b, 4c,
15, 20** as #122)
Filmed: 1 November 1894 (**18: 82**).
See also 12, 16. Hendricks lists this as
"Alcide Capitaine".
No known copy, but 32 frames appear in
33: 31.

Mlle. Capitaine

THE MONROE DOCTRINE (**30: 62**)
Filmed: shortly before 23 April 1896,
when it was one of six films projected at
Koster & Bial's music-hall for the
introduction of the Vitascope projector.
30: 62 describes the action: "Referring to a
recent incident in South America, this
political cartoon on film showed John Bull
and Venezuela fighting. 'Uncle Sam appears, separates the combatants and knocks John
Bull down.'" Although seldom used now, "John Bull" is to Great Britain as "Uncle
Sam" is to the United States. No known copy.

132. <u>A MORNING BATH.</u> THIS SCENE PRESENTS A DARKY AFRICAN
MOTHER IN THE ACT OF GIVING HER STRUGGLING PICKANINNY A BATH
IN A TUB OF SUDS. THIS IS A CLEAR AND DISTINCT PICTURE IN WHICH
THE CONTRAST BETWEEN THE COMPLEXION OF THE LATHER AND THE
WHITE SOAPSUDS IS STRONGLY MARKED. A VERY AMUSING AND
POPULAR SUBJECT. (**2, 4b, 4c, 5, 20, 16b**)
A delightful film of an appealing young mother. It takes several viewings of the film to
notice that she turns her head several times to listen to instructions from a "director".
Filmed: shortly before 31 October 1896, when it was copyrighted.
Copies: AMMI; AMPAS; EH; GCH; GH; MOMA "Films of the 1890s"; MG "Films
of the 1890s" (16mm rental).

A Morning Bath (Notice that the subject is glancing at the "director".)

134. <u>MORNING FIRE ALARM.</u> THIS SHOWS THE FIRE DEPARTMENT LEAVING HEADQUARTERS FOR AN EARLY MORNING FIRE. THE SCENE IS REMARKABLE FOR ITS NATURAL EFFECT. THE OPENING OF THE ENGINE HOUSE DOORS. THE PRANCING OF THE HORSES, AND EVEN THE STARTLED EXPRESSION UPON THE FACES OF THE SPECTATORS ARE ALL CLEARLY DEPICTED. (**4b, 4c, 5, 16c**)

Morning Fire Alarm (Library of Congress)

Also probably the same as *Morning Alarm* and *Starting for the Fire*.
Filmed: 14 November 1896 (?) and copyrighted on 27 November 1896 as *A Morning Alarm*. A 150' version is numbered 183 (**4b**, **4c**, **5**). The camera is pointing up the street, with the fire station on the left. A ladder-wagon comes out of the station and turns towards the camera, followed by other pieces of fire-fighting equipment.
Copies: MOMA; John E Allen Primitives, Roll #2 (23858).

137. <u>MOUNTED POLICE CHARGE.</u> A TROUPE OF MOUNTED POLICE, IN FULL DRESS UNIFORM, ARE SEEN APPROACHING THE AUDIENCE AT FULL GALLOP: WHEN WITHIN BUT A FEW YARDS OF THE CAMERA THEY SUDDENLY HALT AND EACH HORSE AND RIDER APPEARS FULL LIFE SIZE. (**2**, **4b**, **4c**, **5**, **16b**)
Filmed: probably a few days before its being copyrighted on 2 November 1896. The words "appears full life size" show that the film anticipated its being projected – the writing was on the wall for the "peep-show" Kinetoscope!
Copy: GH.

Mounted Police Charge (Library of Congress)

139. MOUNTED POLICE DRILL. MOUNT AND DISMOUNT! THE ABOVE TWO FILMS PRESENT A FULL BATTALION OF NEW YORK'S FAMOUS MOUNTED POLICE, WITH A SERGEANT IN COMMAND, DRILLING IN PREPARATION FOR THE ANNUAL HORSE SHOW HELD AT MADISON SQUARE GARDEN. (**2**, **4b**, **4c**, **5**).
Filmed: shortly before copyright date of 31 October 1896.
No known copy.

138. MOUNTED POLICE DRILL. PARK POLICE-LEFT WHEEL AND FORWARD. (**2**, **4b**, **4c**, **5**)

Filmed: shortly before copyright date of 31 October 1896.
No known copy.

Muscle Dance. (31)
An as-yet unidentifiable title.
The lack of titles on Edison's Kinetoscope films causes a researcher all sorts of problems, and this is one. It was not at all uncommon for distributors to give films names other than those provided by Edison. The reason could have been to give a film more of what used to be called "sex appeal". This was the case with the advertisement in the *Adelaide Register* in Australia, where this film was called the "Naughty Muscle Dance". I am sure that in other circumstances a distributor or exhibitor would change a title to make it appear that he had a new film. Other examples of titles which I have not yet been able to attach to otherwise-identified Edison films are "High Kicking" and "French Ballet".

   After watching *Sandow* several times, I feel that "Muscle Dance" is an "exhibitor's title" for it. In the film, Sandow strikes a pose, then makes a slight turn, perhaps a quarter-turn, strikes another pose and continues this to the end of the film. When projected at a faster than normal speed, the result is astonishing. The otherwise dignified Sandow really does appear to be dancing! Two likely candidates for "High Kicking" are *Amy Muller* and *Ruth Dennis*. "French Ballet" might be *Carnival Dance*.

NEW BAR ROOM. SHOWING A QUARREL IN A BAR ROOM AND A POLICEMAN TAKING A GLASS OF BEER ON THE SLY. $12.50 (12; 4b, 4c, 5 as #37)
Filmed: before 15 December 1894 (18: 82, 186). The latter reference states: "two barroom scenes, one in existence by June, 1894 and a new one made in December". Copy: see entry for BARROOM SCENE.

NEW BARBER SHOP. REPRESENTS THE INTERIOR OF A "TONSORIAL PALACE", WITH CUSTOMER GETTING A "SHAVE"; MEANWHILE "NEXT" IS HAVING HIS SHOES POLISHED BY THE USUAL DARKY ATTENDANT. (15, 4b, 4c, 12, 5 as #36)
Filmed: 17 January 1895 (18: 135).
According to 12, by late spring 1895, the original *Barber Shop* negative had worn out and a new one was taken "which is superior to the old one". (While there may have been other reasons in 1894, one is most apparent in 1994: the original film is severely lacking in contrast; the "new" version is a great improvement.)

   In the new version, the waiting customer is having his shoes shined rather than being handed a newspaper. It seems strange to us now that duplicate negatives were not made, but that appears not to have been the practice. As a matter of fact, only a few subjects warranted a second negative.
Copies: AMPAS: a copy of the NFTVA print; GCH; NFTVA (#160134 A[d]): this modern copy (1963) was made from the original print now owned by the author; SAF, #33158. This film is on its original film stock and, except for many torn sprocket-holes, is in spectacular condition. The images are clear and bright; the film strong and not brittle. P: the above description also applies to the author's copy, purchased 2 October 1992 with Kinetoscope #141 (see page 15). The author also has a modern print from a negative made by the NFTVA.

   Viewing the film (which has an "R", standing for "Raff & Gammon", in the right foreground), at left is a man getting a shoe shine. At the right is the barber and his customer. Three men enter from the right rear and drink from a bottle. An excellent film.

Australian researcher Chris Long found the following in the *South Australian Register* published in Adelaide, 27 January 1896: "The tonsorial artist is seen lathering his customers and during the whole of the scene is to be heard addressing the usual small talk to his victim." This would seem to indicate that an enterprising Kinetophone showman had recorded a cylinder to play with this film.

(New) Black Diamond Express (2, 4b, 4c, 5, 16c)

Filmed: April 1897.

This date is outside the scope of this work but because of the possibility of confusion with the 1896 version and the fact that it is an interesting film *and* a good copy exists, I am including it. Note that 2 calls it simply "Black Diamond Express", while the NFTVA labels it "New Black Diamond Express". Here is a description of the films that I saw at the NFTVA.

First is its film #601.144A. Two men work on the track with picks. There is a group of men on the bank at the left. The train comes by on the right with people waving from the windows. After the train passes, four men from the group on the left start to put a handcar on the track. The film, when projected, is quite unsteady. It would be adequate on a Kinetoscope, but unpleasant to watch projected. It appears that this is the first portion of a "150'" film which has been cut off for a "50'" length.

NFTVA film #600465-A continues the scene. The four men put the handcar on the track and madly propel it out of the scene. Men walk onto the track and exit right. The NFTVA showed me the second film first, and I was puzzled when the film, labelled "New Black Diamond Express", showed only a handcar! When I saw #601.144A, it finally made sense! The "New" film can be distinguished by the larger number of people in the scene and the handcar in the background which shows, even if only the first segment is viewed.

Copy: NFTVA.

Note the photograph (illustration 10) in the description of the Kinetograph (camera) (page 24) showing the crew with its cameras at this scene.

39. NEW BLACKSMITH SHOP (19, 4b, 4c; 5 as #39; 15)

These references say "Blacksmith Shop", but because they date from mid-1895 to early 1897, they almost certainly refer to "New Blacksmith Shop", as the original "Blacksmith Shop" negative was worn out and destroyed by the end of 1894. 4b, 4c, 15 give the following description of "Blacksmith Shop"; however, the description is actually of the film "New Blacksmith Shop": "Shows two men at anvil. A third is repairing a wagon wheel. Incidentally a little liquid refreshment is passed around as the work progresses. $12.50."

Filmed: between 25 January and 18 April 1895 (18).

Viewing "Tyring a wheel in Blacksmith Shop," #458086 at SAF reveals that it may be "New Blacksmith Shop". This film shows a man carrying a wagon wheel across the scene while two men alternate hammering a piece of metal held on the anvil. One man tends the forge. SAF's #35370 is one of the two Blacksmith Shops. My notes say "nice *old* film, perhaps original Kinetoscope stock". As I could not view it, I am not sure which film it is.

Copy: possibly SAF, as described above.

NEW NIAGARA FALLS SERIES. **See** individual films as follows:

161. AMERICAN FALLS (FROM ABOVE, AMERICAN SIDE)
162. AMERICAN FALLS (FROM INCLINE RAILROAD)
163. AMERICAN FALLS (FROM CANADA SHORE, BELOW)
164. HORSE SHOE FALLS (FROM LUNA ISLAND)
165. HORSE SHOE FALLS (FROM TABLE ROCK)
166. RAPIDS AT "CAVE OF THE WINDS".
167. WHIRLPOOL RAPIDS.

These films were advertised as follows: "The following subjects were all taken on the latest and most improved clear stock during December 1896, and should not be confounded with former negatives, which were not entirely satisfactory". Edison put it even more bluntly: "The above negatives are not the old ones originally made for the Kinetoscope, but were all taken on special Edison projecting stock on December 11th, 12th and 13th, 1896 and are the sharpest pictures of Niagara ever made". Thus, by the end of 1896, where this *Index* also ends, it is clear that the "peep-show" Kinetoscope was on its way to history, and projection was the wave of the future.
Note: MG has a film. It has a sequence of Niagara in winter, but I am not sufficiently familiar with the Falls to identify it as any particular one of the above.

New York <u>World</u> Sick Baby Fund (**27, 16a**)
Filmed: July or early August 1896.
Children of poor people enjoying themselves in swings or on hobby-horses. Apparently, a special film taken for charitable purposes. Not catalogued, but the fact that it is listed in **16a** would mean that it was released commercially.
No known copy.

Newark Fire Department.
Filmed: 14 November 1896 (**18: 7**).
The above reference gives two films with this title as being in Hendricks' Collection, but they appear in no catalogue. These 16mm films are now at the LOC, and may be available for viewing.

Niagara Falls
Filmed: **18: 81** says "April 1896", while **30: 66** says "late May or early June" 1896.
18: 81n15 says "a trip by Heise for Raff & Gammon". **30: 66** says the Edison crew took a dozen different scenes but that the results were "somewhat disappointing", and that only four scenes were actually distributed; that the best received was *Niagara Falls, Gorge*, and that it was a panoramic picture taken from the rear of a swiftly moving train on the Niagara Gorge railway, a 150' film. Two others were of the American Falls from the east and west sides. In December 1896, a new set of films was taken, as described in the following entry.
No known copies.

Opera Scene
Filmed: before March 1895.
No known copy.

OPIUM DEN. SCENE REPRESENTS SECTION OF THE INTERIOR OF A
CHINESE OPIUM DEN. $10.00. (4, 4b, 4c, 15, 16d)
Filmed: before August 1895 (15).
Also known as CHINESE OPIUM DEN, ROBETTA AND DORETTO, ETC.
Listed in 12 as ROBETTA AND DORETTO, CHINESE OPIUM DEN. This 12 was
probably issued in spring 1895, and therefore it is likely that the film was made earlier
than August 1895. Also in 4b as #67.
No known copy, but one frame is shown in 33: 47.

Organ Grinder and Monkey see Hear Me, Norma

68. OUTING OF THE BABIES. SHOWING BABIES ON BOARD AN EXCURSION
STEAMER (4b, 4c)
No known copy. No other information.

PADDLE DANCE, BY FIJI ISLANDERS WITH BARNUM AND BAILEY'S
"GREATEST SHOW ON EARTH". $15.00 (4b, 4c, 12, 14, 15)
Filmed: 27 April 1895 (18: 137).
14 has it as "Danza del remo" (English: "Paddle Dance"), and suggests a cylinder called
"Marcia di Nozze Africana (Dal Museo di Barnum e C.)" (English: "African Wedding
March (from the Barnum and Company Museum)"). Not in the Edison cylinder
catalogue. It could well have been recorded by the Barnum and Company Museum. It
was almost as simple to make cylinders and copy them, in those days, as it is to make
tapes today. In 4b as 19. PADDLE DANCE. BY NATIVES OF THE SAMOAN
ISLANDS. (Fiji and Samoa are *only* 400 miles apart!)
See DANCE OF REJOICING; the two sound suspiciously similar, but Hendricks gives
each a listing. No known copy.

Parisian Dance (Library of Congress)

PARADE OF BICYCLISTS AT BROOKLYN, NEW YORK **see** BICYCLE PARADE. ON THE BOULEVARD, NEW YORK CITY.

187. PARISIAN DANCE. A TYPICAL DANCE BY TWO WELL-KNOWN VAUDEVILLE ARTISTS, REPRODUCED EXACTLY AS PERFORMED BY THEM AT HAMMERSTEIN'S "OLYMPIA" NEW YORK CITY. THIS IS A FULL LIFE-SIZE PICTURE, AND SHOWS CLEARLY THE COMBINATION OF BLACK AND WHITE COLORS, MAKING A VERY STRIKING AND BEAUTIFUL EFFECT. THE DANCE PERFORMED IS THE FAMOUS CAN-CAN. **(4b, 4c)**
Filmed: copyrighted on 15 January 1897, but may have been shot in 1896.
One catalogue listing suggests that it is "AN EXCELLENT SUBJECT FOR COLORING". It was filmed in the Black Maria.
Copy: LOC.

PARK POLICE DRILL. LEFT WHEEL AND FORWARD. **(16b)**
See following entry.

PARK POLICE DRILL. MOUNT AND DISMOUNT. THESE TWO FILMS SHOW A FULL BATTALION OF NEW YORK'S FAMOUS MOUNTED POLICE, COMMANDED BY SERGEANT EAGAN, DRILLING IN PREPARATION FOR THE ANNUAL HORSE SHOW, HELD AT MADISON SQUARE GARDEN. **(16b)**. These two films are International Film Company "dupes" of Edison's *Mounted Police Drill* subjects with the names slightly altered.

Advertising card for *Pas Seul No. 2*
Front and back; probably late-1894.
(Collection of Lawrence A Schlick)

PAS SEUL NO. 1 (DANCE) BY MISS MURRAY OF THE "GAIETY GIRL" COMPANY. $15.00 **(12)**
Filmed: 1 November 1894.
Also listed in **14** as LUCY MURRAG (sic). It suggests cylinders "Ridda irlandese" (English: "Irish Reel"), a piccolo solo on Edison cylinder #2806, and "Indugia più a lungo, Lucy" (English: "Linger Longer, Lucy"), possibly Edison #572, "Linger Longer Lou Schottische", by the Edison Symphony Orchestra. **15** lists it as LUCY MURRAY, OF THE "GAIETY GIRL COMPANY" IN AN ATTRACTIVE SKIRT DANCE. $15.00." **4c** has 17. LUCY MURRAY. SKIRT DANCE BY A MEMBER OF THE "GAIETY GIRLS". This is probably either PAS SEUL #1 or #2.
No known copy.

PAS SEUL NO. 2 (DANCE) BY MISS LUCAS OF THE "GAIETY GIRL" COMPANY, $15.00. (12, 14)
Filmed: 1 November 1894.
14 lists this as MAE LEUAS FANCIULLA GAIETY and suggests "Ridda irlandese" (English: "Irish Reel"), a piccolo solo on Edison cylinder #2806, "Danza di Nozze Africana" (English: "African Wedding Dance"). I cannot find a cylinder by this or a similar name. "Polka Eloisa" (English: "Eloise Polka") is Edison cylinder #671 by the Peerless Orchestra. 15 lists this as MAY LUCAS. ECCENTRIC SKIRT DANCER OF THE "LONDON GAIETY GIRL COMPANY". $12.50.
No known copy.

Passion Dance see 170. DOLORITA'S PASSION DANCE. A CHARACTERISTIC MIDWAY DANCER.

70. PAT VS POPULIST. A HUMOROUS SCENE BETWEEN AN IRISH HODCARRIER AND A POLITICIAN. (4b, 4c, 16a)
16a calls it PAT AND THE POPULIST. SHOWING THE POPULIST ENDEAVORING TO CONVERT PAT TO HIS OWN POLITICAL VIEWS.
Filmed: before November 1896.
34 gives a clearer description of the action. Pat ascends a ladder with a hod of bricks, is approached by a Populist politician, and shows his displeasure by dumping bricks on the politician.
No known copy.

69. PATERSON FALLS. THE FALLS OF THE PASSAIC RIVER (4b, 4c, 5).
Filmed: before 31 July 1896 (Hendricks in *Image*).
The name of this falls is somewhat confusing. They were also called the "Passaic Falls", and the film can that Hendricks saw carried the title of "Yosemite Falls". Unfortunately, not all falls survive, but this one does, in a park in Paterson, NJ, and can be seen from the same spot that Edison's camera must have used.
Copy: AMPAS; EH; GCH; GH; P.
A still appears in 35: ill. 14.

PEDRO ESQUIREL AND DIONECIO GONZALES – MEXICAN DUEL see MEXICAN KNIFE DUEL. BETWEEN PEDRO ESQUIREL AND DIONESCO GONZALES. FULL OF ACTION.

Pennsylvania State Militia – Double Time. (10)
Filmed: shortly before copyright date of 8 January 1897.
4c lists 181. PENNSYLVANIA STATE MILITIA-GOVERNOR'S GUARD; also 182. PENNSYLVANIA STATE MILITIA – INFANTRY MANOEUVRES. Either one could be this film by a different name, but I thought it worthwhile to list this film by its copyrighted name.
No known copy.

Pennsylvania State Militia – Single Time

Pennsylvania State Militia – Single Time. (10)
Same information as previous entry.
No known copy.

Pettit & Kessler **see** WRESTLING MATCH BETWEEN PETTIT AND KESSLER, THE WELL KNOWN ATHLETES.

PICKANINNIES. BY 3 LIVELY NEGRO BOYS, FROM "THE PASSING SHOW", A CHARACTERISTIC DANCE. $12.50. (**4, 4b, 4c, 5, 12, 14, 15**)
Filmed: 6 October 1894 (**18: 80**).

Pickaninnies

The dancers were: Walter Wilkins, Denny Tolliver and Joe Rastus. **14** has it as "Danza Pickainnies" (English: "Pickaninnies Dance") and suggests "Danza del ventaglio" (English: "Fan Dance"), "Polka Eloisa" (English: "Eloise Polka"), "Barkies [sic] Tukle" (English: "Darkies Tickle") and "Piccolo Kenkies". I cannot find any Edison cylinder listing under "Fan Dance", but "Eloise Polka" is Edison cylinder #671, played by the Peerless Orchestra. "Darkies Tickle" does not appear on Edison lists, but appears as #2503 on Columbia's 1896 list, played by Issler's Orchestra. "Piccolo Kenkies" does not translate into anything identifiable. In **4b** as 20. A JIG AND BREAKDOWN BY THREE COLORED BOYS. An "R" in the right foreground of the stage would indicate a filming for Raff & Gammon, and the **4b** reference would indicate a later purchase by Maguire & Baucus.

Copies: AMPAS; GCH; NFTVA – an excellent copy and a delightful film of three young blacks in ragged costumes dancing. One plays the harmonica at the same time. Filed under the title "Three man dance", #602935A; P. Both an original film of this scene and a print from the NFTVA copy of 1963 accompanied Kinetoscope #141, bought by the author at Sotheby's on 2 October 1992.

PIER AND WAVES, TAKEN AT CONEY ISLAND DURING THE GREAT STORM OF OCT. 6, 1896. A TREMENDOUS HIT. (**16a**)
Almost surely a "dupe" of Edison's *Surf Scene*.

71. POCAHONTAS. THE INDIAN PRINCESS SAVING THE LIFE OF CAPTAIN JOHN SMITH. (**4b, 4c**)
See RESCUE OF CAPTAIN JOHN SMITH BY POCAHONTAS

180. POLICE PATROL. A SCENE IN WHICH A NUMBER OF MEN ENGAGE IN A ROUGH AND TUMBLE STREET FIGHT. THE POLICE APPEAR, THE PATROL WAGON DASHES UP AND THE COMBATANTS ARE ARRESTED AND DRIVEN OFF TO THE POLICE STATION. A REALISTIC PICTURE, SHARP, CLEAR AND SURE TO EXCITE INTEREST WHEREVER EXHIBITED. (**4b, 4c, 5**)
Filmed: shortly before copyright date of 8 January 1897 (**10**).

No known copy.

95. POLITICAL CARTOON. BLACKMAN [sic] SKETCHING. 150'. (4b, 4c)
Filmed: July 1896 (27).
J Stuart Blackton must have cringed when he saw his name mis-spelled! The
International Film Company promptly "duped" this film, and described it as NO. 2
SHOWING THE ARTIST DRAWING PICTURES OF McKINLEY AND PRESIDENT
CLEVELAND.
No known copy.

POLITICAL DEBATE. REPRESENTS MESSRS. TOPACK AND STEELE IMPERSONATING CLEVELAND AND HARRISON IN A LIVELY POLITICAL DISCUSSION, WHICH PROGRESSES FROM WORDS TO BLOWS. BURLESQUE. $15.00. (15). See also TOPACK AND STEELE. (LIVELY POLITICAL DEBATE, REPRESENTING CLEVELAND AND HARRISON) (12)
Filmed: autumn 1894 (18: 82).
No known copy.

72. PONY RACE. (4b, 4c)
No further information; no known copy.

PRINCESS ALI ORIENTAL DANCER (14) Probably same as 11. EGYPTIAN DANCE (see that entry).
Filmed: 9 May 1895 (18: 7).

Princess Ali, Oriental Dancer

Has letter "C" on stage, apparently indicating that it was made for the Continental Commerce Company of New York, which was organised by Maguire & Baucus to handle overseas business. I do not presently know the connection, if any, between the Continental Commerce Company and the Continental Phonograph Kinetoscope Company of Milan, Italy. "Principessa Ali" appears on this latter firm's "Lista delle films accordate coi cilindri musicati da adoperarsi nel Kinetofono" (English: "List of films matching with musical cylinders for use in the Kinetophone") of January 1896, which suggests a cylinder called "Danza del Ventre" (English: "Belly Dance") be played to accompany the film. The "Lista delle films" would be expected to recommend Edison cylinders, but a list of Edison cylinders of this period gives no title similar to this. However, some of the cylinders on the list are almost certainly Columbia Phonograph Company cylinders, and an 1896 Columbia cylinder catalogue shows selection #1002 as the Washington Military Concert Band playing the "Midway Medley March (The Coochi Coochi)"! This is likely the cylinder referred to.
Copy: EH; GH.
A still appears in 18: ill. 28.

PROFESSOR ATTILA. THE WORLD FAMOUS ATHLETE AND STRONG MAN TRAINER. In **12** and **15** as "ATTILA".
Filmed: 27 April 1895 (**18: 137**).
18: 137 states that Professor Attila was part of the Barnum and Bailey circus, and that "two subjects depicting feats of strength by 'Professor Attila'" were filmed.
No known copy.

Rapids above American Falls (**2**)
Filmed: most likely shortly before the copyright date of 12 December 1896.
Possibly issued under a different title.
No known copy. No other information.

166. RAPIDS AT "CAVE OF THE WINDS". A SCENE TAKEN FROM THE AMERICAN SHORE BELOW THE FALLS, SHOWING SWIRLING WATER AND ICE BACKGROUND. (**4b, 4c, 5**)
Filmed: 11-13 December 1896 (**11**).
See NEW NIAGARA FALLS SERIES.
No known copy.

RAT KILLING
Filmed: several "takes" – 20 September 1894, 21 September 1894 (same) and 22 September 1894 (**18: 79**).
Until October 1996, no contemporary listing of this subject was known. Hendricks felt that faulty punching doomed the negative; **30: 42** felt that the problem was rats "too small"! However, collector Allen Koenigsberg has just found an advertising piece from the first gallery, at 1155 Broadway, apparently from autumn 1894, and listing a film under the above name. Its description is as follows: "'Dick, The Rat' and his rat-terrier. The dog is turned loose among a lot of big, live rats, and kills them in lightning order."
No known copy.

RESCUE OF CAPTAIN JOHN SMITH BY POCAHONTAS
Filmed: summer 1895 (**18: 140**).
Noted as "taken in a forest", but apparently not catalogued until listed as 71. POCAHONTAS in **4b**.
No known copy.

THE RIXFORDS, ACROBATIC FEATS (HEAD BALANCING, A DIFFICULT AND INTERESTING FEAT). $15.00 (**4b, 4c, 12, 15** [$12.50], **20** [#126])
Filmed: 26 November 1894 (**18: 82**).
The Rixfords were brothers. Two subjects were taken (**18: 82**).
One film later appeared in **4b** and **4c** as a 150' film, 128. RIXFORDS, DIFFICULT FEATS OF STRENGTH. Until recently, I would have assumed, because of the 150' length, that this film was not taken until at least 1896. However, Charles Musser informs me that 150' films were taken as early as June 1894, and therefore I feel that it is likely that this was a Raff & Gammon film that was numbered when (I am assuming without concrete evidence) Maguire & Baucus bought Raff & Gammon's film library in early 1897.
No known copy.

ROB ROY see 15. JAMIES. A BURLESQUE SCOTCH DANCE, IN FULL
HIGHLAND COSTUME, BY RICHARD CARROLL AND THE JAMIES, FROM
THE WHITNEY OPERA COMPANY'S "ROB ROY".

ROBETTA AND DORETTO. CHINESE OPIUM DEN. (12)
See also OPIUM DEN. SCENE REPRESENTS SECTION OF THE INTERIOR OF A
CHINESE OPIUM DEN.
Filmed: autumn 1894 (18: 82).
See 4b and 4c as #67, OPIUM DEN.

Roosters (18: 55) see Cock Fight

73. ROSEDALE. PLEASURE BOAT STEAMING DOWN THE HARBOR. (4b, 4c,
16a)
16a gives the title as THE STEAMER ROSEDALE. SHOWING THE ILL-FATED
STEAMER, WHICH, WHILE LOADED WITH PASSENGERS, WAS RECENTLY
SUNK IN NEW YORK HARBOR IN COLLISION WITH THE FERRY BOAT
OREGON. Perhaps this accident (and International Film Company's "duping" of the
film) took place after Edison's title and description had been established?
Filmed: before November 1896, when 16a was published.
No known copy.

ROSS see 116. GLADIATORIAL COMBAT
See also BROADSWORD COMBAT. BETWEEN THE FAR FAMED CAPT.
DUNCAN ROSS, CHAMPION OF THE WORLD, AND LIEUT. MARTIN. AN
EXCITING CONTEST IN FULL ARMOR.

RUNAWAY. SHOWS A HORSE AND CARRIAGE APPROACHING AT A
FURIOUS RATE PURSUED BY A MOUNTED POLICEMAN. THE LATTER
SUCCEEDS IN CATCHING THE RUNAWAY, BUT DOES NOT STOP IT UNTIL
PAST THE POINT AT WHICH THE CAMERA WAS LOCATED. (4b, 4c, 2, 16b as
RUNAWAY IN THE PARK)
Filmed: shortly before its copyright date of 2 November 1896.
No known copy.

Ruth Dennis
Filmed: autumn 1894 (14; 18: 83).
Nature of subject not given, but almost certainly a dance. Ruth Dennis was later known
as "Ruth St. Dennis". and gained fame as a dancer. There is no known American
catalogue listing, but 14 lists "60. Ruth Dennis". In illustration 32, a list of films posted
on the wall lists "High Kicking". This could well be Ruth Dennis, since she was later
called "High Kicker of the World".
No known copy.

THE SAILING OF THE AMERICAN TRANSATLANTIC STEAMSHIP ST. LOUIS
FOR SOUTHAMPTON, ENGLAND. SHOWING ONE OF THE FASTEST
TRANSATLANTIC STEAMERS AFLOAT SAILING DOWN THE RIVER AS SHE
STARTS ON HER LONG VOYAGE. (16a)
A "dupe" of Edison's Steamship St. Louis.

Salem Nassar and Najid Sword Combat **see** Arab "Sword Combat"

SANDOW, THE STRONG MAN.
Also listed as SANDOW, THE MODERN HERCULES (**4, 16**)
Filmed: 6 March 1894 (**18: 53**).

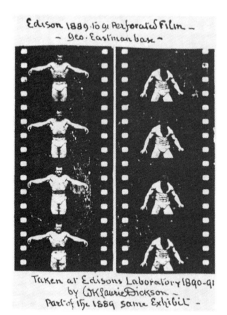

Edison 1889 16 g1 Perforated Film —
— Geo. Eastman base —

Taken at Edisons Laboratory 1890-91
by W.K.Laurie Dickson —
Part of the 1889 same Exhibit —

Sandow, on a Dickson film clip.
Hendricks believes this film was taken in 1894.

Eugene Sandow's visit to the "Black Maria" was widely publicised, as might be expected for anything to do with a protégé of Florenz Ziegfeld! **18: 53-54** quotes the *Orange Chronicle*: "The party arrived at the Phonograph works about 11 o'clock, and were there met by William K.L. Dickson, head of the photo-kinetographic department of the laboratory, and head of the electric ore milling department as well...Mr. Edison was not present when the party arrived, having worked all night and lain down at 7.30 in the morning for needed rest. He reached the building soon after 12 o'clock and was introduced to Mr. Sandow. Sandow had previously stated that he would charge $250 for coming out to give the exhibition, but would gladly come for nothing for the privilege of shaking the hand of Edison, the greatest man of the age...special pictures of various poses were taken... [One was] of Mr. Edison feeling Sandow's muscles with a curiously comical expression on his face...Sandow asked Mr. Cline [business manager of Koster & Bial's Music Hall in New York] if he would mind being 'chucked' out of the door...Mr. Cline demurred but quicker than a flash Sandow caught him with one hand and sent him sailing through the air and out of the door...Sandow...said that he would have to bring out next time some man that liked to be 'chucked'...".

Dickson said that the Black Maria's lighting and stage were so great an improvement that he repeated scenes that he had taken earlier in the 1889 studio, including *Sandow*. It would therefore appear that more than one film of Sandow was taken. *Sandow* was one of the ten films shown on 14 April 1894 at the commercial introduction of the Kinetoscope.

The Northern Queensland Herald, Townsville, Australia, wrote on 4 September 1895: "Sandow (the strong man) in a most vivid and convincing exhibition of his marvellous muscular power and physical strength, wherein every gesture of this world famed athlete, every twist and twito [sic] of his almost preternatural muscular fibre is depicted with an almost uncanny lifelike verisimilitude. Sandow appears within the vision of the mind and eye at once. Every feature of his bodily power, every expression of his face, the firm compression of his lips when straining to produce some tremendous force, is reproduced before the beholder's rapt gaze with absolute fidelity to nature just as these things were done, and but a little while ago by Sandow himself in Mr. Edison's weird, wonderful and magical theatre in America. And though Sandow may – nay, must – in the course of nature pass away, his living personality has been thus fixed for all time and will live for ever." **(31)**

In July 1988 I found the HFM copy in its original film can, lying on a shelf, with some others, in a damaged Kinetoscope in storage. It had been there since at least 1929. The Museum sent it to MOMA for copying, so each has a copy of that print.
Copies: AMPAS; EH; GCH; HFM; MCL; MOMI; P; SAF, #PMU12914.22858".
Stills appear in **33: 34-36**.

74. SCALPING SCENE. A SETTLER PURSUED, OVERTAKEN AND SCALPED BY INDIANS. **(4b, 4c)**
Filmed: between 30 September 1895 and 14 October 1895 **(18: 140)**.
Described as having been "taken in a forest" **(18: 140)**. It seems never to have been offered until it appeared in the Maguire & Baucus catalogue in April 1897.

SCOTCH REEL. SHOWS LADDIE AND LASSIE DANCING, IN COSTUME. **(24)**
Filmed: before April 1894 as, under the title "Highland Dance", it was one of the ten films shown at the first commercial exhibition of the Kinetoscope in New York on 14 April 1894. In the 22 May 1894 copy of a children's magazine, *Harper's Young People*, is an article entitled "Edison's Little Men. Working the Kinetograph", by Barnett Phillips. As part of an interview with Edison, he shows 65 frames of this film – the 65 frames noted as being copyrighted by Dickson. A copy of this article is in the Charles Clarke Collection of the Library of AMPAS.
No known copy. However, if the experiment with *Buffalo Bill Shooting a Rifle* produces an acceptable result, perhaps a short sequence can be re-created.

SERPENTINE DANCE – ANNABELLE see ANNABELLE – SERPENTINE DANCE

Sheik Hadji Tahar-Somersaults, etc. **(16)**
26 lists this act as being from "Primrose and West's Minstrels".
Filmed: 6 October 1894 **(18: 80)**.
Hendricks may have seen this film in the 1960s, as his notes refer to it, but he claims that the subject is really Tojou Kichi! However, Dickson's 1895 book on the Kinetoscope gives pictures and the Tahar name. The film does not appear in any catalogue of the 1890s.
Copy: AMPAS; GCH; GH; P; SAF, under the title "Acrobate Arab", #PMU22864.
There is an "R" in the lower right-hand corner. The film (SAF's copy) is an original, not a later copy, is in excellent condition, and is 37'6" long – just right for a Kinetoscope loop!
Stills appear in **33: 44**.

76. SHOOTING THE CHUTES (AT CONEY ISLAND) **(4b, 4c, 5)**
Filmed: 22 June 1896 or earlier **(21)**.
Maguire & Baucus film #96 was a 150' film, whereas the above was only 50'. The difference was that the 50' film showed only the slide down the chutes, whereas in the 150' film you also saw the car hitting the water! *Shooting the Chutes* is what we would now probably call a "log ride". In the film's foreground, a slender boat full of passengers slides down a water-filled chute. Behind the chute are two tracks. On the farther one, a cable-drawn wagon full of passengers is being pulled up, almost reaching

the unloading dock. On the nearer one, an empty passenger-wagon is descending.
Copies: AMPAS; EH; GCH; GH; P.
A still appears in **35: ill. 12**; **30: 68**.

SHORT STICK DANCE, BY NATIVES OF INDIA, FROM BARNUM'S SHOW. $15.00. (**4b, 4c, 12**)
Filmed: 27 April 1895 (**18: 137**). Originally Raff & Gammon, this appeared in **4b** and **4c** as Maguire & Baucus film #22.
No known copy.

Short Stick Dance (Natural History Museum of LA County)

110. SIDEWALKS OF NEW YORK. A SCENE IN THE OLD BOWERY. VERY GOOD. 150' $45.00. (**4b, 4c, 5, 16a**)
16a gives a more complete description: THIS VIEW IS TAKEN IN MOTT STREET, NEW YORK CITY AND SHOWS A BUSY THRONG OF PEOPLE.
Filmed: probably autumn 1896.
No known copy.

SILVER DANCE BY CINGALESE IN NATIVE COSTUMES, FROM BARNUM & BAILEY'S SHOW. $15.00 (**4b, 4c, 12**)
Filmed: unknown, but the *Paddle Dance* was filmed on 25 April 1895, and it is likely that the two films were filmed the same day, or nearly so.
The film appeared in **4b** and **4c** as #21.
No known copy.

SIOUX GHOST DANCE. (A VERY INTERESTING SUBJECT, FULL OF ACTION AND TRUE TO LIFE.) (**12, 15, 16, 20**; also **4b** as **14. GHOST.**)
Filmed: 24 September 1894 (**18: 80**).
From Buffalo Bill's "Wild West Show". About fifteen Indians in war paint and costume dance and brandish weapons. This film and *Buffalo Dance* are sometimes confused, but the number of Indians in the scene is the governing factor. The film begins with the Indians standing facing the camera, then they dance clockwise in a circle. At the lower right of the frame is a hand-painted banner with the following in script: "BUFFALO BILL'S WILD WEST S". The last few letters of the banner cannot be seen, but apparently the last word should be "Show". The entire film is terribly dark. The action can hardly be discerned. AMPAS is going to attempt to make a lighter copy.
Copies: the original dark version is at EH, GH, MOMA and SAF, under the title *Dance des Esprits Sioux*; the lighter version is at AMPAS, GCH and P.
Stills appear in **33: 23**.

97. SKETCHING MR. EDISON. BLACKMAN (sic), THE "WORLD" ARTIST AT WORK. A 150' film. (**4b, 4c**)
Filmed: July 1896 to early August 1896 (**21, 27**).
I am sure that J Stuart Blackton did not appreciate his name being so seriously mis-

spelled! The Library of AMPAS has a fragile brown manuscript in its "locked case" section. It is titled "Early History, a lecture by Commodore J Stuart Blackton". It is the text of a lecture given by Blackton at the University of Southern California (USC) on 20 February 1929. It was too fragile to photocopy. I was able to copy down the following:

Blackton was sent out by the *World* newspaper as a young reporter of 19 to interview Edison. Edison apparently found the young man pleasant to talk to, and finally asked him:
'What is that you have got under your arm?' I told him it was my sketch book. Then he asked me to draw something for him. I drew Levi P. Morton and several other men he knew and then he asked me if I could make a sketch of him. I said I would and he sat for me while I made a sketch of him. He was pleased with it...Then he asked me if I could draw that picture of him on a big paper, on a board. I told him that I could and he said, 'You come on out to the 'Black Maria' and we did, and he had them get boards and wide white paper and some charcoal, and right there and then he had the camera recording your humble servant drawing a picture of Thomas A. Edison. He said, 'Put your name on that board,' and 'This will be a good ad for you, it will go all over the country in the show houses.'

The film shows Blackton drawing a sketch of Edison, and at the end Blackton turns and bows to the audience. The New International Film Company promptly "duped" the film, as well as other Edison films, and advertised it in the first issue of *The Phonoscope*, which began publishing in September 1896. As a result of this and other duplication of his uncopyrighted films, Edison began copyrighting his films starting on 23 October 1896. They were copyrighted by sending an actual positive paper print of the entire film to the LOC. This was one of the procedures followed by Edison and others until about 1912, and led to the preservation of many early films that would otherwise have disappeared. Thanks to Kemp Niver and others, these prints in recent years have been restored and many of them copied back into films. Indeed, the University of California at Los Angeles continued to copy these paper prints for the LOC until quite recently. Copy: MOMA. I believe that I saw this film as part of a series of films on motion-picture history in 1939 or so, when I was a student at UCLA.

SKIRT DANCE DOG. A SERPENTINE DANCE IN COSTUME, PERFORMED BY ONE OF PROF. TSCHERNOFF'S MARVELOUS TRAINED DOGS. (FROM KOSTER & BIAL'S)
$10.00 (**4, 15**; **12** asks $12.50)
Filmed: 17 October 1894 (**18: 82**).
See also 10. DANCING DOG. SKIRT DANCE BY A TRAINED DOG, A FILM FOR CHILDREN
No known copy.

The Sneeze
Filmed: 7 January 1894 (**2**).
34: 82 describes the occasion:

Fred Ott, the home talent comedian of the Edison staff, who had posed for the camera through the years of experimental work, was called to the stage.

Ott rejoiced in a handsome moustache of the magnificent Texas pattern, with symphonic curves. Ott was robust, cheery and abundant. His sneeze was the pride of the Edison works. He could, and did, sneeze louder than any other white man born east of the Rockies.

Dickson placed Ott before the camera, stepped to the starting switch and ordered the star to sneeze. Nothing occurred.

The first studio property man was then and there sent out to acquire the first of all motion picture accessories – a box of snuff.

The snuff did not work, so they tried pepper. Ott's sneeze refused to ignite. They doubled the dose and mixed snuff and pepper. Again, failure. Ott coughed, choked, gagged and melted into tears, but sneeze he could not. They struck the set and called it a day. The next day it worked.

The Sneeze lasts approximately five seconds, but it is still famous. At the 1990 Academy Awards® ceremony, it was incorporated into a five-minute montage called "One Hundred Years at the Movies", a remarkable production in which extracts of 350 motion-pictures were included. *The Sneeze* has been used in illustrations many times. It was one of the first – if not the first – films copyrighted by W K-L Dickson in 1894; later the copyright was assigned to Edison. Edison did not copyright films until 23 October 1896: I am sure that Edison felt that he could safely avoid the expense of copyrighting, and that (as was the case for some time) no one else would have any incentive to copy his films. This was the case until about September 1896, when the International Film Company began selling copies under its label.
Copies: ENHS #E156-271 (16mm?); GH; LOC; and probably some film anthologies of 19th-century films.
Stills appear in **33: 39**.

SOMERSAULT DOG. PROF TSCHERNOFF'S, FROM KOSTER AND BIAL'S. THIS TRAINED ANIMAL TURNS BACKWARD SOMERSAULTS IN THE AIR. A WONDERFUL PERFORMANCE. $10.00 (**4, 12, 15**)
Filmed: 17 October 1894 (**18**).
No known copy, but sixteen frames are in **33: 12**.

Special Photographing Train (**2**)
Filmed: copyrighted on 12 December 1896 (**10**).
No known copy. No other information. I strongly suspect that this had something to do with the filming of 162. BLACK DIAMOND EXPRESS, and with the still photograph (see illustration 10) of the cameramen with their cameras and crew. The fact that *Black Diamond Express* was also copyrighted on 12 December 1896 might be considered as "circumstantial" evidence.
No known copy.

134. STARTING FOR THE FIRE. SHOWS ENGINE LEAVING HOUSE. (**20, 2, 4c** as 135)
Fortunately, **20** adds the description to the title; nowhere else does it appear, and sometimes this title and *Going to the Fire* are confused; particularly when, as is the case with **4c**, where for number 135 (the correct number for *Going to the Fire*), the title *Starting for the Fire* is given in error. The two films are not at all similar.

Hendricks says that three films were taken on the occasion of the filming of *Going*

to the Fire, which was one of them. **2** lists only one possibility for the second, *Starting for the Fire,* and both were copyrighted on 16 November. *Morning Fire Alarm,* although it was not copyrighted until 27 November (**10**), is almost surely the third film, as its "action" – engine house doors open; a fire engine comes out – is the same as *Starting for the Fire.*
Filmed: c.14 November 1896 (**18**).
See 135. <u>GOING TO THE FIRE.</u> and 134. <u>MORNING FIRE ALARM.</u>
No known copy.

77. STEAMSHIP ST. LOUIS. (**4b, 4c,** "dupe" in **16a** as THE SAILING OF THE AMERICAN TRANSATLANTIC STEAMSHIP ST. LOUIS FOR SOUTHAMPTON, ENGLAND. SHOWING ONE OF THE FASTEST TRANSATLANTIC STEAMERS AFLOAT SAILING DOWN THE RIVER AS SHE STARTS ON HER LONG VOYAGE)
For a description of the "action", see entry for THE SAILING.
Filmed: its being in **16a** would suggest autumn 1896.
No known copy.

214. STORM ON THE SEA COAST. SHOWING A RAGING SURF DASHING OVER AN OLD PIER, AT LONG BRANCH, N.J. DURING THE EQUINOCTIAL STORM, SEPTEMBER, 1896. THE WATER EFFECTS IN THIS FILM ARE PRONOUNCED TO BE ABSOLUTELY PERFECT. OUR BEST SURF SCENE. (**4b, 16b**)
The filming date is apparent. The number is a puzzle. As far as I can tell, Maguire & Baucus numbered their films approximately in sequence, possibly filling in some unused numbers with Raff & Gammon films after they purchased the Raff & Gammon "library". I feel that they crossed over from 1896 into 1897 at *about* number 183 or

Streets of Cairo (Library of Congress)

184, but this film is given a number some twenty numbers later than those, even though it was taken in September.
Copy: NAC has a film matching this description under the title of "Surf Scene".

Street Sprinkling and Trolley Cars.
Mentioned in **30: 68**. Almost certainly 47. EDISON LABORATORY.
Filmed: 1896.
No known copy.

141. STREETS OF CAIRO. FOUR EGYPTIAN GIRLS PERFORMING THE FAMOUS "MIDWAY" DANCE. (**2, 4b, 4c, 5, 16b**)
Filmed: shortly before the copyright date of October 1896 (**10**).
No known copy.

THE SUBURBAN HANDICAP (**30**)
Filmed: 23 June 1896.
Shows Navarre winning the horse race at Gravesend Race Track (**30**).
No known copy.

SUN DANCE – ANNABELLE see ANNABELLE – SUN DANCE. BY THE FAMOUS "ANNABELLE". THESE DANCES, (SERPENTINE, BUTTERFLY AND SUN) ARE AMONG THE FINEST FOR THE EFFECTS OF COSTUME, LIGHT, AND SHADE, AND ARE VERY POPULAR.

149. SURF AFTER STORM. A 150' film.
4b and **4c** say "See description of 50' film", but do not list a 50' film by this name.
No known copy. No other information.

Surf at Long Branch
Filmed: copyrighted on 23 October 1896.
See 142. SURF SCENE. PHOTOGRAPHED AT LONG BEACH JUST AFTER A SEVERE STORM. SHOWS A HEAVY SURF SPLASHING ALONG A PIER AND BREAKING ON THE BEACH CLOSE TO THE CAMERA. AN EXCELLENT SUBJECT FOR WATER EFFECTS, THE GLITTERING SPRAY BEING DISTINCTLY REPRODUCED.

78. SURF AVENUE. A STREET SCENE AT CONEY ISLAND. (**4b, 4c**)
Filmed: 18-23 June 1896.
The camera looks across a street lined with small buildings. Pedestrians and horse-drawn vehicles go in both directions.
Copies: EH; Smithsonian Collection, Misc. Primitives Subject A-39280:719:1.

142. SURF SCENE. PHOTOGRAPHED AT LONG BEACH JUST AFTER A SEVERE STORM. SHOWS A HEAVY SURF SPLASHING ALONG A PIER AND BREAKING ON THE BEACH CLOSE TO THE CAMERA. AN EXCELLENT SUBJECT FOR WATER EFFECTS, THE GLITTERING SPRAY BEING DISTINCTLY REPRODUCED.
Filmed: 6 October 1896 (?). Copyrighted on 23 October 1896 as *Surf at Long Branch* (**10**).

This is not the same film as #214.
Copy: NAC.

98. SWIMMING SCHOOL. A LIVELY BATHING SCENE IN A FIFTH AVENUE SWIMMING SCHOOL. A 150' film (**4b, 4c, 5**).
Listed separately because it gives a bit more information in the description.
No known copy. No other information.

75. SWIMMING SCHOOL. THE SCENE SHOWS MANY BATHERS SWIMMING, DIVING AND TURNING SOMERSAULTS IN THE WATER. VERY GOOD. (**4b**)
There was also a 150' version, #98 (**4c, 5**).
No known copy. No other information.

173. TALLY-HO, THE ARRIVAL. ANOTHER SCENE TAKEN AT THE BUFFALO COUNTRY CLUB, IN WHICH ARE SEEN MANY OF THE ELITE OF BUFFALO DRIVING UP AND ALIGHTING FROM THEIR FOUR-HORSE DRAG AT THE DOOR OF THE CLUB HOUSE. INTRODUCTIONS, HAND-SHAKINGS AND GREETINGS, MAKE A LIVELY AND ATTRACTIVE SUBJECT. (**2, 4b, 4c, 5, 16d**)
Filmed: shortly before the copyright date of 24 December 1896 (**10**).
4b says that the next film "IS SOMEWHAT THE MORE ATTRACTIVE SUBJECT"!
No known copy.

172. TALLY-HO, THE DEPARTURE. (**2, 4b, 4c, 5, 16d**).
Filmed: shortly before the copyright date of 24 December 1896 (**10**).
This is a truly delightful film. More than most it evokes the *joie de vivre* of the "gay" 1890s! **16d** describes it as: "SHOWS THE FOUR HORSE DRAG LEAVING THE CLUB HOUSE, THE OCCUPANTS WAVING ADIEUS TO FRIENDS AT THE HOUSE".
Copy: National Archives, Washington, DC. Unfortunately, this 40' film is attached to about 400' of early 1900s films of the Orient! By now, a copy may be at LOC.

79. TELEPHONE APPOINTMENT. THE GAY YOUNG MAN AND THE PRETTY TYPEWRITER. (**4b, 4c**)
Filmed: unknown, and no copyright, at least under this name.
Included because some numbers in the 70s were taken in summer 1896.
This film is interesting for a particular reason. It seems to be the first and only Kinetoscope film, with the exception of boxing matches (which had a series of rounds, each on a separate film), that had two films, short as they were, with the second film continuing the story-line of the first. The second film is 80. THE INTERRUPTED SUPPER. Incidentally, there is no reason to conclude that the young man was "gay" in the current sense of the word, and he was certainly not "weird" enough to take what we would call a "typewriter" out to dinner. That was the common name, in the gay 1890s, for a typist or stenographer!
No known copy.

Texas Cowboy Throwing Lassos (**16**) **see** Vincent Oro Passo

TOPACK AND STEELE. (LIVELY POLITICAL DEBATE, REPRESENTING CLEVELAND AND HARRISON). $15.00. (**12**)

See also POLITICAL DEBATE. REPRESENTS MESSRS. TOPACK AND STEELE IMPERSONATING CLEVELAND AND HARRISON IN A LIVELY POLITICAL DISCUSSION, WHICH PROGRESSES FROM WORDS TO BLOWS. BURLESQUE. No known copy. No other information.

Toyou Kichi. Japanese Tumbler.
Filmed: 18 October 1894 (**4, 18: 7**).
Something must have happened, as this film appears only in **4**, of December 1894. Copy: EH.

99. TRAIN SCENE AT ORANGE. SHOWING MR. BRYAN ADDRESSING A CROWD OF PEOPLE FROM THE REAR PLATFORM OF A MOVING TRAIN. 150' (**4b, 16d**).
Filmed: unknown.
William Jennings Bryan (1860-1925) was a popular and active politician in the late 1800s. His most famous oration was the "Cross of Gold" speech, which ended with "You shall not crucify mankind on a cross of gold!" or similar words. In 1908, Edison recorded ten wax cylinders of Bryan speeches.
See also 99. BRYAN TRAIN SCENE AT ORANGE. 150' (**4c**).
No known copy.

"A trained bear subject" (**18: 55**).
Filmed: "before the opening on April 14 [1894] of the Kinetoscope parlor at 1155 Broadway" (**18: 55**).
Not only was this film was taken, but also a second one in the fall of 1894.
However, neither appears in any catalogue or film list. On page 316 of *The Life & Inventions of Thomas Alva Edison* (copyrighted 1892, 1893, 1894), W K-L Dickson gives this description:

"A trained bear subject" (photo by W K-L Dickson)

One day chronicled the engagement of a troupe of trained bears and their Hungarian leaders. The bears were divided between surly discontent and a comfortable desire to follow the bent of their own inclinations. It was only after much persuasion that they could be induced to subserve the interests of science. One furry monster waddled up a telegraph pole, to the soliloquy of his own indignant growls...a third rose solemnly on his hind legs and described the measures of some unclassified dance, to the weird strains of his keeper's music. Another licked his master's swarthy face, in deprecation of the invitation to move, while another accepted his keeper's challenge, and engaged him in a wrestling match, struggling, hugging and rolling on the ground.

No known copy.
A still appears in **18: ill. 21**.

TRAINED BEARS.
Filmed: autumn 1894 (**18: 83; 14**).

While no American source lists a trained bear film, **14** lists one as "49. Orsi ammaestrati", which is most likely this film.
Copy: SAF has a film of a bear wrestling with his trainer, while a man wearing a straw hat and carrying a furled umbrella watches. While possibly it is this film, to me the scene just does not look "American". Moreover, the film "rolls over" while being viewed. It may well be a similar subject by a later European source.

Trapeze
Filmed: before 14 April 1894 (**18: 56**).
One of the ten films shown on that date at the first commercial showing of the Kinetoscope. Not further identified in **18** and not identifiable in any known catalogue. MLLE. CAPITAINE. "THE PERFECT WOMAN" EXHIBITING IN A GRACEFUL TRAPEZE PERFORMANCE (see that entry) performs on a trapeze, but her filming date was not until 1 November 1894.
No known copy.

87. TRICK BICYCLE RIDING (**14c**) **see** BICYCLE RIDING. BY RICHARDSON, CHAMPION TRICK RIDER.

TRILBY
Trilby was a "fantastically successful Du Maurier drama" (**18: 136**).
Filmed: April 1895.
There were four subjects taken. See the separate entries.

23. TRILBY DANCE. BY THE FAMOUS LEIGH SISTERS. (**4b, 4c, 5**)
Filmed: April 1895.
No known copy.

TRILBY HYPNOTIC SCENE.
SVENGALI HYPNOTIZES EVERY ONE
IN SIGHT, AND CAUSES THEM TO
GO THROUGH SUNDRY BURLESQUE
PERFORMANCES. VERY POPULAR.
$15.00. (**15**)
See 66. HYPNOTIC SCENE
(BURLESQUE).
Filmed: April 1895 (**18: 136**).
No known copy.

Trilby Hypnotic Scene
(From woodcut in Hendricks Collection)

TRILBY QUARTETTE. THE LATEST. BURLESQUE FROM DAVID HENDERSON'S "ALADDIN, JR." A DECIDED HIT. $15.00. (**15**)
Filmed: April 1895 (**18: 136**).
No known copy.

TRILBY'S DEATH SCENE. FROM DAVID HENDERSON'S BURLESQUE. REPRESENTS TRILBY, SVENGALI AND THE LAIRD. SVENGALI HYPNOTIZES TRILBY AND THE LAIRD, THEN FALLS DEAD ACROSS A TABLE. VERY FUNNY. THE DRAMATIS PERSONAE OF THIS ACT ARE MADE UP IN EXACT IMITATION OF THE ILLUSTRATIONS GIVEN IN DU MARIER'S [sic] BOOK.

$15.00. (**15, 4b, 4c** as 45. DEATH SCENE)
Filmed: April 1895 (**18: 136**).
No known copy.

TRIO. A LIVELY ECCENTRIC DANCE BY FRANK LAWTON AND MISSES WILLIAMSON AND FRANCE, OF HOYT'S MILK WHITE FLAG. ATTRACTIVE COSTUMES. $15.00 (**15**). Also listed in **12** as DANCE. FRANK LAWTON, etc. **See also** listing under 64. MILK WHITE FLAG, ASSEMBLY MARCH (**4b, 4c** under #24. TRIO.).
Filmed: autumn 1894 (**18: 83**).
Listed in **14** as TRIO, WHITE MILK FLAG (English: "Trio, Milk White Flag", and suggests cylinders "Marca Arcadica" (English: "Arcadian March") and "Danza del ventaglio" (English: "Fan Dance"), each played by "Orchestra". I could find neither of these in the Edison catalogue.
No known copy.

81. TUB RACE. DEPICTING THE DIFFICULTIES OF PADDLING IN WASH TUBS (**4b, 4c, 5**)
Filmed: other numbers near 81 were filmed in summer 1896. However, strangely, the first and only listing, by copyright dates, in **2** is 1903.
No known copy. No other information.

Turkish Harem
(Natural History Museum of LA County)

30. TURKISH HAREM. A CHARACTERISTIC TURKISH DANCE IN COSTUME. 150', $45.00. (**4b, 4c**)
The illustration is from a film clip only a few frames long from the Earl Theisen Collection in the Natural History Museum of Los Angeles County. It is not identified (none of their film clips is), but I think the subject can be safely identified as *Turkish Harem*.
No known copy. No other information.

25. UMBRELLA DANCE. BY LEIGH SISTERS. (**4b, 4c, 5, 22**)
Filmed: 23 April 1896 (**22**).
See also Leigh Sisters
No known copy. No other information.

U.S. CAVALRY DRILL AT WEST POINT. VERY SHARP, THE GLISTENING OF THE SABRES IS SHOWN. (**16b**)
Filmed: *Cadet's Charge* was copyrighted by Edison on 27 November 1896, and most probably filmed within the preceding ten days. It would seem likely that this film and the following entry were made on this occasion, but neither appears on any "Edison" lists.
No known copy.

PALMER'S THEATRE.

Mr. A. M. PALMER. .... SOLE LESSEE AND MANAGER

OVERTURE—EVENINGS AT 8.00.   MATINEE SATURDAY AT 2.

2D WEEK OF THE SUMMER SEASON.

Monday, May 22, to Saturday, May 27, 1893,

ENGAGEMENT OF THE MAGNIFICENT ORGANIZATION,

RICE'S SURPRISE PARTY (80 IN ALL,)

who will appear for as long a period as the public will stand it in a jolly evening's entertainment yclept an historical extravaganza in three acts, burdened with the fascinating numerical title

1492 UP TO DATE, OR VERY NEAR IT. 1492

Libretto by R. A. BARNET.   Music by CARL PFLUEGER.

Which will be presented with the following carefully selected Cast:

FERDINAND OF ARAGON, King of Spain	
CHARLEY TATTERS, a fringe on the edge of the crust of society	Mr. WALTER JONES
ALONZO DE QUINTANILLA, royal treasurer	Mr. EDWARD M. FAVOR
DON JUAN, the King's son, aged four.	
FELIX, of the tribe of coppers	Mr. WILL. H. SLOAN
CAPTAIN MARTIN PINZON } Conspirators of the	Mr. CHAS. F. WALTON
DON PEDRO MARGARITE. } Old-fashioned type,	Mr. JOHN C. SLAVIN
CHARLES VIII., King of France	Mr. LOUIS DE SMITH
DON FERDINAND ALLEGRO.	
ADOLPHUS FITZFOOZLE, a regular "chappie" up to date,	Miss YOLANDE WALLACE
MAID MABEL, a sailor lassie.	
MAID MARION, a sailor lassie.	Miss EILEEN KARL
THE ROYAL HERALD.	
WARD KNICKERBOCKER, cacique of the 400	
JIM CONFIDENCE, of the tribe of buncoes.	Mr. C. J. ALDEN
BOB, a New York newsboy	Mr. JAMES LEE
ERASMUS, a vender of maize	Mr. FREDERIC HOWARD
ISABELLA OF CASTILE, Queen of Spain	Mr. RICHARD HARLOW
FRAULIEN, a German waif	Miss THERESA VAUGHN
INFANTA JOANNA, in love with Columbus.	
INFANTA CATALINA, her sister.	Miss HATTIE WILLIAMS
MARY ANN KEHOE, Of the Royal Household of the new world	Miss EDITH SINCLAIR

——— AND ———

CHRISTOPHER COLUMBUS .... Mr. MARK SMITH

Courtiers, Ladies, Peasants, Students. Ballet. Amazons, Newsboys, Moors, Sailors, Bull Fighters, Soldiers, Pages, Standard Bearers. etc., by a full and efficient chorus.

Walton and Slavin

U.S. CAVALRY WATERING HORSES. (16b)
Filmed: see comments for U.S. CAVALRY DRILL AT WEST POINT. VERY
SHARP, THE GLISTENING OF THE SABRES IS SHOWN.
I have seen a few seconds of what must be this film, but cannot recall where.
Copy: location not known.

31. VERNONA JARBEAU. AS CALVE IN CARMEN. (4b, 4c) A 150' film.
Filmed: the 150' length would indicate the latter half of 1896.
No known copy.

Vincent Oro Passo **see** LASSO THROWER. VINCENTE ORO PASSO. THE
CHAMPION LASSO THROWER, GIVES AN INTERESTING EXHIBITION OF
LASSO TWIRLING AND THROWING, FROM "BUFFALO BILL'S WILD WEST."

WALTON & MAYON-BURLESQUE BOXING (22)
Filmed: 23 April 1896 (22), although Hendricks gives a date of 5 October 1894.
No known copy. No other information.

WALTON AND SLAVIN, "THE LONG AND SHORT OF IT". COMICAL AND
MIRTH EXCITING BURLESQUE BOXING CONTEST FROM RICE'S "1492",
REPRESENTING A BURLESQUE BOXING TEST BETWEEN 6FT 4 AND 4 FT. 6.
VERY AMUSING. $15.00. (Also in 16)
Filmed: 6 October 1894 (18: 80).
No known copy, but 32 frames are in 33: 45.

WAR COUNCIL. REPRESENTING BUFFALO BILL AND A NUMBER OF HIS
INDIAN WARRIORS IN COUNCIL SMOKING THE FAMOUS PIPE OF PEACE.
$12.50. (15)
See INDIAN WAR COUNCIL, SHOWING SEVENTEEN DIFFERENT PERSONS-
INDIAN WARRIORS AND WHITE MEN-IN COUNCIL.

WARING & WILSON (4b, 4c, 5) **see** JOHN W. WILSON AND BERTHA
WARING-"LITTLE CHRISTOPHER COLUMBUS", ECCENTRIC DANCERS.

107. WASHINGTON MARKET. (STREET SCENE) THE FAMOUS OLD MARKET
PLACE. (4b, 4c, 5)
Filmed: 1896 (?).
No known copy. No other information.

83. WATERMELON CONTEST. TWO
NEGROES EATING WATERMELON
FOR A PRIZE. (4b, 4c, 5)
Filmed: 1896 (?).
Copy: MOMA.

Watermelon Contest (MOMA)

WAVES AT FAR ROCKAWAY. **16a** says that this is the same film as *Pier and Waves*.

YOUNG WEIMER. THE CHAMPION LIGHT-WEIGHT DUMB BELL LIFTER OF
THE WORLD, PUPIL OF ATTILA. $15.00. (**12**, in **15** as WEIMER etc.)
Filmed: 27 April 1895 (**18: 137**).
From Barnum and Bailey's Circus (**18: 137**).
No known copy. No other information.

167. WHIRLPOOL RAPIDS. SHOWING THE PLACE WHERE CAPTAIN WEBB
MET HIS TRAGIC DEATH: THE MOST TURBULENT AND DANGEROUS SPOT
IN THE ENTIRE GORGE. (**2**, **4b**, **5**)
Filmed: 11-13 December 1896, and copyrighted on 24 December 1896. Also known as
Whirlpool Rapids from Bottom of Canadian Shore in late spring 1897 Edison
"Supplemental List".
See NEW NIAGARA FALLS SERIES.
No known copy.

82. WHITE WINGS. NEW YORK STREET CLEANERS ON PARADE. (**4b**, **4c**, **5**)
Filmed: 1896.
No known copy. No other information.

The Widder **see** Miss Isabelle Coe as "The Widder"

150. WINE GARDEN. A SCENE AT A NOTED GERMAN WINE GARDEN. (In **2**
as WINE GARDEN SCENE) (**4b**, **4c**, **5** and a 150' film, $45.00; **16b**, **16d**)
Filmed: copyrighted 23 October 1896 (**10**), therefore filmed a few days earlier and
"duped" by International Film Company soon afterwards.

Wine Garden (Library of Congress)

4b gives a fuller description: "A scene at a noted German wine garden in Harlem showing a number of people seated at tables drinking, smoking and playing cards. Incidentally, there is a lively flirtation going on between a pretty waitress and one of the guests."
No known copy.

Wrestling. (13) Two men wrestle in front of a white picket fence. (1)
Filmed: before October 1892 (18: 56).
Several frames from this film, and those from *Boxing* and *Fencing*, were published in the October 1892 issue of Edison's house organ for his phonograph dealers, *The Phonogram*. These seem to be the earliest published stills from films taken in a vertical 35mm format, the type still in common use today.
No known copy.

WRESTLING DOG. (WRESTLES WITH HIS TRAINER). $10.00. (12, 15)
Filmed: autumn 1894 (18: 83).
31 lists "J.K. Emmett and his Wrestling Dog" as being shown in Sydney, Australia, beginning 3 January 1895, The *Sydney Morning Herald* of 17 January 1895 describes the film as follows: "The wresting match between the great St. Bernard and the man. The dog, which was the property of the late American comedian M.T.K. Emmett, is a magnificent creature in his way. He bounds about the stage with joyous energy; we can even see his tail wag. Now the man and now the dog has the best of it, and during the performance a lady, evidently the mistress of the dog, comes on occasionally, her face wreathed in smiles, and urges the faithful creature to fresh efforts."

Chris Long, from whom this quotation comes, has done a great service in providing several of these descriptions, which in many cases provide the only description of films which have not survived.
No known copy.

Wrestling Match. Evans and Ryan. (25)
Filmed: by early April 1894 (26).
Wrestling was one of the ten films shown on 14 April 1894 at the first commercial showing of the Kinetoscope and its films.

Wrestling Match. Leonard vs. Stephens. **see** AMERICAN WRESTLING: LEONARD VS. STEPHENS

WRESTLING MATCH BETWEEN PETTIT AND KESSLER, THE WELL KNOWN ATHLETES. ($12-$12.50, **20** as #119) (**15** describes the film as A GRAECO-ROMAN MATCH BETWEEN PETTIT AND KESSLER. (THE FORMER IS CHAMPION OF NEW JERSEY. $12.50) In **4b** and **4c** as #119.
Filmed: by April 1895 (**18: 137**). This is possibly a match in autumn 1894 (**18: 83**).
No known copy.

YOSEMITE FALLS **see** <u>69. PATERSON FALLS.</u> THE FALLS OF THE PASSAIC RIVER

Dickson, W K-L and Antonia Dickson. *History of the Kinetograph, Kinetoscope & Kinetophonograph* (originally published 1895; 1984 reprint available from Ayer Company Publishers Inc, Salem, NH).

————————————————. *The Life & Inventions of Thomas Alva Edison* (London: Chatto & Windus, 1894).

Hendricks, Gordon. *The Beginnings of the Biograph: The Story of the Invention of the Mutoscope and the Biograph and Their Supplying Camera* (New York: The Beginnings of the American Film, 1964). Reprinted in an omnibus edition, *Origins of the American Film* (New York: Arno Press and The New York Times, 1972).

————————. *The Edison Motion Picture Myth* (Berkeley; Los Angeles: University of California Press, 1961).

————————. *The Kinetoscope: America's First Commercially Successful Motion Picture Exhibitor* (New York, 1966) [self-published].

Musser, Charles. "American Vitagraph: 1897-1901", *Cinema Journal* 22: 3 (spring 1983): 4-46.

——————. *Before the Nickelodeon: Edwin S. Porter and the Edison Manufacturing Company* (Berkeley; Los Angeles; Oxford: University of California Press, 1991).

——————. *The Emergence of Cinema: The American Screen to 1907* (New York: Charles Scribner's Sons, 1990).

——————. *Thomas A. Edison and His Kinetographic Motion Pictures* (New Brunswick, NJ: Rutgers University Press, 1995).

—————— (ed). *Thomas A Edison Papers: A Guide to Motion Picture Catalogs by American Producers and Distributors, 1894-1908: A Microfilm Edition* (Frederick, MD: University Publications of America, 1985).

Niver, Kemp R. *Motion Pictures from the Library of Congress Paper Print Collection 1894-1912* (Berkeley: University of California Press, 1967).

Ramsaye, Terry. *A Million and One Nights: A History of the Motion Picture*, volume I (New York: Simon and Schuster, 1926).

Singer, Ben. "Early Home Cinema and the Edison Home Projecting Kinetoscope", *Film History* 2: 1 (1988): 37-69.

Academy Film Archive
Academy of Motion Picture Arts and
    Sciences (AMPAS)
333 South La Cienega Blvd
Beverly Hills
CA 90211
USA
tel +1 310 657 3449
fax +1 310 657 5431

Cinémathèque Française
4 rue de Longchamps
Paris 75116
FRANCE
tel +33 1 53 65 74 74
fax +33 1 53 65 74 97

Edison National Historic Site (ENHS)
Main Street and Lakeside Avenue
West Orange
NJ 07052
USA
tel +1 201 736 0550
fax +1 201 736 8496

Flaherty Brothers Collection
Audio Visual Public Service
National Archives of Canada
395 Wellington Street
Ottawa
ON K1A ON3
CANADA
tel +1 613 995 5138
fax +1 613 995 3074

George Eastman House
(International Museum of
    Photography)
900 East Avenue
Rochester
NY 14607
USA

tel +1 716 271 3361
fax +1 716 271 3970

Greenwood Press
88 Post Road West
Westport
CT 06881-5007
USA
tel +1 203 226 3571
fax +1 203 222 1502

Henry Ford Museum (HFM)
PO Box 1970
Dearborn
MI 48121
USA
tel +1 313 271 1620
fax +1 313 982 6244

Library of Congress (LOC)
Motion Picture, Broadcasting and
    Recorded Sound Division
Washington
DC 20540
USA
tel +1 202 707 5709
fax +1 202 707 2371

Margaret Herrick Library
Academy of Motion Picture Arts and
    Sciences (AMPAS)
333 South La Cienega Blvd
Beverly Hills
CA 90211
USA
tel +1 310 247 3035
fax +1 310 657 5193

Museo Nazionale del Cinema
Palazzo Chiablese
Piazza San Giovanni 2
10122 Turin
ITALY
tel +39 11 436 1148
fax +39 11 521 2341

Museum of Modern Art (MOMA)
11 West 53rd Street
New York
NY 10019-5498
USA
tel +1 212 708 9400
fax +1 212 708 9889

Museum of the Moving Image
    (AMMI)
3601 35th Avenue
Astoria
NY 11106
USA
tel +1 718 784 4520
fax +1 718 784 4681

Museum of the Moving Image
    (MOMI)
National Film Theatre
South Bank
London SE1 8XT
UK
tel +44 171 928 3535
fax +44 171 815 1419

National Film and Television Archive
    (NFTVA)
British Film Institute
21 Stephen Street
London W1P 2LN
UK
tel +44 171 255 1444
fax +44 171 580 7503

National Museum of Photography,
    Film and Television
Pictureville
Bradford
W YORKS BD1 1NQ

UK
tel +44 1274 203300
fax +44 1274 723155

A R (Ray) Phillips Jnr
12337 Landale Street
Studio City
CA 91604
USA
tel +1 818 984 2615
fax +1 818 508 7717

Service des Archives du Film (SAF)
7 bis rue Alexandre Turpault
Bois d'Arcy 78395
FRANCE
tel +33 1 30 14 80 00
fax +33 1 34 60 52 25

UCLA Film Archive
1015 N Cahuenga Blvd
Hollywood
CA 90038
USA
tel +1 213 462 4921
fax +1 213 461 6317

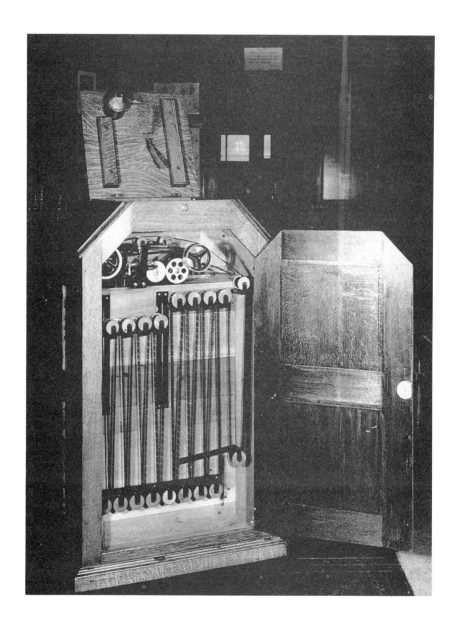

Kinetoscope #1018, c.summer 1896
Used for an experiment in coin-operation, it was never sold. See further information on page 98. The serial number is interesting, as there is no indication that as many as 1000 Kinetoscopes were produced.

ISBN 0-313-30508-0

EAN

9 780313 305085

90000>

HARDCOVER BAR CODE